Hedgehogs and Foxes

Hedgehogs and Foxes

Character, Leadership, and Command in Organizations

Abraham Zaleznik

HEDGEHOGS AND FOXES
Copyright © Abraham Zaleznik, 2008.

First published in 2008 by PALGRAVE MACMILLAN® in the US - a division
of St. Martin's Press LLC, 175 Fifth Avenue, New York, NY 10010.

Where this book is distributed in the UK, Europe and the rest of the world,
this is by Palgrave Macmillan, a division of Macmillan Publishers Limited,
registered in England, company number 785998, of Houndmills, Basingstoke,
Hampshire RG21 6XS.

Palgrave Macmillan is the global academic imprint of the above companies and
has companies and representatives throughout the world.

Palgrave® and Macmillan® are registered trademarks in the United States, the
United Kingdom, Europe and other countries.

ISBN-13: 978-0-230-60623-4
ISBN-10: 0-230-60623-7

Library of Congress Cataloging-in-Publication Data

Zaleznik, Abraham, 1924–
  Hedgehogs and foxes: character, leadership, and command in organizations /
by Abraham Zaleznik.
    p. cm.
  ISBN 0-230-60623-7
  1. Political leadership. 2. Power (Social sciences) 3. Control (Psychology)
  4. Leadership—Psychological aspects. 5. Decision making. 6. Political
leadership—United States—Case studies. 7. Leadership—Case studies.
  8. Executives—Psychology—Case studies. I. Title.

  JC330.3.Z34 2008
  658.4'092—dc22   2007052840

A catalogue record of the book is available from the British Library.

Design by Macmillan India Ltd.

First edition: August 2008

10 9 8 7 6 5 4 3 2 1

Printed in the United States of America.

In commemoration of the 100th anniversary of the founding of the
Harvard Business School

Contents

Preface

This book is a product of a personal odyssey in search of a method for the study of leadership and command in organizations. It began formally in 1947 when I became a research assistant at the Harvard Business School immediately after I earned an MBA degree there. My job initially was to go into factories and offices to research and write case studies to be presented in various classes of the MBA program. One of the perks of this job allowed me to study for a doctor's degree, which I completed with the acceptance of my dissertation on the role of the foreman in a factory. The director of the Division of Research read the dissertation immediately after my defense of the thesis and decided to offer it to a wider audience in the division's book publication program.

As a case writer I became aware that I had certain talents, particularly in interviewing officials in offices and factories. It was almost second nature to me to listen carefully and to build a framework for writing the case study. I also discovered that I enjoyed writing and never felt offended at the critical comments my drafts received. I was blessed with enthusiasm for the work I was doing and also with a certain freedom in writing, so that the malady of writer's block was a stranger to me.

As I progressed in my career at the Harvard Business School, I took advantage of the school's liberal policy of time off from teaching to pursue research and writing. The early focus in my research was group behavior with emphasis on the role of the formal leader of the group. I read extensively in social anthropology and in the structure of groups, particularly in the relationship between formal and informal organization. The formal organization establishes roles and relationships according to the logic of purpose, but alongside this structure, roles and relationships emerge sometimes to support the goals of the organization, but frequently to meet human needs that exist apart from the design and purposes of the organization. Even in the most tightly knit organization, especially in factories, an underlying mistrust of authority pervades the informal organization. Norms of behavior, particularly restriction of output, are strongly adhered to, enforced through various forms of group punishment such as isolating the deviates from the rituals of group membership. The norm, unstated but almost universally recognized, is to avoid behavior that would make group members look bad in the eyes of authority.

My research focus gradually shifted from the factory floor to the office and the executive suite in corporations. My reading also shifted from treatises on social anthropology and sociology to psychoanalysis, starting with Ernest Jones's three-volume biography of Sigmund Freud. At the same time, I read Freud's essays on the unconscious, the psychoneuroses, and group psychology. Harvard's Department of Social Relations, under the leadership of luminaries such as Talcott Parsons, Clyde Kluckhohn, and Henry Murray, sought an integration of the human sciences in which psychoanalysis was a major building block. The Boston Psychoanalytic Institute offered a program for academics to study psychoanalysis, but short of working with patients. It was an academic program with exposure to clinical material through seminars, but candidates in this program signed a pledge not to represent themselves as psychoanalysts and accept patients in a clinical practice.

I became a candidate in this program (we were under the pledge designated as "C" candidates) in 1960 and began a training analysis that year. In 1961 I began the seminar program that included in due course clinical seminars in which patients in analysis were the subjects of presentation and discussion. My participation in these seminars led a number of senior analysts in the faculty to urge me to apply for a waiver of medical and psychiatric prerequisites so that I could begin full training. The waiver had to be approved by a committee of the American Psychoanalytic Association. I received a waiver and began clinical work under the supervision of senior analysts. My supervisors, mostly European trained psychoanalysts, included Joseph Michaels, M.D., Helen Tartakoff, M.D., Arthur Valenstein, M.D., and Grete Bibring, M.D. I completed the formal program, graduated, and became an active member of the American Psychoanalytic Association, the International Psychoanalytic Association, and the Boston Institute. Certification for the practice of psychoanalysis came in 1978.

Throughout my training and subsequent career, I continued teaching, conducting research, and writing at the Harvard Business School while engaged in a psychoanalytic practice. I was invited to join the faculty of the Boston Institute and gave the required course on psychoanalytic theory. I joined colleagues from Harvard Business School at seminars in the Philippines, Japan, and Israel in consulting with organizations, and maintained a lively consulting practice throughout my career.

I began writing for a general business audience in 1968 with the publication of *Human Dilemmas of Leadership* and later *The Managerial Mystique*. A number of my articles appeared in *The Harvard Business Review,* including "Managers and Leaders: Are They Different?"—which won the McKinsey prize for the best article of the year. Another article I wrote for the *Review* entitled "Real Work" also received the McKinsey Award.

Except for my work in consulting, I generally avoid a prescriptive stance. I continue to believe that the proper study of mankind is man in all his complexity, especially in the study of leadership and command. In accepting a leadership role, a person brings to bear intellect and character. Intellect grows out of intrinsic ego capacities, or talents, that can be honed through self discovery, education, and the quality of mind called imagination. If an individual pursues a life path that does violence to intrinsic ego capacities, he or she will experience the discomfort of depressive reactions.

While I never accepted students in my classes as patients (in fact I always introduced the course with the admonition that they should check their neuroses at the door as they entered the classroom), I did encourage them to come to my office to discuss the course and problems they had with the material. Many students took advantage of this invitation, and besides discussing the course, students often gravitated into their worries about jobs and career. One student, I recall, felt at odds with his experience at the Harvard Business School. He had applied to the school at the urging of his father, and while his academic performance was acceptable, he felt estranged from the experience. In due course he revealed to me his concern that perhaps he was not suited for a career in business, that he was complying with his father's wishes, and that he was fated for work that seemed at a distance from his real interests and talents. He had artistic interests and in describing these interests to me, he came alive. He really wanted to work in a museum and saw the possibility of linking his work at the Harvard Business School with a career in museum management. Ego interests and talents make a demand on the individual who is fortunate to discover what these interests and talents are and to make a life in pursuing them. Perhaps he needed the permission of an authority figure to follow his inclinations.

In his book *Childhood and Society*, Erik Erikson reports on George Bernard Shaw's decision to abandon his career in banking, not because he would fail, but because he would succeed. Business and banking were alien to his talents and ego interests. He left banking and began writing, following the discipline of five pages a day for five years. He became a writer.

Perhaps it is unfair to hold individuals in positions of responsibility in organizations to a standard of creativity exemplified in the life and work of George Bernard Shaw. Few in life will meet this standard. But I suspect many labor with unfulfilled desire, especially in organizations overweighted with repetitive routines. This has long been a problem in blue-collar work, but it has invaded high-status white-collar and executive work as well. Ask yourself how long it will take for the routine of preparing annual budgets and forecasts before boredom takes over. Even at the highest reaches of executive responsibility, boredom threatens the integrity of work. To escape boredom, how often will executives seek adventures in acquisitions, where caution is thrown to the winds? Add to boredom, the lure of high executive compensation packages of salary, bonus, and stock options, incentives to suppress the demands of ego interests and talent.

Holding fast to one's ego interests can result in a loss of flexibility and a fixation on the product of one's imagination. An Wang, the founder of Wang Laboratories, was born in China and emigrated to the United States where he studied at Harvard and joined Howard Aitken's applied engineering group. Wang had an idea for the application of computer memory to the design of a small calculator. He formed Wang Laboratories and created this product, which was a smashing success. But Wang foresaw the eventual demise of the handheld calculator analogous to the fate of the ballpoint pen. When it first appeared, the ballpoint pen competed as a high-priced luxury product. Soon imitators took over, and while the ballpoint pen has a place in the luxury pen market, it is also a commodity used as a giveaway in banks or sold as a low-cost pen in chain stores. The same fate awaited the handheld calculator.

Wang called his key executives to a meeting and announced that Wang Laboratories was going to change course to enter the word-processing market in place of the handheld calculator market. His colleagues thought he had lost his mind to give up a successful product in order to concentrate on word processing. Although the word processor was initially successful, the personal computer rendered obsolete the word processor. Wang did not foresee this development, and

Wang Laboratories failed. One cannot become fixated on a product or an idea at the risk of being rendered obsolete by innovations that improve functions and thereby create new markets.

Henry Ford, the founder of the Ford Motor Company and the father of the Model T, enjoyed phenomenal success with the T, a product for the mass market priced to enable middle- to low-income workers to own an automobile. Like An Wang, Ford had become fixated on the Model T and refused to change the product despite the apparent success of Alfred Sloan and General Motors in segmenting the market and offering automobiles from low-price products to luxury vehicles. Without consulting his father, Edsel Ford brought a group of engineers and designers together to create a mock-up of a new design. If introduced, this car would abandon the elder Ford's insistence that he will offer cars in any color as long as it was black.

Organizations operate in a competitive environment. Fixations undermine the capacity for command, where the primary responsibility is to lead organizations in anticipating changes in customer preferences. This principle applies equally to business and government organizations. When Alfred Sloan devised the form for the organization structure in the 1920s with centralized financial controls and decentralized operations, he also sidelined his technical genius, Walter Kettering, among whose innovations was the electrical starter that allowed drivers to start the engine from the inside ignition instead of hand-cranking the engine from the outside. Kettering was intent on the invention of an air-cooled engine. Sloan and the heads of factories feared work on this invention would shift factory emphasis on mass producing cars with water-cooled engines, thereby reducing immediate productivity and profits. Sloan's solution to this dilemma was to create a new organization to design and build a product with an air-cooled engine with Kettering at its head. This move placated Kettering's supporters on the board of directors and Kettering himself, who, while seemingly given the go-ahead signal to develop the air-cooled engine, found his talents and passions ill-suited to managing an organization. The air-cooled engine encountered numerous technical problems and never became the star in the General Motors firmament. The top management of General Motors lost interest in this potential new product, and with the high consumer demand for the existing water-cooled engines, General Motors prospered in its marketing strategy of product segmentation. But the story does not end here. In 2007 General Motors, along with Ford and Chrysler, is struggling to reverse its loss of market share to Japanese car makers. To reverse this ominous trend, perhaps U.S. car companies need to renew the search for product excellence and innovation in the spirit of Charles F. Kettering.

Leaders in the public and private sectors must avoid the malady of the repetition compulsion: repeat the policies and practices that have succeeded in the past. The repetition compulsion, first discovered in the experiments of behavioral psychologists, found that pigeons would find, by random trials, that a button, when pressed, would produce a pellet of corn. Once they discovered the button that produced the reward, the pigeons continued to return to it. Leaders in organizations live in a dynamic world in which the reward goes to the individual who stands above the crowd and is able to anticipate change.

At this writing, the newspapers are filled with stories about the crisis in Pakistan where lawyers have taken to the streets to protest General and President Musharraf's declaration of martial law, firing the chief justice, and suspending the election of a new president. As a steadfast ally in the battle against the resurgent Taliban, Musharraf has enjoyed the support of the American government with billions of dollars in arms and aid. This crisis calls for the leadership of a fox instead of a hedgehog, one schooled in foreign affairs and the antithesis of a leader enamored of slogans and bereft of imagination.

Acknowledgments

Many people helped in preparing this manuscript for publication. Paula Alexander and Jan Simmons applied their computer expertise in working on the successive drafts of the manuscript. Eileen Hankins, also of the Cumnock 300 staff, typed drafts on to the computer before returning to school to complete her degree. Besides their practical help on the manuscript, these three ladies displayed their enthusiasm for the book and were a constant source of encouragement for which I am grateful.

Erika McCaffrey of the Baker Library reference staff tracked down references with speed and thoroughness, and I thank her for her patience and help. Ann Menashi and Steven Mirandi, the librarians of the Boston Psychoanalytic Institute, were also helpful in answering my queries regarding psychoanalytic source material.

Professor Alan A. Stone of the Harvard Law School faculty read an earlier draft of the manuscript and offered valuable suggestions. The history luncheon group of the Tavern Club of Boston discussed the Eisenhower chapter of this book, and I thank them for their interest and responsiveness. Many members of the Tavern Club responded with interest as I described the book in our Monday evening informal gathering over drinks before dinner.

Melody Lawrence provided expert editorial help in improving one of the last drafts of the manuscript. She worked rapidly and with exemplary patience and tact, even when I did not take some of her suggestions.

My colleagues and friends of the psychoanalytic community have enriched my understanding of both clinical and applied psychoanalysis. Dr. Robert Michels and I have cochaired a discussion group, Psychodynamic Problems in Organizations, for more than 30 years during the winter meetings of the American Psychoanalytic Association in New York. It was a stimulating experience working with Dr. Michels and gaining the benefit of the group's clinical acuity. I thank all of the participants over the years and look forward to meetings in the future.

I have reserved for concluding these acknowledgements my special gratitude to my wife, Elizabeth Anne Zaleznik. Our marriage, approaching 64 years, has sustained me in more ways than I can acknowledge, including, especially, her help in reading my books and articles and applying her gifts as a professional editor to improve clarity and eliminate unnecessary verbiage.

In dedicating this book in commemoration of the 100th anniversary of the founding of the Harvard Business School, I want to express my gratitude to that institution and to the university of which it is a part for the spirit of adventure that permeates the school and the university.

Abraham Zaleznik

I

Introduction

The idea of command is a victim of a bad press. The scars remaining on the American psyche from the debacle of Vietnam, and the fresh wounds from the ill-advised war in Iraq, call into question the legitimacy of command in a democracy. President Bush has lost the confidence of the American electorate and, as commander in chief, he no longer speaks with authority. Command is the projection of one's character in solving problems and making decisions that gain the support of followers. Once support is lost, the quality of the leader's character and his fitness for command are called into question.

This book is a psychoanalytic study of command, using the concept of character as the lens through which to focus on the ways individuals in positions of authority use power. Character, in its derivation from psychoanalysis, refers to two functions of the mind. The first function is directed inward to regulate anxiety. The second is directed outward to present a constant representation of the person that is relatively unchanged over time. This representation can be described further as character traits—on a scale, for example, of introverted to extraverted, or impassive to expansive in personality.

An important component of character is the style the individual habitually uses to solve problems and arrive at decisions. Cognitive style is not simply intellect, but also habits of the mind. Individuals in positions of authority approach problems differently. For some, the habit is thinking, discussion, examination of alternatives, and being directly involved in the decision-making process. For others, it is as though the mind consists of an in-basket and an out-basket. When presented with a problem, the habit is to decide where and to whom to delegate the issue. Once the delegation has been made, the issue is transferred from the in-basket to the out-basket, and the mind is cleared. One typical way to transfer a problem is to engage outside consultants. However, if such consultants are used excessively, subordinates may be demoralized, and their identification with the leader may weaken as a reciprocal defense.

Freud's essay on group psychology posits the leader of the group as the force for group cohesion. The leader becomes the object of identification for members who, with this ego ideal in common, in turn identify with one another. The leader stands apart from the members in that he loves no one but himself, and this independence from the group solidifies the identification. The leader maintains his independence by showing no favoritism. In Freud's theory of social organization, membership in many groups creates identifications that solidify the individual's link to society. In differentiating the leader from the group, Freud suggests that the leader, who has a share in many group minds and is susceptible to the influence of many group and institutional identifications, "can also raise himself above them to the extent of having a scrap of independence and originality."[1]

There is ample evidence, in the literature on experimental social psychology, of the effects of group pressure on members to conform to the norms of the group. Members are pressed to think alike, to accept opinions and preferences arrived at through group pressure. As Freud suggested, a scrap of independence frees the individual from group thinking. In the case of the leader, it makes it possible, through example, for innovation and new ideas to take hold. Thus, a healthy dose of narcissism is a valuable addition to the character of leaders, just as a healthy dose of paranoia helps a leader stand apart from group pressure and question advice received for solving problems. This scrap of originality, in turn, stimulates thinking and improves the quality of group effort.

An individual's character develops slowly through the relatively successful mastery of the tasks of infancy and early childhood through to adulthood. Sensitive parents understand not only the importance of providing gratification of appetites, but also the timing of transition from one stage of childhood to the next as the tasks of infancy change and the relationship to caregivers also changes.

The story of character development is far from idyllic. In its own way, it is a story of learning about power. The omnipotent parent can be the source of pleasure, but can also be the agent who frustrates desire in the interest of moving the infant along from simpler desires to more complex wishes that involve a larger cast of characters. Infancy begins with a sense of omnipotence, only to become an experience of limitations (e.g., learning to gain control over bodily functions). The expanded existence, for the infant, that is brought about in the consciousness of the infant by the presence of a father, provides a new and intensified experience with power. The infant is no longer the center of the universe and begins to experience both loss and new challenges of adaptation. The birth of a sibling complicates the story, increasing the sensitivity to power in the experience of sibling rivalry.

The legacy of early development is the formation of character traits that ultimately define the person and establish the repertoire of ego defenses. Character also defines the individual's orientation to power. For some, power is problematic, and to seek and have power arouses anxiety, since, in the unconscious mind, rivals are just waiting for the opportunity to attack the would-be power holder. One becomes an object of envy, a target of aggression, and an uneasy incumbent when in a position of responsibility. The defense against this type of anxiety—call it power envy—is to abdicate responsibility in subtle ways such as distancing oneself from the center of problem solving and decision making. Instead of command, the result is laissez-faire leadership.

The opposite of this detachment from power and command is to seek power actively and aggressively as a compensatory motive. The individual feels deeply and unconsciously inadequate and, as a defense, turns this sense of injury and inadequacy into its opposite and becomes power hungry. This ego defense is incorporated as a character trait and prevents the individual from applying reason and subtlety in the quest for power. Peers and subordinates recognize the workings of the hunger for power, while the individual appears oblivious to the effects, in the extreme, of his or her own power mania.

There is no rule book to guide leaders in the consolidation and uses of power in command. The lessons to be learned are personal, they come from and constitute the foundation of character, they educate the mind. Some individuals are lucky and find a teacher who, in on-the-job training, helps them cultivate an educated mind. When Dwight D. Eisenhower received a transfer to Panama to work under General Fox Conner, he began a tutorial on command and leadership that altered a lackluster career into a path of upward mobility, ending in his command of the Allied forces during World War II.

Uninterrupted success in early career years is not necessarily the foundation for character development. Overcoming disappointment, experiencing a setback or impasse, can put the individual into a mode of introspection, which, with the help of an authority figure, can result in an alteration of character, however small, that propels that person into accelerated learning.

Socrates' advice to "know thyself" often falls on deaf ears. This advice appeals to people who have cultivated a vertical pattern of thinking as opposed to a horizontal pattern. Thinking horizontally can be likened to a vessel skimming the surface of the sea completely oblivious to the depths and the life contained below the surface. Vertical thinking, on the other hand, ranges from observation of the environment to plumbing the depths of one's psyche to explore connections in the mode of free association as a stimulus to one's imagination. In vertical thinking, psychological defenses relax and permit a kind of playfulness that enables the solution of problems the same way a dream can solve the residue of conscious mental activity, with its link to the past. (As a poet once reminded leaders, "relax your grip, let go your hold, so all that glitters may be gold.") A sense of humor is a companion to vertical thinking and has the further advantage of enhancing the respect one has for authority figures. Putting it another way, vertical thinking deepens individuals' identification with leaders who display imagination, central to the capacity to solve problems, in ways that appear like pulling a rabbit out of a hat. The technical term for this imaginative form of thinking is regression in the service of the ego.

Some things get in the way of the process of thinking vertically. Anxiety about performance is a common impediment. Laurence Olivier, one of the finest character actors on the British stage, suffered from stage fright, a manifestation of performance anxiety. A person suffering from this form of anxiety has an unconscious fear that he will be uncovered as an imposter, that he will appear as if naked and be destroyed by ridicule. In the case of actors, the anxiety disappears as the actor merges with the character he or she is portraying and the audience merges with the performer in a reciprocal loss of identity to rise above the mundane. To defend against the equivalent of performance anxiety in command, authority figures try to prevent subordinates from getting too close. The instinct is to create distance by becoming unknowable, but the fear of humiliation cannot be warded off. A powerful chief executive officer (CEO) who harbors the fear of humiliation might cite having been reduced to tears earlier in his career when a leader in the community humiliated him in response to his overreaching in asserting his solution to a problem beyond his scope and practical possibility. This same CEO might weep as he recounted the many instances when his father humiliated him for his brashness and overreaching. His defense is to hide and become unknowable to his subordinates and associates. He manages this by indirection and uses others as a screen to his visibility.

Writing in the sixteenth century, Niccolò Machiavelli offered advice to princes to adopt the ways of both the lion and the fox as models for command. Model yourself after the lion for its courage, he said, and the fox for its cleverness. Although Machiavelli is often scorned as amoral, thinking only of advising princes on how to survive amidst a mankind of mixed motives and vulgar natures, his thinking still has far-reaching validity. He was an early advocate of clear vision about leadership and command, emphasizing the acceptance of human nature as it is, rather than encumbering oneself with a superstructure of ideas about what it should be. Today, Machiavelli's thinking has been extended to apply to reflections on how leaders might change human nature or at least appeal to higher motives. This latter idea has become pivotal in a certain current philosophy of leadership by empowerment. But although it might be self-satisfying, it can impose a burden on others, who may still be engaged in a struggle to know and accept themselves, warts and all. To foist ideals on others, as if one were their parent, is to produce a sense of shame in them from the constant reflection that they are less than perfect.

The use of the animal kingdom in analogies to illuminate styles of thinking and behavior did not end, if indeed it began, with Machiavelli. Isaiah Berlin, the twentieth century historian and philosopher, used the analogy of the hedgehog and the fox when he discussed the imaginations of great writers and thinkers. Extended to character, particularly to cognitive style, this imagery sets up a dichotomy that is useful in examining styles of leadership and command in organizations. The hedgehog knows only one great thing, it has a single overarching idea that controls its view of the world and human nature. The fox knows many things and is prepared to adapt to a complex view of the world.

> [T]aken figuratively, the words [describing the hedgehog and the fox] can be made to yield a sense in which they mark one of the deepest differences which divide writers and thinkers, and, it may be human beings in general. For there exists a great chasm between those, on one side, who relate everything to a single central vision, one system less or more coherent or articulate, in terms of which they understand, think and feel a single, universal, organizing principle in terms of which alone all that they are and say has significance and, on the other side, those who pursue many ends, often unrelated and even contradictory, connected, if at all, only in some *de facto* way, for some psychological or physiological cause, related by no moral or aesthetic principle; these last lead lives, perform acts, and entertain ideas that are centrifugal rather than centripetal, their thought is scattered or diffuse, moving on many levels, seizing upon the essence of a vast variety of experiences and objects for what they are in

themselves, without consciously or unconsciously seeking to fit them into, or exclude them from any one unchanging, all-embracing, sometimes self-contradictory and incomplete, at times fanatical, unitary inner vision.[2]

It is not uncommon, especially in academic circles, to attack dichotomies on the grounds that they oversimplify. Yet the two opposing worldviews of the hedgehog and the fox may be useful in thinking about human nature. In particular, this dichotomy provides a thrust into the character and cognitive style of individuals engaged in positions of authority in organizations.

In late December 2006, President George W. Bush faced a decision about changing course in the U.S. military strategy in Iraq. Four years after his dramatic landing on a carrier with the banner "Mission Accomplished" raised high on the bridge, and in the aftermath of the repudiation of the Republican control of Congress and a historically high disapproval rating of his presidency, President Bush offered, in an address to the nation, a supposedly new program to deal with the civil war in Iraq and the crumbling of U.S. prestige in the Middle East and the world. Evidently, he was not lacking in advice. The Baker-Hamilton Commission report had been submitted and confirmed the mishandling of the mission in Iraq. Top policy makers and military leaders were divided. Should the United States increase its military presence in Iraq and take a more active stance in quelling the insurgency? Or should the military presence be diminished, which would call the attention of the Iraqi government to the fact that the problem was theirs to face and resolve, thus acknowledging that the U.S. military presence had made matters worse and that withdrawal would leave it up to the Iraqis to solve their political problems as a prelude to ending the civil war? President Bush had dispatched to Iraq his new secretary of defense on a mission to assess the situation in the government and on the ground and, presumably, to develop recommendations on changing course in Iraq. Members of Congress were also weighing in with their opinions on changing course in Iraq.

At issue in this debate about Iraq is Bush's character. He abhors introspection. The press speculates on the psychodrama of his relationship to his father, with the underlying premise that he is engaged in an oedipal drama with the intention of using Iraq to best his father—who refused to go forward after the military victory and refused to depose Saddam Hussein. George W. Bush's response to questions about his father's authority is to state that God is the higher authority. (Paradoxically, James Baker the cochair of the commission on Iraq, was an insider in the first President Bush's administration and is credited with steering the route to the Supreme Court that gave George W. Bush the presidency in 2000.)

President Bush's aversion to introspection solidifies a defensive structure that relies on denial and beyond. He does not accept responsibility for the false intelligence that Saddam Hussein harbored weapons of mass destruction, which became a central rationale for the war. His cognitive style of bifurcating issues into good and evil, the tendency associated with an obsessive-compulsive personality structure, goes beyond a single mechanism of defense such as denial. It has its roots in the stage in his development that led to his religious conversion under the persuasive influence of the Reverend Billy Graham. He became a born-again

Christian to overcome an addiction to alcohol, after having been arrested on charges of driving while intoxicated.

There is no known cure for alcoholism. Individuals with this perversion in their character are dry drunks—a view held both by Alcoholics Anonymous (AA) and religious fundamentalists. As dry drunks, they cannot drink and are prevented from drinking by the 12 steps of AA or by the acceptance of a sense of sin when they become born-again Christians. But the underlying compulsion remains, a mark in character. Thought patterns become tainted, held fast to defining issues in the extremes of black and white, good and evil. Bifurcation in cognition defends against the anxiety aroused when faced with ambiguity, complexity, and the subtlety behind most policy questions. (This defense should not be confused with its opposite: the inability to bring debate to an end and reach conclusions and decisions.)

Psychoanalysis refers to complexity as the reality principle. The task of the ego is to refine the cognitive process so it can take account of complexity and counteract the effects of the compulsion to seek safety in repetition. In behavioral psychology, the repetition compulsion is a well-known law derived from experiments with pigeons that learn by the repetition of success which button to peck at to get food. The experiments show that the pigeons' success, arrived at randomly, results in learning that has been reinforced by success. Leaders who deny complexity fall victim to the repetition compulsion. In the repetition, in the present, of the successful formula from the past, a failure in vision takes hold. Technological change, shifts in consumer tastes, and innovations in product design all favor the entrepreneur who renders past practice obsolete. The institutional cure for the compulsion toward repetition is ceremonial patricide, killing off the legacies of father figures whose early successes gave rise to the compulsion.

The story in back of a leader's life of thought and action is always a mixed bag. If the proper study of mankind is man, the enduring lessons of leadership will emerge from the study of lives, of men and women who, with an often tenuous grasp of command and less than perfect clarity in inner visions, dependent on the strength and mobility of their character, search for the courage to lead. Leaders present their life stories as a text, calling upon readers to engage in vertical thinking as a way of identifying with that text.

This book contains five parts. Each part consists of two narrative chapters on the life and work of individuals caught up in the trappings of power and struggling to make it meaningful in their lives and the lives of others who become part of their story. The third chapter in each part is thematic and uses the stories to sharpen the portrayals of character in action when in positions of responsibility.

Part I

The Optimists

The Propensity for Risk: Eisenhower in the Military and the Presidency

On May 7, 1945, at 0241 local time, General Eisenhower sent a message to his command announcing Germany's unconditional surrender. His superior officer, General George C. Marshall, wrote in reply to Eisenhower's last wartime message:

> You have completed your mission with the greatest victory in the history of warfare. You have commanded with outstanding success the most powerful military force that has ever been assembled. You have met and successfully disposed of every conceivable difficulty incident to varied national interests and international political problems of unprecedented complications. Through all of this, since the day of your arrival in England three years ago, you have been selfless in your actions, always sound and tolerant in your judgments and altogether admirable in the courage and wisdom of your military decisions.
>
> You have made history, great history for the good of mankind and you have stood for all we hope and admire in an officer of the United States Army. These are my tributes and my personal thanks.[1]

The historian Stephen E. Ambrose, Eisenhower's principal biographer, offers an appraisal of Eisenhower's generalship. He ranks high Eisenhower's commitment to his work. Alongside commitment, he values Eisenhower's brains, talents, and leadership. He noted, following these attributes, the importance of luck, calling it "Eisenhower luck" but not dumb luck. He noted, for example, Eisenhower's attention to detail, as shown by his numerous meetings with the chief weather forecaster before deciding to go forward with the Normandy invasion. Ambrose also praised Eisenhower's ability to get into the mind of the enemy and to be flexible. While, for Eisenhower, plans were essential, once the battle was joined, flexibility and the willingness to override plans were also important. Ambrose cites the taking of the railroad bridge at Remagen as an example. General Omar Bradley recommended that the division cross over to the east bank and establish an offensive foothold there. However, Bradley pointed out that the intelligence officer had advised against the crossing because of terrain difficulties, and that the crossing was not part of the plan. Eisenhower's response was, "To hell with the planners. Sure, go on, Brad and I'll give you everything we got to hold that bridgehead. We'll make good use of it even if the terrain isn't too good."[2]

According to Ambrose, Eisenhower was exceedingly cautious during the North African campaign. Eisenhower had no experience with command prior to his appointment as head of the Allied forces. His success as a wartime general depended upon a balanced approach to taking risks. For him, recklessness meant wasting lives, but excessive cautiousness meant missed opportunities to engage with and defeat the enemy.

Among the mistakes attributed to Eisenhower was his tendency to appease Field Marshall Montgomery to the consternation of Generals Bradley and Patton. Montgomery was cautious in his approach to battle. Montgomery objected strenuously to Eisenhower moving his headquarters from England to the Continent, urging Eisenhower to maintain a lofty and far view of the war. A hero among the British, he pressured Eisenhower to put all the Allied armies in France under his field command instead of the arrangement then in place of having Bradley and Montgomery each in command of an army group and both reporting to Eisenhower as the supreme commander.

Eisenhower did not accede to Montgomery's desire to command the entire armies in the field, but he compromised, giving Montgomery the air command and priority in supplies. Both Generals Patton and Bradley were very critical of Eisenhower and his willingness to placate Montgomery.

Eisenhower's actions with regard to the Battle of the Bulge and the encirclement of the 101st Airborne Division are a case in point. He viewed the German counterattack as an opportunity to destroy the German armies and thrust rapidly into Germany. Eisenhower ordered Montgomery to attack. Montgomery promised do so no later than January 1, but that date passed without an offensive being launched. Eisenhower was furious and drafted a letter to Montgomery ordering him to attack, stating that if he refused he would be relieved of command.

Montgomery's aide prevailed on Eisenhower to hold the letter while he conferred with his chief. But Montgomery held fast and argued again that there should be no offensive, that he should be given command of all the armies, that Patton should be ordered to stand still, and that the proper strategy was to await the exhaustion of the German offensive and then to attack. He even issued a directive for Eisenhower's signature that would have authorized a plan and command arrangement exactly as Montgomery wanted. Eisenhower refused, issuing his own directive contrary to Montgomery's plan, and sent a letter to Montgomery. As presented in Ambrose's biography:

> In a covering note to Montgomery accompanying the directive, Eisenhower was simple, direct, and forceful. "I do not agree," Eisenhower said, referring to Montgomery's contention that there should be a single ground commander. He said that he had done all he could for Montgomery and did not want to hear again about placing Bradley under Montgomery's command. "I assure you that in this matter I can go no further." He added, "I have planned an advance" to the Rhine on a broad front, and ordered Montgomery to read his directive carefully. All the vagueness of earlier letters and directives to Montgomery was now gone.

Ambrose continues,

In conclusion, Eisenhower told Montgomery that he would no longer tolerate any debate on these subjects. "I would deplore the development of such an unbridgeable gulf of convictions between us that we would have to present our differences to the CCS (Combined Chiefs of Staff)," he said, but if Montgomery went any further that was exactly what he would do. "The confusion and debate that would follow would certainly damage the goodwill and devotion to a common cause that have made this Allied Force unique in history," Eisenhower admitted, but he could do nothing else if Montgomery persisted.[3]

Freddie de Guingand, Montgomery's aide, had acted as go-between after persuading Eisenhower to withhold his letter and directive to Montgomery. De Guingand convinced Montgomery of the seriousness of the situation, including the fact that Eisenhower and his staff had a replacement for Montgomery. This ended the crisis. De Guingand had prepared a letter for Montgomery's signature, which, in keeping with the code of the military, displayed submission to authority. Montgomery followed this formal acquiescence with a personal, handwritten note to Eisenhower that said, "Dear Ike, You can rely on me to go all out 100 percent to implement your plan." Montgomery then launched an attack on January 3, 1945, that managed to destroy the mobility of the German army, although Eisenhower had anticipated greater results.

The Battle of the Bulge was decisive in more ways than just the destruction of German mobility and heavy casualties. According to Ambrose, in the final dash to defeat the Germans and end the war, in fact as well as in name, the commanding general would be Dwight David Eisenhower.[4]

In his hesitation, even vacillation, in confronting Montgomery, Eisenhower had suffered a perception on the part of key subordinates such as Generals Bradley and Patton that he was indecisive and fearful of taking on Montgomery. To Bradley and Patton, Montgomery was an obstacle, harmful to their efforts, their commands, and the waging of the war with the German armies. In addition, he continued to be a bane to them. He incensed them by holding a press conference after the decisive Battle of the Bulge claiming he had won this battle. He was arrogant during the press conference, taking all the credit for the victory and comparing this battle to El Alemein, where he had been the victorious commander.

Eisenhower's tendency to avoid conflict and to compromise, particularly in political relations with Allies, proved costly according to Ambrose. Ambrose writes, concerning an offensive called Market Garden designed to take Arnheim at the expense of taking Antwerp, a much-needed port, to augment the supplies available:

But of all the factors that influenced Eisenhower's decisions—to reinforce success, to leap the Rhine, to bring the underutilized paratroopers into action—the one that stands out is his desire to appease Montgomery. At no other point in the war did Eisenhower's tendency toward compromise and his desire to keep his subordinates happy exact a higher price.[5]

Montgomery had pressured Eisenhower to abandon, or postpone, the plan to take Antwerp. The plan to move on Antwerp was part of the overall offensive in the original war plans, but Montgomery pressed Eisenhower to cross the Rhine at Arnheim, which required diverting supplies from other armies. The operation was not successful and delayed taking Antwerp and the estuaries necessary for port operations.

Eisenhower's willingness to placate Montgomery made Patton and Bradley furious over Eisenhower's wavering on the assignment of the American First Army to Montgomery. Patton suggested that they both submit their resignations. Bradley would not agree to that drastic step. Instead, he went to Eisenhower to protest the transfer. His meeting with Eisenhower yielded another compromise to maintain Bradley's command of the First Army, but to give Montgomery the authorization to go through Bradley to coordinate Montgomery's Second Army actions with Bradley's First Army. According to Ambrose, "that decision, and its sequel, strengthened Montgomery's . . . —and Bradley's and Patton's—conviction that Eisenhower always agreed with the last man he talked to."[6]

One should reach conclusions about the propensity for risk, especially in the military, with the utmost caution. Risk taking is surely an aspect of character, as is the tendency to compromise, and the tendency to be influenced by the last person who presents an argument. In warfare, one calculates risk in terms of human lives. Those who see calculated risk as the essence of strategic planning in warfare will justify taking risks and even abandoning plans to exploit opportunity with the argument that sustaining casualties in one risky action is designed to minimize casualties in the long run. There are some analysts who believe that the war was prolonged as a result of some of the decisions, or avoidance of decisions, ascribed to Eisenhower and the high command. The point of this discussion of Eisenhower as a wartime leader is to suggest that this low propensity for risk was encompassed in a character trait, or character constellation, that habitually caused Eisenhower to search for compromise, particularly in the areas involving political considerations alongside military issues. One of Eisenhower's jobs was to forge unity among the Allies. He had a large and complex constituency to deal with. First came his superior officer, General George C. Marshall. Both Eisenhower and Marshall, along with other generals, had internalized the code of the military and its surrounding mystique. The core of this mystique exists in the concept of subordinacy. Those officers who have been successful in their role as subordinate can count on the support of the mystique, the sense of belonging that enables an individual to subordinate his aims to higher authority regardless of the personality of the authority figure. But subordinacy is not to be equated with passivity, or blind acquiescence to the aims and desires of the authority figure. Indeed, the record of command during World War II suggests that to advance one's career and to succeed at any level of the hierarchy one requires initiative and the display of independent thinking. Certainly, during the European campaign, subordinates to Eisenhower, not only Montgomery, felt it important to take issue with directives and to show initiative in viewing operational plans. Eisenhower encouraged subordinates to debate plans. Purportedly, he never ended a meeting without consensus. He also recognized and encouraged initiative in the field, where the officer assumed responsibility for altering plans when the opportunity presented itself. Obedience and initiative both are at the heart of subordinacy and present a subtle balance.

A subordinate who loathes initiatives is useless. In as cohesive an organization as the military, there is ample opportunity to observe character, ability, and resourcefulness. One of Eisenhower's gifts was his ability to select subordinate commanders and to rely on them just as his superior officer, General Marshall, observed the qualities in Eisenhower that propelled him into the position of supreme commander of the Allied forces. Once selected, the superior provides support, guidance, and counsel.

In his reminiscence entitled *At Ease,* Eisenhower describes his service under General Fox Conner in Panama. George Patton urged Eisenhower to apply for service under Conner. At the time, Eisenhower was discouraged about his prospects in the army. He had had no combat experience during World War I and seemed destined in the peacetime army to the job of coaching football. The army rejected his application for a transfer to Panama, leaving Eisenhower possibly facing a dead end. Not long after, his son Icky fell ill with scarlet fever and died, leaving the Eisenhowers desolate in their grief. Miraculously, or so it seemed, shortly after this tragedy, Eisenhower received orders assigning him to Fox Conner in Panama. Eisenhower learned that General Conner, who was a close friend and former aide to General Pershing, had arranged the transfer.

Perhaps nowhere in *At Ease* is Eisenhower more eloquent than in his chapter on Fox Conner. General Conner organized tutorials on military strategy and tactics, on history, and on the career of former great military figures. Equipped with a splendid library, General Conner assigned reading to Eisenhower and spent hours in discussion with him. Eisenhower writes,

> Our conversations continued throughout the three years I served at Camp Gaillard. It is clear now that life with General Conner was a sort of graduate school in military affairs and the humanities, leavened by the comments and discourse of a man who was experienced in his knowledge of men and their conduct. I can never adequately express my gratitude to this one gentleman, for it took years before I fully realized the value of what he had led me through. And then General Conner was gone. But in a lifetime of association with great and good men, he is the one more or less invisible figure to whom I owe an incalculable debt.[7]

Eisenhower's estimation of his debt to General Conner suggests that successful subordinacy enhances prospects for personal growth, laying the foundation for command. We should also note the psychological impact of this tutorial with Conner at the time when Eisenhower was mourning the loss of his firstborn son. General Conner became Eisenhower's father figure and Eisenhower revisited earlier periods in his life when he was son to his father, although the record is far from clear on the nature of his relationship with his father. Eisenhower entitled a chapter on growing up in Abilene, Kansas, "Life with Mother." The main impression one gains from this chapter is the life of a secure, Kansas boy, growing up in a large family, all boys, who learned much from an outdoor life, relatively free from hardship, and who was cultivating an optimistic outlook on life.

If Eisenhower displayed a tendency in the military to avoid interpersonal risk, to play the part of a mediator, one could argue that that was the definition of the job for which General Marshall had selected him. In his character, he displayed optimism.

His smile was infectious, and along with his ability to work closely with subordinates both in staff and in the field, he was able to stimulate subordinates to go forward, overcoming doubt and even distress at his tendency to avoid confrontation.

High propensity for risk seems to be the lot of individuals who want to promote change. When in positions of power, the urge to take risks is usually aligned with the desire to bring about change, often in the face of ambiguous circumstances. In Eisenhower's command during World War II, the aims were clear, friend and enemy sharply defined, and even strategies easily articulated if not subject to doubt. Churchill appeared reluctant to support Overlord, the plan to invade France in a cross-channel operation of huge magnitude. Churchill prevailed in the decision to fight in North Africa and in Italy, but finally acquiesced in support of Overlord. According to Eisenhower, Churchill's concerns stemmed from his experience in World War I and the brutal casualties Britain endured, losing the cream of its youth. He felt a slower route through Italy and the Balkans would finally wear down the enemy. The American side felt it had to be Overlord, the thrust through France and into Germany to destroy the enemy. Eisenhower led the way in meetings with Churchill in convincing the British. Eisenhower's optimism, goodwill, and the absence of ego proved convincing.

Whatever changes he sought to bring about within the military, such as his alliance with George Patton to convince the army to change its theory of tank warfare, there were no radical notions underlying their efforts. It was change well within the traditions and history of the military. The caution he later displayed and his unwillingness to force confrontation displayed his faith that discussion, consultation, and persuasion would result in consensus and unity of purpose and methods. While this faith was based on his conviction in how he should lead to achieve results, at a deeper level it also reflected a deep-seated aversion to confrontation and interpersonal conflict.

One might interpret Eisenhower's low propensity for risk, especially interpersonal risk as in the case of his dealings with Montgomery, as a reflection of political astuteness. But when that same caution, or hesitancy, comes face-to-face with the office and person of the presidency, the incumbent's character now becomes center stage. Is the hesitancy, or caution, necessary to assure deliberation, or does it reflect indecisiveness and the unwillingness to make decisions?

Politics in America is divisiveness, seldom broad consensus. The divisiveness goes beyond the simple fact of a two-party system. The divisions within each of the parties are impressive. Seeking a centrist course, a mediator's interpretation of presidential power is a formidable task, particularly thout the deep institutional support such as that which the military provided Eisenhower in its mystique—the concept of subordinacy and the unity of purpose in winning the war.

After the war Eisenhower was the answer to the moderate Eastern Republican struggle for power and control against the forces of isolationism and deep conservatism at the base of the Taft wing of the Republican party, which sought to overturn the New Deal and the legacy of Franklin Delano Roosevelt. Thomas Dewey had won the nomination in 1948 only to lose the election to Harry Truman. The Eastern moderates saw in Dwight Eisenhower their chance to assert their dominance over the Taft wing of the Republican Party.

While maneuvering to enlist Eisenhower as their candidate, Senator Henry Cabot Lodge and Governor Thomas Dewey, two leaders of the moderate wing of the Republican Party, did not know what party Eisenhower favored. He could have had the Democratic Party's nomination for the asking, as President Truman practically guaranteed him the nomination. After much persuasion, including a dramatic rally at Madison Square Garden, Eisenhower declared himself a Republican and agreed to have his name submitted in nomination. The convincing arguments for Eisenhower were, first, that it was his duty to run, and, second, that he could preserve the internationalist foreign policy against the isolationists such as Senators Taft, Knowland, and others who were dominant in the conservative wing. At the time the moderates were pressuring Eisenhower to stand for the nomination, he was the military head of the North Atlantic Treaty Organization (NATO) and an advocate of international cooperation. The call to duty was deeply embedded in his personal sense of responsibility. But the record fails to show in Eisenhower a strong desire for power or a mission either in political reform or in policy, except in international cooperation and, later, perhaps, fiscal conservatism in balancing the budget. Even here, the objective of balancing the budget derived from Eisenhower's family background and the ideas advocated by "his gang," the business millionaires who were his golfing, bridge, and vacation companions, rather than from a deeply schooled understanding of economics and fiscal policy.

Before venturing further in reaching conclusions on Eisenhower's risk profile in the presidency itself, let us look at three critical incidents in his run for the presidency and his actions while in office. The incidents reflect a lack of conviction and uncertainty in Eisenhower as he faced controversial issues. The first is the challenge Senator Joseph McCarthy evoked in Eisenhower's loyalty to George Marshall. The second is his budget for the fiscal year 1958. The third is the decision to send troops into Little Rock following Governor Orville Faubus's challenge to the Supreme Court decision in *Brown v. The Board of Education* overturning the doctrine of "separate but equal" in the education of black children. These three critical episodes in Eisenhower's run for office and while in the presidency highlight the problem of risk and the orientation to power he displayed as president.

Of the first critical incident, the McCarthy challenge, the journalist Emmet Hughes writes, in his book *The Ordeal of Power: A Political Memoir of the Eisenhower Years,* about the problem Eisenhower faced while campaigning for the presidency. Senator Joseph McCarthy had launched a vicious campaign to "ferret out" Communists and sympathizers in the government. He accused Marshall of communist sympathies in allegedly protecting appointees in the State Department. Eisenhower was scheduled to speak in Milwaukee with McCarthy sharing the platform. What would Eisenhower say? Would he defend his former superior officer and attack McCarthy?

Here are the words Emmet Hughes wrote for Eisenhower and that Eisenhower kept in his pocket as his train approached Milwaukee:

> To defend freedom is to respect freedom. This respect demands, in turn, respect for the integrity of fellow citizens who enjoy their right to disagree. The right to question a

man's judgment carries with it no automatic right to question his honor. Let me be quite specific. I know that charges of disloyalty have, in the past, been leveled against General George C. Marshall. I have been privileged for thirty-five years to know General Marshall personally. I know him as a man and a soldier, to be dedicated with singular selflessness and the profoundest patriotism to the service of America. And this episode is a sobering lesson in the way freedom must not defend itself.[8, 9]

Eisenhower did not read this text. Hughes interpreted this dramatic omission of defense of General Marshall as follows:

The event gave warning that certain qualities in the man, even virtues in themselves, could be wrenched in the play of politics and made to seem misshapen. Clearly there was in him a profound humility—a refusal to use the full force of his personal authority or political position against a critical consensus. He saw himself realistically as a man of military affairs, a stranger to political affairs, surrounded by Republican leaders who—by their testimony, at least—were political "experts." He would have abhorred any image of himself as a man-on-horseback, crudely importing military discipline into a civil arena. Hence, even if the self-denying constraint drove him close to a teeth-grinding anger, he must shun the merest suggestion of martial arrogance. He must show and prove himself, in short, a modest enough member of the "team." He would use this phrase through the years, long after it grew stale, to describe or to commend all his political associates be they his cabinet or his White House staff, his Administration, or his party. I am sure that the word "team" genuinely expressed for him a set of virtues transferred from the military life: coordination and cooperation, service and selflessness. Yet I often wondered if the simple, terse exhortation were not addressed, perhaps only half-consciously, as much to himself as to others.[10]

Whether intentionally or by allusion, Hughes adds his voice to those of Patton and Bradley, to suggest that Eisenhower's inhibitions arose from his distrust of his own impulses, and, in particular, of aggression. To submerge himself in the "team" is to create a barrier to self-assertion, however admirable this may seem to team players. The failure to take on McCarthy is further confounded by the real possibility that Eisenhower had long repressed hostile feelings toward Marshall that existed side by side with gratitude and respect for his superior officer. In any case, he was mute in defending a highly regarded general later to become famous for the Marshall Plan for the reconstruction of Europe.

The second critical incident in viewing Eisenhower's risk profile as president is the uncertainty surrounding the submission of the 1958 budget during 1957. The budget called for an expenditure of about $72 billion. It provided for some increases in defense spending and foreign aid and several domestic initiatives including school construction and welfare. The political scientist Richard Neustadt uses the fiscal 1958 budget to chronicle the lack of awareness on the part of Eisenhower of his powers and of the need of other people, notably in the Congress, to use presidential power.[11]

Briefly, the Eisenhower budget for the fiscal year 1958 went to the Congress on January 16, 1957. Secretary of the Treasury Humphrey, with Eisenhower's blessing, held a press conference in which he read a statement expressing some unhappiness with the size of the budget. In response to a question following his prepared remarks, Humphrey said, evidently with considerable heat:

> If the government cannot reduce the "terrific" tax burden of the country, I will predict that you will have a depression that will curl your hair, because we are just taking too much money out of this economy that we need to make jobs that you have to have as time goes on.[12]

To add to the confusion about what the president stood for, Eisenhower held a press conference shortly after Humphrey's press conference. Eisenhower supported his secretary of the treasury, seemingly unmindful of the fact that his support went against his own budget. The doubts about Eisenhower appeared greatest among his supporters in the Congress who believed he was committed to "modern republicanism," a new party stance counter to the old image of the reactionary, isolationist Republican Party. Indeed, on the eve of his reelection in 1956, Eisenhower had addressed the nation, proclaiming that modern republicanism had arrived and was the wave of the future. While these events caused confusion about what Eisenhower believed in his definition of modern republicanism, later he sided strongly with conservatives. If one defines the presidency as an opportunity to create a vision, as with the concept of modern republicanism, and to lead the party in making this vision real, then the direction and aims of the president become clear in the call to enlist support among his constituents. Eisenhower switched positions and became more like the conservative wing of his party. For those who promoted his candidacy in the hopes of creating a new Republican Party, he must have been a disappointment.

The events surrounding the fiscal 1958 budget showed a tendency in Eisenhower to confuse his friends and foes alike. Was this tendency reflective of a certain political astuteness and Machiavellianism in which the object of the political exercise is to placate potential adversaries while maintaining the loyalties of friends and associates? His initial budget proposal was aligned with "modern republicanism." Through Secretary Humphrey, and later his own statements to the press, the criticism of the budget was meant to solidify his relationship with the people from whom he had wrested the nomination. Perhaps the answer is that, as president, Eisenhower held few beliefs consciously, and as issues evolved, he became aware of a deep conservatism that finally held sway. The case of his confrontation with Governor Orville Faubus in Little Rock, Arkansas, provides another incident critical to a political understanding of the Eisenhower presidency.

The facts of the case are simple enough. The Supreme Court had ruled that "separate but equal" was unconstitutional and that schools had to integrate so that blacks and whites would sit together in the nation's schools. Governor Faubus defied the Supreme Court order and refused to integrate the schools in Arkansas. He called out the state's National Guard and prevented black students from entering the high school in Little Rock. Eisenhower agreed to meet with Faubus in Newport, Rhode Island, where the president was vacationing. Evidently, he believed he could persuade Faubus to comply with the court order without the necessity of his interventions. This was not the case and a specific court order was issued.

Faubus withdrew the state's National Guard following the court order, and rioting ensued. After much vacillation and in direct response to a plea from the Mayor of Little Rock, who feared the rioting crowds, President Eisenhower placed the National Guard under federal control and ordered federal troops into Little Rock, forcing compliance with the law. Eventually, blacks sat with whites in the high school, but after the school had remained closed for a year while the issue of compliance played itself out. Once again, the question of President Eisenhower's beliefs and commitments were unclear.

Eisenhower's problem in the Faubus case was his ambivalent position regarding civil rights. He steadfastly refused to meet with a delegation of black leaders during bombings of churches in the South. But uncertainties about his position heightened when he issued the following statement to the press: "I can't imagine any set of circumstances that would ever induce me to send federal troops . . . into any area to enforce the orders of a federal court, because I believe that [the] common sense of America will never require it."[13]

Evidently, Eisenhower failed to persuade Faubus to comply with the law, but instead set the stage for the withdrawal of the National Guard and the ensuing riots, which forced Eisenhower to make a decision in favor of compliance with the law and send in federal troops to Little Rock.

With the Arkansas events in mind, Ambrose concluded as follows:

> With regard to civil rights, an area in which the depth of commitment of the American people was considerably less than the commitment to civil liberties, Eisenhower's refusal to lead was almost criminal. Who can say what might have been accomplished in dealing with this most permanent of problems had President Eisenhower joined Chief Justice Warren in enthusiastically supporting racial equality and justice? But he did not; and by putting the problem off, by leaving it to his successors, he just made it worse.[14]

While most biographers and commentators treat Eisenhower kindly, as did the American people, the critical comments, such as Ambrose's, offer rather thin explanations of why Eisenhower acted as he did both in the military and the presidency. There seems to be general agreement that America liked Ike and there was little he could do or avoid doing that would damage this affection. Writers attribute this affection to Ike's personality. He was warm, his smile engaging, and he rarely confronted another person, even indirectly, to diminish that person's self-esteem. Even in the case of McCarthy, whom he purportedly disliked, he avoided the negative. In dealing with his personality, authors attribute Eisenhower's behavior principally to the need to avoid conflict and to be liked.

To conclude merely that Ike's low risk profile reflected a need to be liked is unsatisfactory. Or, to evaluate Eisenhower's presidency in the simplistic terms of Herbert Parmet, "to label [Eisenhower] a great or good or even a weak President misses the point. He was merely necessary."[15]

This evaluation suggests that there was extraordinary compliance between the man as he was and the nation he was elected to lead. While true, this fit between the person and the situation still leads to the fundamental question of character formation, of what makes the man who fits the times so well.

Human beings are all recognizable to themselves and others. The stability of character, the window of recognition, is revealing. In Eisenhower's case, what was recognizable was his optimism and his fund of goodwill. He was an organizer who imposed a plan of order on the jobs he held and the tasks at hand. As a military officer, he responded strongly to the staff system that he established and he continued doing so during his presidency. He was comfortable with an organization chart and the presence of a chief of staff to arrange the order of issues to be brought to his attention. He functioned through staff meetings with subordinates. The rule of these meetings was deliberation and consensus. He delegated. He defined jobs and chains of command. He expected issues to be brought to him with recommendations. Besides needing to be liked, he needed order. This need could be seen solely as a reflection of experience. But the need for order was an aspect of his character, the familiar and habitual responses to external and internal stimuli.

Another aspect of his character was his aversion to interpersonal conflict. He could easily delay responses and avoid confrontations, in the interests of turning away from conflict. His aversion to conflict translates itself into a low propensity for risk. In general, he maintained few strong beliefs about substantive issues, a frame of mind that played into his desire to avoid conflict and, hence, to avoid risk.

There is a paradox in the Eisenhower story. Eisenhower achieved extraordinary personal popularity. Yet he was unwilling, or unable, to perceive this esteem as power to be used in the service of ideas and ideals. Power for chief executives both in elective politics and in business is personal power. It begins with the institutional framework of office that provides various elements of authority. The foundation of the role is the legal terms by which a person is designated to assume authority and to function with the legitimacy of command in the superior-subordinate relationships contained in the hierarchy. But beyond these elementary facts of office, wide expanse exists in how the role is to be enacted and the programs and policies to be defined and implemented. At some point, institutional authority leads to personal power, with the risk attendant to an individual becoming corrupted by personal power. If an individual eschews power, as in Eisenhower's case, erosion occurs, and there is no chance for subordinacy to work its wonders, permitting other people to advance programs and policies the chief executive initiates. The critical element in the transformation of institutional authority into personal power is a phenomenon of the mind called internalization.

Who we are and how we come to recognize ourselves and, in turn, are recognizable to others is an outgrowth of development, from infancy on to adulthood. It is one thing to be governed by outside agencies. It is another to be governed by our own internal standards. This transformation from external to internal control is the result of the incorporation into the psyche of representations of parents and subsequent power figures who play an important part in development. Over time, the internal standards and expectations become abstract and relatively independent of the internalized power figures from the past. Thus, General Fox Conner had a lasting effect on Eisenhower and, presumably, remained important as a representation of ideals of the military. It would not be stretching the limits of psychological interpretation to suggest that Fox Conner entered into the processes of internalization and therefore had a lasting impact on Eisenhower as a man and a military officer.

If we accept the descriptions of Eisenhower as averse to interpersonal risk, a man who needed to be liked, who sought consensus, who was subject to the influence of the last person who spoke to him, and, above all, who resisted making decisions until forced by circumstances, the psychological profile that emerges is one of an individual who had difficulty dealing with aggression. This interpretation may seem odd given the fact that Eisenhower's entire career before becoming president was rooted in warfare. But, having noted this fact, we should also recognize that Eisenhower was an organization man, attached to warfare in a much different way than a field general such as George Patton.

The transformation from institutional authority to personal power requires a wide tolerance of aggression. It is here that Emmet Hughes's comment, quoted earlier, about Eisenhower's fervor for the "team," his exhortations about cooperation and selflessness, is apt. Hughes wondered if Eisenhower's exhortations "were not addressed, perhaps only half-consciously, as much to himself as to others."[16]

Eisenhower displayed a rebellious streak in his cadet days at West Point. He was somewhat older than the average cadet, and he managed to accumulate demerits as he violated rules about smoking and the like. He was not the model cadet either in deportment or in academics. But, somehow, he suppressed these rebellious tendencies and even managed to endure the years when his career was on dead center. Even during the years with MacArthur in the Philippines, Eisenhower, for the most part, contained his aggression in the face of the astonishing egoism MacArthur continually displayed. He served with MacArthur for ten years, five in Washington when MacArthur was chief of staff, and five in the Philippines. Of his work with MacArthur in the Philippines, Ambrose wrote:

> Nothing he did [in the Philippines] met any of the criteria he himself had set down for a happy life. His work was neither rewarding nor suited to his age and abilities. It was also terribly frustrating and, when the test came, proved to be worthless, as the Japanese in 1941 easily conquered the Philippine Army he had labored to help create. His close and warm relationship with MacArthur became distant and cold. His best friend died in an accident. Mamie was ill and bedridden much of the time. John was the only member of the family who enjoyed the Philippines and prospered there. The best that can be said for Eisenhower's years with the Philippine Army was that he gained some experience in juggling and cutting national budgets.

Perhaps gaining experience in juggling budgets was second best in appraising what Eisenhower learned during his frustrating years in the Philippines. He also learned to endure and to contain frustration with the aid of a defense mechanism of the ego called reaction formation. This defense turns anger into tolerance of frustration, but also impassiveness that observers often take for a genial personality. Enduring and containing frustration and its complement, anger, affect the ego. Eisenhower offered his own sense of the need to contain anger. In a rare run in with General Marshall, while Eisenhower served on Marshall's staff in Washington, Eisenhower lost his temper. Marshall informed Eisenhower that he intended to keep him in Washington and deliver promotions to field officers rather than staff. Eisenhower softened his outburst as he was leaving Marshall's office, but soon felt an upsurge of frustration and anger that he would once again be deprived of field command and promotions. Eisenhower confided to his diary, after he destroyed the angry pages he had written the day before, "Anger cannot win, it cannot even think clearly. . . . I blaze for an hour! So, for many years I've made it a religion never to indulge myself, but yesterday I failed."[17]

The face Eisenhower presented to the world gave no hint of the degree to which he had to labor to control his aggression. As with all human beings, this control came at a price. And perhaps Emmet Hughes caught the aspect of Eisenhower's personality that suppressed anger at frustrating circumstances and repressed aggression in ways that went beyond particular circumstances to become an integral part of his character and the definition of a presidency marked by passivity. Whether he was placating Montgomery, avoiding confrontation with McCarthy, playing into Treasury Secretary Humphrey's violation of the power of the presidency, or miscalculating the intent of Governor Faubus, who, in the end, forced Eisenhower's hand, the man could not take a chance on himself. Thus, he avoided risk and confrontation until it was too late. The end result was the sacrifice of the most important aspect of executive leadership: the transformation of institutional authority into personal power.

The argument could be made that Eisenhower's true beliefs were those of a conservative belief system in which the principle to follow is to do no harm, or to avoid making a bad situation worse. The measure of the man, especially as president of the United States, could include certain criteria that were center stage at the time he was being courted to accept the nomination of the Republican Party. His advocates were Eastern Republicans with a history of centrism, of acceptance of the changes that occurred during the New Deal, and the recognition that the United States was inevitably a player on the world stage. He undoubtedly disappointed his supporters. He could not bring himself to become the leader of his party and to carry through lasting transformations into what he once called modern republicanism.

3

A Disengaged President: Ronald Reagan and His Lieutenants

Donald Regan had been in office for less than two months as secretary of the treasury under President Ronald Reagan when he wrote a note to himself:

> To this day I have never had so much as 1 minute alone with Ronald Reagan! Never has he, or anyone else, sat down in private to explain to me what is expected of me, what goals he would like to see me accomplish, what results he wants. Since I am accustomed to management by objective, where people have *in writing* what is expected and explicit standards are set, this has been most disconcerting. How can one do a job if the job is not defined? I have been struggling to do what I consider the job to be, and let others tell me if I'm wrong, or not doing the right thing. (So far no one has said!) This . . . is dangerous.[1]

At the beginning of President Reagan's second term, Donald Regan and James Baker switched jobs. Regan became chief of staff and Baker secretary of the treasury. There was little discussion when Baker, Regan, and Michael Deaver met with the president to consider the change, although Regan gave the president ample opportunity to consider, discuss, and think about going forward with the new assignments. Reagan simply accepted the proposal and it was a done deed. The meeting on this important decision lasted about 30 minutes.

In 1989, Nancy Reagan published a memoir, entitled *My Turn*. The title is apt, reflecting Nancy Reagan's need to explain herself and, possibly, to get even with the press and, particularly, Donald Regan, whom she despised. Mrs. Reagan had taken on the assignment of protecting her husband. Her anxiety in carrying out this assignment, self-chosen as it was, heightened whenever the president was in trouble. For President Reagan, the trouble peaked during the Iran-Contra affair, and Donald Regan became the focus of Nancy's anxiety. After he was fired under pressure from her, Donald Regan revealed the fact that he had not been able to schedule activity for the president without consulting with Mrs. Reagan, who, in turn, cleared the proposed dates with her "friend," a California astrologer. In exasperation, Regan had gone as far as hanging up the telephone on Mrs. Reagan, whose frequent calls became more than he could bear.

President Reagan was reluctant to fire Regan (euphemistically speaking, he finally resigned) because he liked him. Besides, he had difficulty with any kind of confrontation. Mrs. Reagan kept after him to fire Regan, but he would not budge. She arranged to have William Rogers and Robert Strauss go to the White House to meet President Reagan in the living quarters to convince him to fire Regan. Rogers was passive and indirect, but Strauss openly criticized Regan for not being effective with the Congress and the press. Even so, President Reagan would not act. Mrs. Reagan did not ease up her pressure on him. Regan submitted a terse and obviously angry letter of resignation on February 27, 1987, because the information leaked that he would resign the following Monday. Mrs. Reagan wrote in her book, "That night, for the first time in weeks, I slept well."[2]

One of the accusations hurled at Donald Regan was that he did not understand his job as chief of staff. He was accused of acting as a "chief operating officer" rather than head of staff. This accusation was meant to indicate that he was usurping the president's position and responsibility. But as we have seen, President Reagan had not defined the job for Regan, and, given the president's passivity, Regan defined the job as he went along.

Specific criticism of Donald Regan's performance came from the Tower Commission established to investigate the Iran-Contra scandal. The commission concluded that Donald Regan should have assured an orderly process in the development of the Iran initiative. Thus, while Nancy Reagan criticized Regan for exerting excessive control over the White House, the Tower Commission faulted Regan for exercising too little control, especially over the activity of the national security advisor and his staff. One could conclude that Regan, in departing from the Treasury, had entered a power world completely foreign to him, given President Reagan's detachment from issues requiring his direct involvement. Unfortunately for Regan, as chief of staff to a passive president, he was in a no-win situation.

Donald Regan was not the only subordinate puzzled by President Reagan's style of leadership. Other key subordinates, particularly those outside the California circle, were also perplexed. David Stockman, the head of the Office of Management and Budget, was at a loss as to how to carry out his job in the face of Reagan's passivity. Stockman's frustration became public in an article in *Atlantic Monthly*,[3] in which he charged Reagan with abandoning supply-side economics. Stockman was a true believer in fiscal conservatism. He saw himself as a warrior in the battle called the Reagan Revolution. Taxes would be cut drastically, defense spending increased dramatically, and social spending, including social security, slashed materially. The net result would be a balanced budget and a diminished role for the federal government—true to Reagan's promise to get government off the backs of the people.

Stockman was a zealot, but, much to his sorrow, he discovered that politics in America, based on interests and emotions, did not follow a revolutionary script. He came up against the brutal reality that the Reagan budget was deeply inconsistent. It called for the first two points—reduction of taxes and increase in defense spending—but it also proposed that social security and other social spending be kept intact. The budget could not be balanced if the administration pursued this program.

Stockman later confessed that he had misunderstood Ronald Reagan. He had believed in Reagan's public pronouncements of revolutionary right-wing ideals. He stated in his book (written in 1986 following his resignation a year earlier),

> The fact was, due to the efforts of myself and my supply-side compatriots, Ronald Reagan had been made to stumble into the wrong camp on the eve of his final, successful quest for the presidency. He was a consensus politician, not an ideologue. He had no business trying to make a revolution because it wasn't in his bones.[4]

Where Nancy Reagan carried the battle to remove Donald Regan, the California triumvirate of Deaver, Meese, and Nofziger were after Stockman's scalp, because, in their eyes (and Nancy Reagan's as well), with the *Atlantic* article, Stockman had violated the cardinal rule of presidential appointments: be loyal. James Baker, the chief of staff, held another view. While Stockman was probably indiscreet, the Reagan administration badly needed him, because he was the only person who understood the budget process. Baker convinced the president, who characteristically hated to fire anyone, to give Stockman a scolding but to retain him. Baker himself gave Stockman a tongue-lashing and prepared him to meet Reagan privately at lunch. Baker's final comment to Stockman was that he wanted to see Stockman's "ass dragging along the carpet floor" as he went into the Oval Office.

President Reagan listened to Stockman's account of his conversion to supply-side ideology with eyes moistening and finally asked Stockman to stay in the job. Nancy Reagan believed the president should have fired Stockman the afternoon the *Atlantic* story appeared. According to Mrs. Reagan, the president later regretted not firing Stockman. She wrote, "If Ronnie had thrown Stockman out when that story appeared in *The Atlantic Monthly,* he would have made an example of him. It would have been a signal to everyone else who worked for Ronnie that he expected their loyalty. And who knows? Maybe we wouldn't have had so many kiss-and-tell books about the Reagan years."[5]

A would-be assassin shot President Reagan on March 30, 1981. Fortunately, the president survived the bullet wound. There was little firm news about his condition. With Vice President Bush on a plane returning to Washington, reporters pressed Larry Speakes, the press secretary, on who was in charge of the government in the face of the president's likely incapacity and the vice president's absence. Speakes could not answer the questions to reporters' satisfaction, and his uncertainty created the risk of public panic. Secretary Haig, observing with other officials this hastily formed press conference on television, evidently became agitated, left the meeting room, and rushed upstairs to where the press conference was being held. More than the words he used, Haig's agitated manner alarmed the press and the viewing public.

Lou Cannon's biography of Ronald Reagan describes the background and events, including Haig's taking over the press conference, leading to Haig's demise as secretary of state. Haig blurted out, "I'm in control here," in an agitated manner that suggested he was out of control. According to Cannon, Haig had a bad temper and easily detected slights, minor or major, to his position and prerogatives.[6] And his resignation, when it came, was over a clash with William Clark, Reagan's then national security advisor, over prerogatives. Haig had issued directives that Clark felt were properly President Reagan's prerogative. Haig offered his resignation unless the President supported him and made clear his preeminent position on foreign policy. After much backing and filling, Reagan arranged to have George Shultz accept the post of secretary of state and immediately called a press conference to announce Haig's resignation and Shultz's appointment.

Another key subordinate who was harmed by the opacity of Reagan's style was Michael Deaver, Reagan's deputy chief of staff. Deaver decided to leave his job at the White House to open a public relations firm. He made this decision in February of 1985, secure in the knowledge that he had helped the president achieve a landslide reelection to a second term. The decision to leave brought to a close two decades of an extraordinarily close relationship that had lasted throughout Reagan's political career. Perhaps of equal significance to his service to Ronald Reagan was his closeness to Nancy Reagan, whose primary, self-defined mission in life was the protection of her husband. Nancy's mission, in a sense, defined Michael Deaver's job, which was mainly in the sphere of public relations and image building for Ronald Reagan.

Deaver's last assignment before becoming a public relations consultant was to prepare for President Reagan's visit to the Bitburg Cemetery to fulfill a promise he had made to German Chancellor Helmut Kohl to participate in a ceremony at the military cemetery as an act of reconciliation. Deaver was not aware, nor was he informed, that Bitburg was the burial site of 49 members of the Waffen SS, the guard unit at the death camps.

In his memoir, *Behind the Scenes,* Deaver takes full responsibility for the firestorm of outrage following the disclosure that President Reagan would attend a wreath laying ceremony at the Bitburg Cemetery. Deaver wrote, "This was one of those periods when no one seemed to be talking about anything else. The economy, Nicaragua, everything else had been moved to the back burner. The president was hurting. I felt like falling on my sword."[7]

Nancy Reagan was furious that her husband was in trouble, and she vented her anger at Deaver. "I could not recall our ever before having been on opposite sides of an issue. But now she was convinced that I had ruined her husband's presidency and perhaps the rest of his life. We had a very painful emotional confrontation."[8]

Deaver managed to overcome the negative public relations fallout, taking advantage of a piece of good luck. General Matthew Ridgeway, the 90-year-old general, who was the only living four-star general of World War II, offered to accompany the president and lay the wreath. Reagan accepted the offer but modified it so that he and the general would lay the wreath together, and the president and the presidency weathered the storm.

The public relations firm Deaver formed after he left the White House in the spring of 1985 was an instant success. He had riches beyond his belief, but trouble was soon to ruin him. His success came from his closeness to Ronald Reagan; clients appeared, presumably expecting his access to the president to work miracles for them in solving their public and government relations problems. Deaver was indicted for and convicted of perjury during a special prosecution's investigations into influence peddling—a federal crime.

Deaver fought another battle, this one against himself. He was an alcoholic. He finally accepted the fact that his drinking was out of control, a precondition for recovery, and sought treatment.

In his memoir, Deaver tells a story that vividly portrays the pain he felt in his fall from power and the loss of his relationship with Ronald Reagan.

> A few weeks earlier [referring to his visit with Bud McFarlane who was recovering from a suicide attempt], at Christmas, Carolyn and I were invited to the White House for a small dinner party. The subject of trading arms with Iran was carefully avoided, but I eagerly brought up another, more promising subject. "I don't want to talk business with you, Mr. President," I said, "but in a few days you are going to give the Citizenship Medal to the *Voyager* crew, out in California." (Pilots Dick Rutan and Jeana Yeager had circled the globe without refueling, sharing for one week a cockpit the size of a phone booth.)
>
> "Why don't you give them the Medal of Freedom?" I went on. "These people epitomize all that you believe in: private enterprise, daring, a new world record without a dime of federal support. Five years out there in a little town in the Mojave Desert, sleeping on the floor, putting it together. It's a feat up there with Lindbergh crossing the Atlantic and Chuck Yeager breaking the sound barrier. It's the American dream."
>
> The president, seated in the chair next to mine, cocked his head and said, "Mike, I've got competent people at the White House who make these decisions."
>
> It seemed as if the twenty years I had worked for him had vanished in the blink of an eye.[9]

Secretary of State George Schultz was, in his turn, subject to the difficulties of working with a disengaged president. His years in the Reagan cabinet tell the story, yet again, of the effect Reagan's style had on his lieutenants.

Schultz felt on a number of occasions that his power and prestige in foreign affairs had been threatened and even undermined by others. On these occasions he told the president he intended to resign. In each case, Reagan gave way and prevailed on him to continue as secretary of state.

In the fall of 1985, Admiral Poindexter, then head of the National Security Council (NSC), promulgated an order under President Reagan's signature, supported by the CIA, the FBI, and the Defense Department, to conduct lie detector tests on federal employees, including members of the cabinet and the vice president. News of the order appeared in the press, causing a furor. George Shultz had long opposed lie detector tests, believing that they were unreliable and would undermine morale, that the order would imply that the president did not trust his staff. When Shultz held a press conference to introduce the members of an advisory commission on South Africa, the conference inevitably turned to the issue of the lie detector tests. "Don Oberdorfer of the *Washington Post* then asked me whether I would take such a test if asked to do so. 'Once,' I answered. 'Once?' he followed up. 'Once,' I repeated. 'The minute in this government that I am told that I'm not trusted is the day that I leave.' I then walked out of the room."[10]

Following this press conference, as Shultz put it, "all hell broke loose." As a reporter for the *New York Times* put it, this marked the first time Secretary Shultz had publicly dissociated himself from a presidential order. Shultz had a meeting with the president in the Oval Office and presented his arguments in opposition to the order Reagan had signed. Reagan backed off, and the order was nullified. Shultz and Poindexter negotiated a press release with Shultz making sure that the president would not be represented as "eating crow."

Schultz was newer than the California group, which included Weinberger, to the counsels of Ronald Reagan. Schultz had come in contact with Reagan first in August 1974, when Reagan, then governor of California, invited him to brief him on the workings of the federal government. Shultz had recently resigned as secretary of the treasury. Evidently, the presidency was much on Reagan's mind, hence the briefing request to Shultz.

When Reagan tapped him for the job of secretary of state, Shultz, unlike Donald Regan, seemed unperturbed by the sudden and seemingly hasty request. Shultz was in London attending an important meeting as president of the Bechtel Corporation (a construction company with worldwide activities). He received a telephone call from William Clark, who asked him to take a call from the president from a secure telephone at the American embassy. President Reagan asked him to become secretary of state to replace Alexander Haig, whose resignation, ambivalently offered, the president had chosen to accept.

> As we talked, it dawned on me that President Reagan wanted me to say yes then and there. "Mr. President, are you asking me to accept this job now over the phone?" "Well, yes, I am, George," he replied. "It would help a lot because it's not a good idea to leave a post like this vacant. When we announce that Secretary Haig has resigned, we'd like to announce that I have nominated you to be secretary of state."[11]

Shultz accepted.

He immediately flew to Washington and was met by James Baker, chief of staff; Edwin Meese, counselor to the president; Michael Deaver, assistant to the president; and William Clark, national security advisor. The group flew to Camp David in a waiting helicopter. It was a Saturday and the president and Mrs. Reagan were spending the weekend there.

> As President Reagan and I surveyed the world from this relaxed country setting, the challenges I faced were daunting. The president and his White House staff talked less about those challenges than about organization and working relationships. I could detect ongoing institutional tensions between the White House and State Department.[12]

Shultz reassured the president and his White House staff that he intended to work for the White House as secretary of state. So far in his presidency, Reagan had been unable to develop and implement a coherent foreign policy. He and his staff seemed to believe that the problem resided in the temperamental personality of Alexander Haig, who wanted to run foreign affairs without White House interference. Shultz was a more subtle person. He did not use his first meeting with the president to establish clear lines of responsibility. He expressed sentiments of cooperation the president wanted to hear, and by saying he wanted to work for the White House, he accepted the primacy of the president without relinquishing his status as secretary of state.

> Washington insiders were saying that the foreign affairs system in Washington wasn't working after a year and a half of the Reagan presidency and Haig's secretaryship. Former National Security advisor Zbigniew Brzezinski had just said in an interview that the United States had a choice in making foreign policy: the president does it all, and he and the NSC (National Security Council) advisor overshadow the secretary of state; or, the secretary of state, in close communication with the president, is allowed to go to work. "What has surprised me about the last 18 months is that we have had neither the first nor the second system." Brzezinski said, "The president has not been actively involved, but the secretary of state has not been permitted to run foreign policy. I hope now, with Mr. Shultz coming on, that the president will decide to let the secretary of state run foreign policy and be recognized as the man in charge."[13]

Whatever President Reagan's intentions, which were not articulated at the time, Secretary Shultz would find himself constantly up against the ideas and power sensitivities of the various incumbents of the office of the national security advisor, the secretary of defense, and the CIA. With Shultz in office as secretary of state, these competitors for influence had a formidable adversary in gaining the attention and support of the president.

As commonly occurred during the Reagan administration, coalitions formed to advance one side or another in forming and carrying out foreign policy initiatives. In one case, Clark and his coalition, which included Weinberger, Casey, and the National Security Office, prepared to mine the Nicaraguan harbor without authorization or support from Congress and without the advice and approval of the State Department. This action, if taken, would have been an act of war and would have been reminiscent of the faulty actions taken in Vietnam. On the other side, Shultz led a coalition including James Baker, Michael Deaver, and, most importantly, Nancy Reagan. Mrs. Reagan wanted Clark fired. When this appeared evident to Shultz, he recognized that Clark's days in the White House were numbered. (In her memoir, Nancy Reagan wrote, "Bill Clark, who came in 1981 as deputy secretary of state, was another bad choice, in my opinion. I didn't think he was qualified for the job—or for his subsequent position as national security advisor. I wasn't the only one who felt that way; he embarrassed himself in front of the Senate Foreign Relations Committee when he couldn't name the prime minister of Zimbabwe. Clark had been in Ronnie's administration in Sacramento, but even then I had never really gotten along with him. He struck me as a user—especially when he traveled around the country claiming he represented Ronnie, which usually wasn't true. I spoke to Ronnie about him, but Ronnie liked him, so he stayed around longer than I would have liked.")[14]

The rivalry between the two coalitions, the ideologues and the pragmatists, continued over the question of who would replace Clark as the national security advisor. The pragmatists wanted James Baker, the chief of staff. The ideologues, including Weinberger and Casey, opposed Baker because he was identified with the pragmatists, and wanted Bud McFarlane. The ideologues won out.

Throughout his tenure as secretary of state, Schultz remained vigilant in defending his role in foreign affairs, and aggressive in overcoming competition from the Defense Department, the NSC and staff, and the CIA. But there was a limit to his capacity, and also his willingness, to do battle to protect the integrity of the State Department's responsibility for foreign affairs.

> On August 5, 1996, I gave the president my letter of resignation. He did not accept it. I did not want to abandon him, but I felt I must correct the indecisiveness and backbiting involved in the current NSC and White House processes. I also knew when it came to anti-communist dictators, he and I were just not on the same wavelength. And I was sick and tired of fighting the same battles on Soviet matters over and over again. "You might be better off without me," I told him.[15]

Donald Regan, then chief of staff, spoke to Shultz on behalf of the president, urging him to remain as secretary of state. Shultz unburdened himself, describing all the frustrations he endured, given the efforts of the national security advisor and staff, the Department of Defense, and the CIA to block him in his approach to foreign policy. Shultz and his staff believed the time was ripe to reach some accords with the Soviet Union leading to the elimination of intermediate range missiles in Europe and a reduction in strategic arms.

Donald Regan believed the president was ready to "bang heads" to solve the problems Shultz was experiencing. Being realistic and knowing the president's inability to deal with conflict among his cabinet officers and advisors, Shultz remained skeptical but stayed in the job, preparing to focus negotiations with the Soviet Union on arms reduction.

Change was under way in the Soviet Union, culminating in the accession of Gorbachev to the position of general secretary of the Communist Party on March 11, 1985. Shultz had been busy preparing Reagan for the new approach to the Soviet Union. A change in Reagan's attitudes and public pronouncements seemed essential to meet the more forthcoming position reflected in the new Soviet leadership. (It was only two years earlier, in March 1983 that Reagan, in a speech to the National Association of Evangelicals, had called the Soviet Union an "evil empire.")

Reagan had been aghast to learn well before he became president that there was no assured defense against nuclear attack. World peace was dependent on the concept of mutually assured destruction (MAD) encapsulated in a treaty signed in 1972. If either the Soviet Union or the United States launched a nuclear attack, retaliation would result in massive destruction of the attacker. To Reagan, the idea that the United States had no primary defense against nuclear attack was abhorrent. For some, the Strategic Defense Initiative (SDI) was a new version of the Maginot Line and Fortress America, visions of a new arms race and general destabilizing of world peace.

Shultz's initial reaction when he learned of the SDI speech two days before it was to be delivered was disbelief and horror. He worked hard to soften the drafts of the speech and tried to convince the president of the true practical significance of what he, Reagan, was proposing to advance as his vision. Tactically, Shultz supported the idea of SDI as a research effort that would be consistent with the 1972 Anti-Ballistic Missile (ABM) treaty and avoid its violation. He did not make a frontal attack on the idea, knowing that Reagan had become impassioned with his vision of a defense against nuclear attack. Reagan's support for this vision and his speech presenting it for the first time came from his science advisor, Edward Teller, and seemingly from the Joint Chiefs of Staff (JCS). For Shultz and his aides, the chiefs lacked credibility to opine on the feasibility of this vision. On purely technical and scientific grounds, the chiefs were out on a limb, even lacking support from the secretary of defense. Indeed, the chiefs backed off from their assurance to Reagan as preparation for his speech continued.

Predictably, the speech declaring an SDI program alarmed the Russians, along with America's allies—including Reagan's friend Margaret Thatcher—Congress, the many experts in foreign affairs, and the political/technological experts on arms control.

As much as MAD appeared to leave the American people vulnerable to nuclear attack, it had maintained the peace precisely because America's main adversary, Russia, had the same fears of preemptive attack and the mutual destruction that would follow. The thrust of American foreign policy, whether led by Republicans or Democrats, was to improve on the treaties underlying MAD, including, especially, movement toward disarmament, both nuclear and conventional. Furthermore, the United States had an obligation to look after the interests of its allies. Hence the anxiety that Reagan's SDI was an extension of the historical isolationist forces in America mostly associated with the Republican Party of which President Reagan was the titular head.

SDI held center stage during the summit meeting in Reykjavik, Iceland (October 11 and 12, 1986). This summit was billed as a nonsummit, a weekend meeting of Reagan and Gorbachev. But it turned into a major substantive negotiation centered on the elimination of nuclear armament through adherence to the ABM Treaty over a ten-year period, with reduction of nuclear weapons in five-year stages. The sticking point, which resulted in the termination of the negotiations, was SDI. Gorbachev insisted on abiding by the ABM Treaty of 1972 restricting SDI to the laboratory, while Reagan fervently held to his position to permit testing and development outside the laboratory. In Shultz's memoir, he claims that Reykjavik was an astonishing success in that Gorbachev had made proposals that moved Russia far toward the American position on nuclear arms. He defends Reagan's insistence on allowing SDI testing outside of the laboratory. At one point in the negotiations, when Reagan and Gorbachev were arguing repeatedly over SDI, Reagan passed a note to Shultz, asking, "Am I right?" Shultz whispered his assent, which firmed even more Reagan's conviction to go forward with SDI both in and outside the laboratory.[16]

During the final press conference, following the break-off that weekend, Shultz and his aides appeared bleak and upset. Shultz's lips quivered, and Max Kampelman, the State Department negotiator, was in tears.[17] The United States and the Soviet Union had come within reach of an agreement to relinquish offensive nuclear weapons over time.

Instead of holding to the image of failure, the Reagan administration went on a public relations blitz to convey the impression that Reykjavik had been a success, disarmament was within reach, and both sides would continue meeting to try to complete an agreement.

The public relations blitz had some success, particularly with the general public, which seemed to accept the interpretation that Reagan was in control and would not relinquish the defensive shield called SDI.

But the professionals in foreign policy, defense, and the Congress were horrified over the specter that a relatively unprepared American negotiating team, including the president, had been on the verge of giving up nuclear offensive weapons. Frances Fitzgerald, in her book on Star Wars (SDI), provides a vivid description of the horrified reactions among the experts and the allies.[18]

> Washington journalists and others following the story were flabbergasted. Had Reagan almost bargained away the entire U.S. nuclear deterrent or only a part of it? The very question sent shock waves through the American defense community. In the weeks that followed, Richard Nixon, Henry Kissinger, James Schlesinger, Brent Scowcroft, Sbigniew Brzezinski, Jim Woolsey, Les Aspin, Dick Cheney, Dante Frascelli, and others took to the airwaves and wrote articles in the major newspapers and foreign-policy journals on the folly of Reykjavik. Members of the House and Senate Armed Services Committees called for hearings and voiced astonishment over what had occurred. If agreement had not fallen apart over Star Wars, Senator Nunn said, "it would have been the most painfully embarrassing example of American ineptitude in this century, certainly since World War II." Reykjavik, Schlesinger wrote, was "a near disaster from which we were fortunate to escape." The "melange of agreements, near-agreements, and contradictory proposals," Kissinger wrote, "run the risk of undermining deterrence and the cohesion of the Western Alliance." But the consternation of the American defense experts was nothing beside that of the NATO allies. "It was like an earthquake," Margaret Thatcher said. "There was no place you could put your political feet, where you were certain that you could stand."[19]

Deeply troubled by the proposal for the total elimination of nuclear weapons, Admiral William Crowe, the chairman of the Joint Chiefs of Staff, called a meeting of the JCS. Admiral Crowe anticipated that he would soon have to testify before a congressional committee and that he would have to answer no to the obvious question of whether he or the JCS had been consulted on the proposal for the elimination of all nuclear weapons. The chiefs agreed with Admiral Crowe that the president should hear the military opinion on the proposal to eliminate nuclear weapons.

At a meeting of the National Security Planning Group, which included the president, Admiral Crowe made a formal statement outlining the chiefs' negative views of the proposals arising from Reykjavik. Admiral Crowe concluded his statement with the following:

> As your chief military advisor, I do not recommend that you submit this proposal, Mr. President. It is not my intention to make your burdens any greater than they normally are, but this subject is of sufficient significance that I feel I would not be carrying out my responsibilities without informing you.

The following was Reagan's response:

> Admiral, I really love the U.S. military. I have always loved it. Those young men and women do a wonderful job for our country, and everywhere I go, I tell people how proud I am of our armed forces. You oversee a superb organization, one that is not adequately appreciated. But I am constantly trying to get the country to recognize and understand the true value of our military.[20]

Despite the controversy over the so-called zero option—the elimination of nuclear ballistic missiles and eventually all nuclear arms—disarmament talks with the Soviet Union continued, following Reykjavik. On May 8, 1987, Reagan and Gorbachev signed a limited disarmament agreement at a ceremony in the White House.

During the Washington summit, which unlike Reykjavik had been well prepared, a strange event took place. As reported in Shultz's memoir, a large meeting had been staged in the Cabinet Room of the White House following the signing ceremony. As a courtesy, Gorbachev spoke first and described perestroika and his reform efforts in the Soviet Union. Reagan interrupted Gorbachev to tell a story to highlight the differences between the U.S. and Soviet societies.

> An American scholar, on his way to the airport before a flight to the Soviet Union, got into a conversation with his cabdriver, a young man who said that he was still finishing his education. The scholar asked, "When you finish your schooling, what do you want to do?" The young man answered, "I haven't decided yet." After arriving at the airport in Moscow, the scholar hailed a cab. The cabdriver, again, was a young man, who happened to mention he was still getting his education. The scholar, who spoke Russian, asked, "When you finish your schooling, what do you want to be? What do you want to do?" The young man answered, "They haven't told me yet."[21]

Shultz reports that Gorbachev colored upon hearing this story and changed the subject to a substantive issue dealing with reduction in conventional weapons. Reagan had no preparation for this subject and was without briefing materials, so he called on Shultz to respond. Shultz reports that he was upset and felt reluctant to respond, believing that, under the circumstances, the president should have been the main participant.

Following Gorbachev's departure, Shultz, Colin Powell, and Howard Baker, the then chief of staff, met with Reagan and criticized his performance. Reagan was apologetic and asked for advice on how to proceed. There would be no more large meetings and he would be supplied with talking points.[22]

On November 3, 1986, an article appeared in *Al Shiraa*, a Lebanese journal, reporting that the United States had sold weapons to Iran, then engaged in a war with Iraq. McFarlane and Oliver North had gone to Teheran on a mission to provide arms for Teheran in exchange for the release of American hostages. The mission appeared bizarre, not only because it had failed, but because McFarlane carried with him as gifts a Bible and a chocolate cake.

To make matters worse for Reagan and his administration, the news broke that Iran had been overcharged for the Hawk missiles and that the excess funds had been diverted to support the Contras in Nicaragua. Schultz learned of this diversion at a meeting of the National Security Planning Group on Tuesday, November 25, 1986.

The sale of arms to Iran, the diversion of funds, and the transfer of money and arms to the Contras were all illegal. Ronald Reagan was in deep trouble and faced possible impeachment.

When first disclosed, the Iranian venture was presented to the American people as the administration's attempt to improve relations with Iran and to support moderate groups there. Reagan resolutely denied that he was trading arms for hostages. He held press conferences and gave a televised talk, but opinion polls indicated that the American people did not believe him.

Throughout the controversy, Reagan loyalists' sole aim was to protect him. Instead of acting forthrightly and telling the truth, the loyalists lied and conspired to cover up what amounted to a conspiracy to do what he wanted—trade arms for hostages and support the Contras despite the explicit restriction that Congress had imposed.

Once the story came out, the damage control was placed in the hands of Edwin Meese, the attorney general, who took on the assignment of investigating the events. Meese tried to maintain that the president had been unaware of the arms shipment to Iran in November 1985 despite what others, including Shultz, McFarlane, Casey, Poindexter, and even Reagan, knew to be the case. Reagan appointed a special review board to investigate the scandal, with John Tower as chairman and Edmund Muskie and Brent Scowcroft as members.

The report of the special review board presented details on both the Iran arms-for-hostages initiative and the diversion of funds to the Contras. The report emphasized the position of the National Security Agency, its staff, and the national security advisor as creatures of the president. It concluded that the activities of the NSC and the national security advisor had failed to follow a process of "vetting" the Iran initiative and the Contra aid, implying that various legal requirements had been overlooked as a result of sloppy work. The report indirectly referred to Reagan's "management style" and the requirement this style demanded for proper vetting of proposals. It treated this matter of presidential style and its consequences in the unfolding of the scandal gently, neglecting to specify what had proved problematic.[23] That the error might lie in the weaknesses in Reagan's style had not become an explicit line of inquiry for the review board.

On December 19, 1986, a federal court appointed Lawrence Walsh as independent counsel to conduct a criminal investigation of the events and the principals involved in the Iran-Contra scandal. The investigation continued until August 5, 1991, when Walsh submitted a three-volume final report to the Court of Appeals in Washington. The conclusion to the investigation, both symbolically and substantively, was President Bush's pardon of Casper Weinberger, who had been indicted for obstruction of justice and for lying. Bush pardoned Weinberger 12 days before he was to go on trial. At the same time, he pardoned five other people, including Bud McFarlane.[24] Poindexter and North, the two principal actors in the Iran-Contra events, were convicted of various counts of perjury, obstruction of justice, and conspiracy, but had their convictions overturned because of the immunity they received while testifying before congressional committees.

A numbers of memoirs, as well as two major biographies, have been written about the Reagan presidency. Lou Cannon's biography presents a detailed narrative of Reagan's political career. Cannon, a journalist, had followed Reagan's career in politics from his California days through the White House years. His biography is straightforward and represents a superb example of the journalist's craft. Edmund Morris wrote a controversial memoir about "Dutch," as Reagan was known in his early years. Morris, who had won a Pulitzer Prize for his biography of Theodore Roosevelt, became an official biographer after Reagan's landslide reelection in 1984.

The controversy surrounding Morris's *Dutch* centered on his use of a fictional device to develop a sense of immediacy and intimacy in his narrative. He sought to find the person behind the role. He was not able to find Reagan in conventional ways, because, as a person, Reagan was inscrutable. Even to his children, he was an unknowable figure. And to his associates, even those such as Deaver and Meese, who had been with him throughout his political career, he revealed little about himself. Nancy Reagan claimed to know him, but little of the person appears in her memoir. When she complained of all the "kiss-and-tell" books about Reagan, she did not recognize the frustration his associates and his children often felt in their relationship with him.

Morris has confessed that to write the Reagan book he had to overcome severe writer's block. Faced with the prospect of returning the $3 million publisher's advance if he could not deliver a manuscript, he hit on the idea of inserting himself in the memoir as a fictional character growing up in Reagan's childhood milieu and beyond. (Despite this unconventional use of fiction, the reader is never confused by the appearance of fictional characters.)

Lou Cannon gave a largely unfavorable review of *Dutch*. He writes, "Ronald Reagan, the most pleasant of modern presidents, was a frustrating interviewee. While usually friendly and invariably polite, he preserved the mystery of leadership by keeping himself to himself."[25] Cannon describes poring over transcripts of interviews hoping to find neglected scraps of information, presumably to clear up the mystery of the man behind the role. He continues, "Edmund Morris . . . soon learned that access did not guarantee learning much about Dutch. . . . After numerous interviews, he found himself wondering, "How much does Dutch really know?"

The authors of the books on Reagan take as their unifying theme his experience as an actor. Cannon subtitles his biography "the role of a lifetime." Garry Wills wrote an intriguing study of Reagan, thematically linking Reagan to the American psyche. Properly titled *Reagan's America: Innocents at Home*,[26] Wills's book shows that Reagan's appeal lay in his optimism, friendliness, and down-to-earth beliefs in the goodness of Americans. These characteristics, which appeared often in his movie roles and carried forward during his political career, created a bond with the American people. Drawing on Reagan's autobiography (written with Richard G. Hubler) *Where's the Rest of Me,* Wills presents a homespun story of a boyhood in small-town America, a driving ambition that took Reagan from radio broadcasting to Hollywood and then to television as a spokesman for the General Electric Company (GE).[27]

In all the biographies of Reagan, there is only one instance reported about Reagan's personal life in which one can find a trace of an upending event associated with the need for introspection. His divorce from Jane Wyman threw him into a state close to despair. In his book with Hubler, Reagan writes,

> I arrived home . . . to be told I was leaving. I suppose there had been warning signs, if only I hadn't been so busy, but small-town boys grow up thinking only other people get divorced. The plain truth was that such a thing was so far from even being imagined by me that I had no resources to call upon."[28]

In Cannon's biography, the breakup appears even more abrupt than Reagan's version. Reagan arrived home one afternoon and Wyman told him the marriage was over and to "get out."[29] Cannon describes Reagan's characteristic way of dealing with bad news. He was not inclined to turn inward for long. Besides his characteristic optimism, Cannon asserts, Reagan was a denier. He took on the Hollywood pose of the time that family life was sacrosanct and embodied all the virtues of American society. The same pattern of denial appeared during the Iran-Contra scandal. Reagan resolutely maintained that he had not traded and was not trading arms for hostages.[30]

Reagan became the spokesman and sometime actor in the GE television program from 1954 to 1962. Besides acting as host of the *General Electric Theater,* he traveled from one GE plant to another meeting with executives, workers, and local chambers of commerce. During this period, he honed his right-wing speech, even taking the Tennessee Valley Authority (TVA) as an example of the misuse of the government. It happened that TVA was a customer of GE, purchasing power generating equipment. In 1962, GE terminated Reagan's contract with only 24–hours' notice.[31]

Reagan's experience of battling to prevent the radicals from taking over the union when he was president of the Screen Actor's Guild alerted him to the threat of communism. These anticommunist convictions culminated during his presidency with his speech characterizing the Soviet Union as the evil empire.

His attacks on "big government" were based on personal experience, including the Justice Department investigation of MCI, a talent and entertainment agency that represented him during his acting career and arranged his contract with GE. This personalization of his political views became entrenched when he had to pay high taxes on his large earnings following the war.

In all his inscrutability, he might be understood by the simplicity of his beliefs: he identified with the venerable values in the American society (free enterprise, distrust of government, and individual initiative) and he attacked perceived threats to these values. His eight years on the GE circuit created visibility for him and the speech he honed was the foundation of his image as a right-wing Republican politician who was ideologically driven.

The opinions Reagan portrayed during his political career were not the enduring beliefs he had developed from childhood on. He was a Democrat for most of his adult life and an admirer of Franklin Delano Roosevelt and the New Deal. His biographers and memoirists had to explain the transformation.

In a study of the relationship between opinions and personality, the psychologists Smith, Bruner, and White pose the question: "What adjustive functions of personality are served by the formation and maintenance of an opinion?"[32]

Reagan's opinions, beliefs, and values were abundantly clear. How they solidified is equally clear. They derived from two sources. The first, as described above, was his personal experience. The second was his practical orientation to life. He was not a sophisticated thinker, was not well educated through formal schooling, associations with others, or inherent intellectual curiosity. The "functions of personality" that gave rise to and that sustained his opinions were his outward orientation and practical bent. When he paid taxes that took a substantial slice of his income, he had a personal grievance against the federal government and could say with conviction that the government should "get off the backs of the American people."

As a practical and ambitious man, Reagan found reinforcement of his beliefs in his success representing GE. His audiences loved his ideologically laced speeches because he spoke with personal conviction. Had he not received the reinforcement of audience approval, it is not likely he would have held his opinions so fervently—especially as his association with GE came at a time in his life when his movie career was at a low point. He had all the more impetus to believe in the values he espoused as the GE spokesman.

As his career moved into politics and public office, he received further reinforcement in his opinions by his association with wealthy businessmen who supported his ambitions with money. While campaigning for president, and during his first term, he held to his formula-driven opinions and they became policies and mandates to his subordinates. Supply-side economics, what George H. W. Bush later called "voodoo economics," could not be tested analytically by Reagan's own knowledge, or the views of experts whose theories had been subjected to the rigors of the academy. In providing the Defense Department with a blank check, he showed his disinclination to subject the defense budgets to controls such as cost-benefit analysis. With the reluctance of Congress, even the Republicans, to cut other spending, including social security, the nation endured astronomical deficits.

Holding fast to opinions, even in the face of evidence casting doubt as to the validity of those opinions, would seem to produce a state of mind called cognitive dissonance.[33] Dissonance produces unease and anxiety. The methods for resolving dissonance include rational investigation and testing, or altering one's opinions. Or irrationally, one might try to ignore contradictory evidence through a defense mechanism, denial. In the case of denial, the discomfiture and anxiety disappear while the beliefs and opinions remain intact.

When Lou Cannon called Reagan a denier, he was naming Reagan's propensity to overlook or ignore reality. When Reagan denied he was trading arms for hostages, he relied on his capacity to alter reality in his own mind. The more he was presented with the evidence, the stronger his denial. Even his admission, finally, that he was trading arms for hostages was evasive. In a television address to the nation on March 5, 1987, after the Tower Review Board report and in response to his low standing in opinion polls, he said,

> A few months ago, I told the American people I did not trade arms for hostages. My heart and my best intentions still tell me that's true, but the facts and the evidence tell me it is not. As the Tower Board reported, what began as a strategic opening to Iran deteriorated, in its implementation into trading arms for hostages. This runs counter to my own beliefs, to administration policy, and to the original strategy we had in mind. There were reasons why it happened, no excuses. It was a mistake.[34]

Reagan was speaking the words of a speech writer collaborating with Reagan's advisors who wanted to reverse the public's adverse views and regain its trust in Reagan the president. After he had given the televised address, public opinion moved in his favor, but he "reverted" to his old stance denying he was trading arms for hostages. This reversion supports the view that Reagan's mind could overcome reality, a characteristic of a chronic denier.

Reagan's Hollywood experience solidified tendencies already at work in favoring his personalization of experience over abstract thinking and reality testing. Movie making is a world of make-believe. Outside of one's movie roles, success for a practical person involves continually working on one's image and appeal to the public. Reagan became one of Louella Parsons's favorites along with Jane Wyman. As Wills points out, gaining the support of Parsons could easily be tallied in dollars and cents. The translation from movie role to public acclaim involves carrying over a fiction that the role is the real person. Hence, working on the role, creating the public persona, and suppressing the real person have practical economic advantages.

Much the same can be said for politics. Reagan cultivated the persona of amiability, optimism, good humor, and constancy. This persona proved itself to be remarkably effective in gaining public support. Even when bad things happened during his years in public office, he could overcome negative perceptions by projecting the image of the well-meaning and optimistic public servant. This art of using image to mask negative evaluations led to the view that Reagan was a teflon president: nothing stuck.

As much as observers of the art of leadership may find it distasteful to apply Freudian ideas in considering what makes power-oriented people tick, they cannot resist the notion that the past determines the present. Wills, Cannon, and Morris all examine the past to uncover some workable conceptions of the man. For Wills, Reagan's years as a lifeguard on the public beach in Dixon, Illinois, where he saved 76 people, seem indicative of his being both a loner and a responsible person. From morning until dark, seven days a week, he worked his summers in Lowell Park, beginning in 1927 and ending in 1932. He was conscientious and appeared not to mind the boredom and inactivity until an emergency occurred. Newspaper articles recorded his exploits as a lifeguard.[35] There is little indication of what went through his mind as he kept a watchful eye on the river.

Reagan liked to tell stories. He tended to repeat stories often, to the consternation of his subordinates. The stories often came in the midst of policy discussions and diverted attention from serious matters. David Stockman vividly portrays the dismay he felt when Reagan would reach for one of his stories to make a point that was often far off the mark of what was being debated in budget discussions. The stories he told had a purpose: they affected his attitudes. He would repeat stories about waste in government during his California years to deflect his attention from the need for decisions to deal with inconsistencies in, for example, his proposed budgets. Diverting attention away from the need to make painful decisions reflected his difficulties in concentrating on complicated policy issues, such as what to do about the horrendous deficits. But the stories also fit into Reagan's defenses against anxiety by denying the reality of painful choice and thereby resolving conflict among his subordinates.

According to Stockman, one of Reagan's favorite stories was about two boys—one a pessimist, one an optimist—getting Christmas presents. The pessimist receives a roomful of toys and worries that there is some catch involved. The optimist gets a roomful of manure, and digs happily believing there is a pony somewhere in the pile.[36]

Reagan loved to tell stories that reinforced his opinions. In one case, he and his aides staged an event that later became a favorite story. At the first summit with Gorbachev in Geneva, Reagan and his aides found a scene to enable Reagan to demonstrate how person-to-person talk can overcome major differences. The scene was a lakeside pool house with a fireplace. Reagan invited Gorbachev to walk to the pool house where a roaring fire awaited them. The way Reagan told the story of this intimate, barrier-breaking conversation, he would ignore the presence of interpreters. He spoke no Russian and Gorbachev no English. Yet the story conveys the impression that it was just the two of them breaking the barriers of mistrust. Indeed, barriers of mistrust had been broken, but largely as a result of the fact that Gorbachev was different from other Soviet leaders. Success in alleviating tensions of the cold war was important for him in moving his program of reform. For Reagan, the former ideologue and cold warrior, changing his image from hard-liner to conciliator in foreign affairs became important to secure his place in history during his second term. The "fireside chat" and the story that resulted from it probably had little to do with progress in ending the embittered conflict between the United States and the Soviet Union. The warmth of the fire could not overcome Reagan's insistence on Star Wars and Gorbachev's refusal to abort or modify the 1972 ABM Treaty. But for Reagan, the scene and the event became part of his usable lore.

Many of Reagan's stories came from movies he had seen or from articles that appeared in *Reader's Digest,* a publication he read avidly. He told them for effect; it was often difficult to separate apocryphal from real events. For example, in talking or writing about his World War II service, he often left the impression that he had gone somewhere, when, in fact, he was near Hollywood making training films. Cannon cites a report in the newsletter *The Near East Report* that in a meeting with Israeli prime minister Yitzhak Shamir in the White House on November

29, 1983, Reagan told a story of photographing Nazi death camps. He told Shamir that he kept a copy of the film so he would later be able to verify to holocaust deniers the authenticity of the existence of death camps. According to the report, Reagan said he had actually shown his copy of the film to doubters—in one instance, a member of his family, and in another instance, a Jew. He repeated this story in a meeting with Simon Wiesenthal and Rabbi Marvin Hier when they were at the White House to discuss the dedication of the Wiesenthal Center in Los Angeles.

Cannon decided after a cautious delay to pursue this story because he knew that Reagan had never left the country during the war. The White House went on "red alert" when Cannon pursued the story, since it raised questions about Reagan's tendency to confuse reality with what he saw in films. The films of the liberation of the death camps had been widely shown in movie houses. Cannon concludes, "His imagined accounts of having filmed the liberation of the death camps showed not only his difficulty in distinguishing actual from cinematic experience but the deep impression the Holocaust had made upon him."[37]

Another story, which Reagan tells in his autobiography, was about his father's alcoholism.

> I was eleven years old the first time I came home to find my father flat on his back on the front porch and no one there to lend a hand but me. He was drunk, dead to the world. I stood over him for a minute or two. I wanted to let myself in the house and go to bed and pretend he wasn't there. Oh, I wasn't ignorant of his weakness. I don't know at what age I knew what the occasional absences or the loud voices in the night meant, but up till now my mother, Nelle, or my brother handled the situation and I was a child in bed with the privilege of pretending sleep.
>
> But someplace along the line to each of us, I suppose, must come that first moment of accepting responsibility. If we don't accept it (and some don't), then we must just grow older without quite growing up. I felt myself fill with grief for my father at the same time I was feeling sorry for myself. Seeing his arms spread out as if he were crucified—as indeed he was—his hair soaked with melting snow, snoring as he breathed, I could feel no resentment against him.
>
> That was Nelle's doing. With all the tragedy that was hers because of his occasional bouts with the dark demon in the bottle, she told Neil and myself over and over that alcoholism was a sickness—that we should love and help our father and never condemn him for something that was beyond his control.
>
> I bent over him, smelling the sharp odor of whiskey from the speakeasy. I got a fistful of his overcoat. Opening the door, I managed to drag him inside and get him to bed. In a few days he was the bluff, hearty man I knew and loved and will always remember.[38]

What is the probability that an 11-year-old boy would have the strength to get a drunken man who had passed out in the snow into his bed? Where were his mother and brother? Here is Michael Deaver's version of the story: "Jack Reagan had been a binge drinker. The president told me one time of a Christmas when his father passed out on the porch in the snow, and he and his brother, Neil, and their mother had dragged him into the house and put him to bed."[39]

The fact that Deaver attributes his version of the story to Reagan lends credence to the view that Reagan once again had indulged himself in storytelling in which he created an effect ("I learned responsibility") while engaging in fantasy. It would not be surprising for Reagan to have been angry at and disappointed in his father (Jack Reagan changed jobs and moved his family seven times while his son was growing up), but Reagan maintained his outward love and loyalty to his father. If there was anger and disappointment, it was repressed. If he repressed this important aspect of his emotional life, he probably repressed other emotions, which would account in part for his powerful tendency to keep himself to himself. No one claimed to know him as a person, but many were attached to his role.

The presidency of the United States is awe inspiring in terms of the authority vested in the office and consequently inherent in the role of the incumbent. Whether this authority ultimately becomes power is subject to the ability of the incumbent to transform authority into personal power. The transformation depends on the work the individual in office does on himself. Part of this work is to have a deep awareness of himself as an object for his constituency. For a leader such as Reagan, becoming an object would depend on the authenticity of his inner beliefs and the congruence of these beliefs with the dominant values of his constituency.

Reagan maintained a love affair with America and its people. He exuded confidence, optimism, a sense of fair play, and a belief that if left to their own devices, the American people would always do the right thing. As effective as these beliefs were in the mutual attachment of the American people to Reagan as their president, the bond was strengthened by Reagan's beliefs in the presence of enemies from within and without. The enemy within was the federal government, which in Reagan's articulation prevented people of goodwill from acting to further their own interests and ultimately the common good. The enemy without was the Soviet Union and its central beliefs in Marxism, Leninism, and Stalinism.

Reagan's vision dealt with both enemies. Hence, he could state very simply the elements of a program to defeat both enemies. Cut federal taxes and the bureaucracy. Reduce federal expenditures while increasing defense spending. The federal cuts would come from domestic programs and entitlements, which in Reagan's system of beliefs stifled individuals and limited their freedom. The ultimate vision was Star Wars, an umbrella of space weapons to protect the United States from its enemy, the Soviet Union and its communist allies of the cold war.

The mutual identification of Reagan and the American people was itself an abstraction. The American people identified with an image and a role. They knew little of Reagan as a person except what he chose to reveal as in *Where's the Rest of Me?* Reagan could become emotional, as he did when Stockman told him of his conversion to supply-side economics. It was also emotion that drove Reagan to trading arms for hostages. He could not tolerate the notion that Americans were being held hostage while the principle of not bargaining with terrorists seemingly tied his hands. Beyond amiability, quips, and stories, he was as detached from his subordinates at a personal level as he was from the issues over which they fought. He avoided confrontation and the intense emotions that surfaced when cabinet officials and staff seriously disagreed. The limitations in his emotional involvement probably had their roots in the repression of his emotions surrounding his father's failure to control his alcoholism and to hold a job.

Reagan's relationship with his subordinates in the cabinet and on the White House staff was a function of practical power issues and to a certain extent the attitudes toward him as a person. To serve the presidency is to serve the nation. What enhances the president's esteem in the eyes of the nation strengthens the power base, which in turn influences Congress to support the president's program and allows subordinates to implement initiatives.[40]

During Reagan's presidency, the issue of loyalty appeared as the quintessential focus of expectations on how a subordinate should behave. But being loyal to Reagan posed numerous problems. There were major differences among his subordinates, in their opposing coalitions, as they sought his support. The hard-liners took him literally in his policies and they were bound together as cold warriors. The moderates seemed to understand the practical issues of domestic politics and statecraft. To be loyal to Reagan, given the fact that he distanced himself from the efforts to work through the gap between a vision and a program, posed serious problems and was further complicated by his tendency to work separately with each of the coalitions. His disengagement from the practical workings of the institutions surrounding the presidency often left it up to subordinates to interpret what he wanted. Thus, one coalition could interpret his feelings for the hostages and engage in making deals for their release, while the other coalition could be left in the dark, or limited to indirect means of finding out what was going on.

Loyalty also posed conflicts between supporting the president and upholding the law. The Iran-Contra initiative broke laws, which made the president vulnerable and also made his subordinates subject to criminal investigation and penalties, particularly if they carried their commitment to engaging in cover-ups and tampering with evidence. Their forms of defense, unlike Reagan's capacity for denial, which allowed him for a long period to disavow that he was trading arms for hostages, were not psychological mechanisms. They were deeply involved in the Iran-Contra initiatives and were plainly dishonest in destroying or withholding evidence or were lying. Others such as Attorney General Meese, or Secretary of Defense Weinberger, were artful in their involvement in protecting Reagan to the point where they appeared to be covering up. In the end, Reagan may have been saved in an eerie sense when William Casey, the head of the CIA, fell into a coma with a brain tumor and died before the independent counsel could seek his testimony.

What did Reagan's subordinates truly think about him as president and as a person? It is clear that they had a deep respect for the role, but how did they feel about the man? In his memoir, George Shultz was frank in describing how difficult it was to function as secretary of state given Reagan's problematic style of leadership. Both Casper Weinberger and Edwin Meese were loyalists and bypassed in their memoirs the problems evident in his leadership style. Nancy Reagan, his fierce protector, seemed oblivious to the problems subordinates encountered working for him.

Perhaps Lou Cannon deserves the last word:

> The sad, shared secret of the Reagan White House was that no one in the presidential entourage had confidence in the judgment or capacities of the president. Often, they took advantage of Reagan's niceness and naïveté to indulge competing concepts of the presidency and advance their own ambitions. Pragmatists and conservatives alike treated Reagan as if he were a child monarch in need of constant protection. They paid homage to him, but gave him no respect.[41]

4

Character and Mood in Presidential Leadership

Presidents operate in two arenas simultaneously. The first is the arena of the staff, cabinet members, and political advisors. The second is the arena of the press and the masses, for whom the president exists in a goldfish bowl. The observers in these arenas assess the president's mood as a backdrop to evaluating his performance. While presidents publicly tend to discount opinion polls and take the position that they will make decisions based upon the merits of the issues, it is the rare chief executive who is truly indifferent to how he is scoring in the minds of constituents. Therefore, presidents are watchful of their own mood when they appear in the arenas of public opinion.

The conventional wisdom favors the optimist, the individual who characteristically views life through rose-colored glasses. Franklin Delano Roosevelt (FDR) epitomized the optimistic spirit. Despite the paralysis that left him physically handicapped, the economic depression of the 1930s, World War II, and the despair following Pearl Harbor, he rallied the nation to identify with his optimism while fashioning a program of economic recovery and mobilizing the nation to combat Nazi Germany and the Japanese military in the battles of the Pacific. Meeting FDR, Churchill recalls, "was like opening your first bottle of champagne, knowing him was like drinking it."[1] When Roosevelt died, *The Times* editorial said, "Men will thank God on their knees a hundred years from now, that Franklin Roosevelt was in the White House." It was not his positive mood alone that rallied the nation. His domestic policies, the New Deal, the mobilization of the defense industries, and the military command's competence during the war amplified the optimism he projected, leading to his reelection to an unprecedented fourth term.

The Times concluded its tribute to the memory of FDR with this story:

Memories like that are a living legacy, and millions share them. A little boy we knew in 1945 had made a little pine flagpole in manual arts class. When F.D.R. died, students were let out of school. The boy went home, lowered his little flag to half-mast, and picked out "Taps" on the piano, over and over again. It was his small reverence to The President.[2]

In 1901–1902 William James, the Harvard philosopher and psychologist, brilliantly distinguished two mood sets embedded in character. Intended as an exposition of character and mood in religion, James's book *The Varieties of Religious Experience*[3] applies, as well, to two types of moods in politics: healthy-mindedness, or optimism; and morbid-mindedness, or pessimism. James was not engaged in studying the developmental precursors of the two moods, but he offers the distinction borrowed from the theologian Francis Newman of the once-born and twice-born personality.

The once-born sees God

> not as a strict Judge, not as a Glorious Potentate; but as the animating Spirit of a harmonious world, Beneficent and Kind, Merciful as well as Pure. The same characters have no metaphysical tendencies; they do not look back into themselves. Hence they are not distressed by their own imperfections: yet it would be absurd to call them self-righteous; for they hardly think of themselves at all.[4]

James quotes Dr. Edward Everett Hale, the eminent Unitarian preacher, for another pointed description of the once-born type of consciousness:

> I can remember perfectly that when I was coming to manhood, the half-philosophical novels of the time had a deal to say about the young men and maidens who were facing the "problem of life." I had no idea whatever what the problem of life was. To live with all my might seemed to me easy; to learn where there was so much to learn seemed pleasant and almost of course; to lend a hand, if one had a chance, natural, and if one did this, why, he enjoyed life because he could not help it, and without proving to himself that he ought to enjoy it.[5]

The twice-born, in James's treatise, a sick soul characterized as morbid minded, is easily recognized as a person with depressive tendencies. Often plagued by an underlying conviction of sin or imperfection, the morbid minded are thrown back into themselves to emerge, if their introspection is successful, with a high degree of independence and a deep concern for reality in all its aspects. As James describes the twice-born's deeper appreciation of reality:

> It seems to me that we are bound to say that morbid-mindedness ranges over the wider scale of experience, and that its survey is the one that overlaps. The method of averting one's attention from evil, and living simply in the light of good is splendid as it will work. It will work with many persons; it will work far more generally than most of us are ready to suppose; and within its sphere of successful operation there is nothing to be said against it as a religious solution. But it breaks down impotently as soon as melancholy comes; and even though one be quite free from melancholy one's self, there is no doubt that healthy-mindedness is inadequate as a philosophical doctrine, because the evil facts which it refuses positively to account for are a genuine portion of reality; and they may after all be the best key to life's significance, and possibly the only openers of our eyes to the deepest levels of truth.[6]

If there is a grain of wisdom in James's conception of how individuals arrive at "the deepest level of truth," one must account for the duality in political life of, on the one hand, the ability to project optimism and, on the other hand, remaining deeply attached to reality in all its manifestations. Is this duality a form of acting, playing a role? Or is it a deeper achievement of character forged from the experience with, and resolution of, inner conflict?

Perhaps the dichotomy between healthy-mindedness and morbid-mindedness is too severe and limiting as applied to politics, even if we take into consideration James's caveat about the significance of being deeply attached to reality.

George F. Kennan, the career foreign service officer and diplomat, provides a good example of the realist who reflects no semblance of morbidity in his character. Kennan is widely known as the author of a famous paper, written in the late 1940s, in which he proposed that communism be kept out of the West containing it, from the outside, in the Soviet Union. Kennan's realism derives from a fundamental view of the fissures in human nature. He refers to man as a cracked vessel, whose

> psychic makeup is the scene for the interplay of contradictions between the primitive nature of his innate impulses and the more refined demands of civilized life, contradictions that destroy the unity and integrity of his undertakings, confuse his efforts, place limits on the possibilities for achievement, and often cause one part of his personality to be the enemy of the other.[7]

Kennan would agree with Isaiah Berlin in his quotation from Immanuel Kant that "out of the crooked timber of humanity no straight thing was ever made."[8] Writing in *The New Yorker,* Nicholas Lemann calls Kennan a provocateur who "has a genius for importing a tragic consciousness from its natural home in literature into the usually hopeful realm of public affairs. . . . In fifty years, I would guess, he will be better known as the father of 'tragic realism' than as the father of containment."[9]

James, in his concern for reality; Berlin, in his deep respect for pragmatism as opposed to ideology; and Kennan, in his acceptance of the dual nature of man as reflected in practical affairs, are all in accord with Freud's views concerning human motivation. In 1921, Freud, extending his findings on individual psychology to the psychology of the group, published an essay in which he explored the forces underlying group cohesiveness and morale. He concluded that the basis of group cohesion is the attachment individuals in the group establish to the leader. The group members share this attachment in the form of a common identification with the leader. If the identification exists as sublimated love of the leader, the psychological experience of group membership is high morale and esprit de corps. If the common identification takes the form of fear of the leader, the psychological mechanism of the group is the control of anxiety in the attachment to the leader. While Freud did not deal specifically with other bases for identification, we should include, besides love and fear, the mutual attachment to common purpose. In any case, Freud concluded, "it is impossible to grasp the nature of a group if the leader is disregarded."[10]

While not disregarding the leader, historians and political scientists favor the view that leadership is essentially a reciprocal relationship. Leaders and followers are bound together in defining and meeting needs. James MacGregor Burns, the noted historian and student of leadership, places the leader's position at the center of the relationship, with this centrality existing to define, activate, and ultimately satisfy the followers' needs and motives.[11] He posits a condition of mutual dependency between leader and follower in which the follower accords power to the leader whose mission becomes the satisfaction of the follower's needs.

But in a democracy as diverse as the United States, the divides make it difficult to achieve consensus about what the needs are and what will satisfy them. Conservatives' needs are often to be left alone to pursue their interests as they define them. For liberals, often the need is for change, for actions that redress perceived injustices in the distribution of power and wealth.

In the realm of politics, it hardly seems reasonable to define the central character of what binds leaders and followers as revolving around needs. It would be more accurate to think of motives more broadly as, for example, the validation of the beliefs individuals hold dear personally and as an integral representation in their group memberships. The leader articulates these beliefs and, in doing so, enhances the self-esteem of followers who, in turn, willingly accord power to their leader.

The problem of power in leadership is even more complicated, according to Burns, who recognizes the conflict of motives among diverse groups, but generally defines the fundamental leader-follower process as "a more elusive one; it is, in large part, to make conscious what lies unconscious among followers."[12]

In its strict usage, the unconscious, as it is described in psychoanalysis, remains unavailable to conscious awareness. Through the process of defense—an important function of the ego—conflicting desires remain safely repressed only to appear in disguised form in dreams and occasional slips of the tongue. The unconscious also finds expression in the appearance of neurotic symptoms and in the formation of character. On occasion, as in the case of the Beatles and their adoring public, unconscious wishes find expression in the relative safety of the group.

To cite Burns again: the unconscious in the definition of the fundamental process in the leader-follower relationship is not the dynamic unconscious of psychoanalysis. It appears to be, instead, a concept derived from need, which can be active or latent in the individual's motivational system, but hardly unconscious. An active need is at the surface of one's consciousness, and the individual has available from experience a repertoire of paths of behavior aimed at satisfying active needs. Satisfying active needs often involves relationships, including relationships with authority figures. An individual who has an active need for job advancement understands that an authority figure can help in satisfying this need. A reciprocal relationship then develops: the subordinate works hard, meets expectations, and is rewarded in time with job advancement and higher pay. The superior in this relationship understands that subordinates who perform well will enhance his or her own performance, which will create favorable performance reviews, advancement, and tangible gains. The unconscious is typically out of the picture in this reciprocal relationship in a power structure. Indeed, there is an underlying premise that unconscious motivation should be suppressed to enable the reciprocal relationship to continue.

Burns's theory of motivation in the relationship of leader and follower derives from the need hierarchy concept formulated by Abraham Maslow, the Brandeis psychologist. According to Maslow, human needs are arranged in a pyramid, with safety needs at the base and self-actualization needs at the apex. As lower order needs are satisfied, higher level needs potentially become activated. The higher order needs in the members of the group may become the focus of the leader's communications and programs. The leader's power derives from his or her ability to activate these higher level needs, which then govern the relationship between leader and follower.[13] The leader activates the need in the follower and then provides the path, through an agenda, for gratifying the need.

The hierarchy of needs differs from unconscious motivation. Needs are dormant until activated. The unconscious in the form of desires, prohibitions, and defenses exists as a complex mental life outside of awareness, but is still operative as a motivational system in the individual. In the example cited earlier of the Beatles' effect on the audience, the motivation was a direct response from the unconscious—in this case a shared response of love, adoration, and sexual desire, encompassed in individuals who suddenly found themselves in a cohesive group. The phenomena were religious and political: religious, in the feeling of being loved by an infinite power; political, in the sense of feeling personal power as a result of being released from inhibitions and melancholy. The feeling of personal power through group cohesion liberates the individual from inhibitions, but often at the cost of judgment and self-control.

Group cohesion and the sense of power achieved in membership are inherently threatened by the possibility of rivalry among group members, who may vie for a special relationship with the leader. Freud observed:

> This transformation—the replacing of jealousy by a group feeling in the nursery and classroom—might be considered improbable, if the same process could not later on be observed again in other circumstances. We have only to think of the troop of women and girls, all of them in love in an enthusiastically sentimental way, who crowd round a singer or pianist after his performance. It would certainly be easy for each of them to be jealous of the rest; but, in the face of their numbers and the impossibility of their reaching the aim of their love, they renounce it, and instead of pulling out one another's hair, they act as a united group, do homage to the hero of the occasion with their common actions. . . . Originally rivals, they have succeeded in identifying themselves with one another by means of a similar love for the same object.[14]

Subordinates in the leader's small group may all identify with the leader, but at the same time compete for his or her attention and approval. The end game for subordinates is to exert direct influence on the leader's thoughts and actions. George Schultz and Casper Weinberger had equal status in Reagan's cabinet: Schultz was centrally situated as head of the moderates and Weinberger as head of the hard-liners. At the heart of this rivalry were two opposing worldviews, which became translated into antagonistic belief systems about the nature of history and politics. Belief systems, termed "operational codes" by Nathan Leites, the psychoanalytically oriented political scientist, have a subtle relationship to decision making. They serve, as it were, as a prism that influences the actor's perception of the flow of political events and his or her definition or estimate of particular situations. The beliefs also provide norms and standards that influence the actor's choice of strategy and tactics and the actor's structuring and weighing of alternative courses of action.[15]

While there may be a significant degree of cohesiveness in the belief system of immediate subordinates, more often than not, a significant cleavage may also exist. The formation of blocs and subgroups represents significant differences in beliefs and hence policy initiatives. These differences can become institutionalized in conflicting views of areas of responsibility between departments, as is often the case between the Department of Defense and the State Department. They cannot remain localized. Rather, they tend to spill over into constituency groups that reflect the conflicting premises underlying opposing operational codes. As a result, subordinates and larger constituent groups tend to limit identification with the leader and instead make him into the object of their pressures and lobbying.

Political leaders grasp intuitively the necessity of creating and maintaining the group feeling among followers. How else does one persuade followers to subordinate their interests in the service of permitting the leader to advance her or his agenda? But leaders often rely on the contagiousness of their optimism and healthy-mindedness to provide the mood needed to maintain their popularity in the face of differences in beliefs and premises on proper courses of action.

While the need hierarchy theory may be ambiguous in its formulation, it is attractive to political practitioners and theorists because it is attuned to the psychology of healthy-mindedness, or the character of optimism. It provides a humanistic credo for the practice of politics, reflecting an abiding faith in the human potential. With this as their credo, leaders can view their actions as building on high-level needs—first, by activating them, and, second, by encouraging their gratification.

In contrast to the optimism of humanistic psychology that can characterize successful political leaders, Freudian psychoanalysis appears pessimistic. Its view of human development is tragic in the sense that it sees various stages of development as involving the less-than-perfect resolution of conflict. Freud believed that the residues of development contain compromises, including the potential for sublimation but also for the appearance of conflict in the form of rigidities in character, if not overt neurotic symptoms. Reflecting this tragic view, Freud offered a definition of the aims of psychoanalysis: to convert neurotic suffering into common human misery.[16]

As mentioned earlier, healthy-mindedness in politics can boomerang. In arousing expectations, the optimist must achieve a substantial measure of success through implemented policies and programs. Where falling short, the political leader faces anger and frustration. While healthy-mindedness tends to produce cohesion among followers, the same principle does not apply in the conversion of promises to programs.

Group psychology in politics operates at two levels in the leader-follower relationship. One level is the masses that make up the electorate. The other is the inner circle of "lieutenants" and confidants, who play an important role in formulating programs and gaining the support of responsible legislative groups.

As we have seen in the case of Ronald Reagan and, to a lesser extent, Dwight Eisenhower, cohesion among the lieutenants was problematic. President Reagan's healthy-mindedness or optimism seems to have prevented him from exercising leadership in the small group of his intimate advisors. To act as leader of the small group would have required his becoming immersed in the substance of policy debate and being firm in making decisions and setting policy in the face of conflicting positions of immediate subordinates. For the optimist, the healthy-minded, this stance is nearly impossible to sustain given the anxiety unleashed in the use of aggression necessary in making decisions. Inevitably, decisions tend to favor the position of one subgroup over another.

While they were both optimists, Eisenhower and Reagan differed in the underpinnings of their healthy-mindedness. Eisenhower had cultivated his approach to command through his experience with subordination under McArthur, Conner, and Marshall, and his experience of his peer relations with Patton and Bradley. Assuming command of the Allied forces represented continuity in career in an organization built on cohesiveness. Even in his final confrontation with Montgomery, Eisenhower could rely on one of Montgomery's staff to allow him to make decisions and realize them, regardless of the inhibition built into his character that precluded confronting interpersonal conflict. His habitual use of the staff system in organizing the presidency put him at a distance from the demands of making decisions.

Eisenhower glided through his two-term presidency with his optimism largely intact and the favorable perception of his use of the office secure. He was truly once-born and functioned as a conservative in his political orientation. In his farewell address, he warned the nation of the threat to stability arising from the military-industrial complex. He had little to lose in issuing this warning. What would have resulted had he issued it and acted on it at the start of his presidency? He would have been faced with a direct and intense involvement with his advisors and staff, which did not fit with his inclinations, his characteristic detachment from the give and take of political leadership. Instead, he left the residues of it to his successor, perhaps leaving behind his less than gracious accession to the office as he refused to join president-elect Kennedy for coffee in the White House before the ride to the inauguration.

Eisenhower feared emotional outbursts of anger as we see in his diary entry in which he chastises himself for his display of rage when General Marshall told him he had to stay in Washington and would not be given command responsibility. It causes one to wonder if Emmett Hughes, who wrote the speech for him to deliver on the platform with McCarthy, had in mind this inhibition against engaging in interpersonal conflict when he wrote as the aftermath to this story, "Yet, I often wondered if the simple, terse exhortation [for teamwork] were not addressed, perhaps only half-consciously, as much to himself as to others."

The human psyche plays tricks to permit one to have gratification without responsibility. Eisenhower, on the platform with McCarthy, perhaps unconsciously had an old score to settle with Marshall over the threat that he would be relegated to a staff position in Washington and, so, did not read the speech Hughes had written for him and bypassed the opportunity to honor the reputation of his one-time superior officer.

Eisenhower presents an integrated picture of the character of the once-born, unlike Reagan, who defies definition. Edmund Morris, who spent three years in close proximity to Reagan as his official biographer, gave up writing a standard biography and resorted to a fictional device to portray a man he called Dutch with a lifeline from childhood to adulthood. This fictional device saved Morris from depression and the need to return a $3 million publication advance, but it did not penetrate the mystery that cloaked the person.

Reagan's children were as mystified by their father as Morris was. They contributed to the books that Nancy Reagan called disloyal show-and-tell stories of Reagan, but even so, the veil remained. One son reported that at his graduation ceremony his father asked him who he was, and was stunned by the reply, "I'm your son."

Reagan's character becomes less mysterious in light of the clinical findings of the psychoanalyst Helene Deutsch in an article on the "as if" personality.[17] The "as if" personality appears completely normal, except that "relationships are devoid of any trace of warmth, and that all the expressions of emotion are formal, that all inner experience is completely excluded. It is like the performance of an actor who is technically well trained but who lacks the spark to make his impersonations true to life."[18]

There is little evidence that Reagan came to terms with his father's alcoholism and failure in his work—including the family's frequent moves as his father went from one failed job to another. Nor is there evidence that he developed a sense of himself separate from his mother, the family mainstay, who used her religion, to which she brought him, to support her family's emotional needs. His failed marriage to Jane Wyman came to confrontation with an inner life, but the "as if" person lacks awareness of an inner life so he was perplexed over Wyman's decision to kick him out of the house with the declaration that the marriage was over. Had he become deeply depressed, he might have found cause to acknowledge that there was more to his psyche than the surface amiability. As we know, he used this amiability in furthering his career as a remote radio sports announcer, and later as a B film actor in Hollywood. And further, we know that as the amiable GE spokesman, he provided the slant needed to satisfy his conservative sponsors (until he went after a prime customer for GE's power equipment business and was fired without notice).

The "as if" personality is strangely adapted to a political career. Reagan converted from a New Deal Democrat to a staunch conservative as a result of having to pay taxes on his earnings as an actor and as GE spokesman. As an amiable politician he made no demands on the voters who elected him governor of California and then president of the United States. His opponent, Jimmy Carter, was a failed president who managed the economy into a disastrous rise in interest rates.

He attached himself, as president, to goals such as tax reduction, large defense expenditures, and aggressive criticisms of communism, but he remained passive as to how these goals were to be met, since they were often in conflict with one another. He was uninterested in resolving conflicts, and left such nuances to subordinates. He would act surprised that subordinates took conflicting stances on policies such as how to reduce taxes and at the same time avoid budget deficits.

Apart from the limitations of typologies in predicting presidential performance, deeper questions persist toward understanding the effects of character on performance. For example, what is the role of intellect in presidential performance? Deficiencies in intellect, or, perhaps more accurately, in intellectual curiosity, could account for the appearance of passivity in presidential style. Ideology may take the place of intellect in establishing positions on public policy. To observers the effect may be passivity in the face of contentions among subordinates. Depending on the sides lieutenants take, the president appears rigid or indifferent, often frustrating those responsible for promoting programs and implementing policies.

Healthy-minded individuals often have little patience for abstractions and subtleties. In declaring the policy of the United States not to bargain or trade for hostages with terrorist governments, the abstract principle was to avoid rewarding illegal behavior. At the concrete level, concern for the safety and safe return of American citizens dominated Reagan's thinking. His willingness to pay ransom for the hostages reflected his compassion and overcame the abstraction of preserving American and Allied policy to avoid rewarding criminal behavior. But as often occurs in the minds of optimists, rationalizations appear to overcome the apparent conflict between emotion and thought. In taking the position, almost to the bitter end, that he was not engaging in ransom, but was instead dealing with friendly third parties, Reagan could, at least in his own mind, overcome the reality that was so apparent to his advisors, the media, and the public at large.

It is characteristic of healthy-minded individuals to believe in their own perceptions and rationalizations. Reality is less important than what feels right. To believe in oneself, even at the expense of reality, can allay anxiety and, to the world at large, appears as optimism, or conviction that following a simple course of action will result in favorable outcomes.

Star Wars is a good example of the strengths and limitations of healthy-mindedness. Start with a simple thought: Wouldn't it be wonderful if the United States developed an antimissile device that would provide an impenetrable shield against nuclear weapons? From infatuation with that idea—call it a vision—to acting as though it were, or easily could become, a reality is the epitome of an unsophisticated intellect. Technological hurdles disappear under the sway of optimism. Problems of alliance politics fade from view if indeed they had ever penetrated consciousness. And so, mutual deterrence could easily be sacrificed even though it had kept the peace for a generation.

Soon, the vision takes on a life of its own, flowing into deeply held beliefs such as the almost religious conviction that there is no problem technology cannot overcome in the hands of U.S. scientists. Those who are believers, the optimists, bring ideology to bear to discredit so-called prophets of doom and gloom. Imbedded in ideology, the discourse on issues of importance in the nation's life fall outside the realm of rational discourse.

"There is a line among the fragments of the Greek poet Archilochus which says, 'the fox knows many things, but the hedgehog knows one big thing.'"[19] Isaiah Berlin's essay portrays Leo Tolstoy as conflicted in his yearning to be a hedgehog, while in his writing he was a fox. But for Berlin, the distinction goes beyond Tolstoy and differentiates between human beings.

> For there exists a great chasm between those, on one side, who relate everything to a single central vision, one system, less or more coherent or articulate, in terms of which they understand, think and feel—a single, universal, organising principle in terms of which alone all that they are and say has significance—and, on the other side, those who pursue many ends, often unrelated and even contradictory, connected, if at all, only in some *de facto* way, for some psychological or physiological cause, related by no moral or aesthetic principle. These last lead lives, perform acts and entertain ideas that are centrifugal rather than centripetal; their thought is scattered or diffuse, moving on many levels, seizing upon the essence of a vast variety of experiences and objects for what they are in themselves, without, consciously or unconsciously, seeking to fit them into, or exclude them from, any one unchanging, all-embracing, sometimes self-contradictory and incomplete, at times fanatical, unitary inner vision.[20]

In public opinion and electoral politics the single vision, the unitary principle, in short the hedgehog, often prevails. In governing, the fox dominates, often causing political opponents to believe that the leader is contradictory or without principle.

The major exception to this generalization is in times of a clear crisis such as economic depression or war. The crisis provides the single, unifying principle. Leaders are sometimes tempted to promote a crisis, as in the case of Ronald Reagan's persistent effort to characterize the Soviet Union as the evil empire even when massive change was under way in that society. Alert to the possibility of change, the fox will find ways to promote the change by actions that will create an alliance with the agents of change. To do so, a leader avoids the temptation to manipulate followers' anxiety. When a leader can objectify a threat and arouse anxiety, and then present a vision or plan of action for dealing with the threat, then the followers will intensify their identification with the leader but at a cost of flexibility.

To describe a politician and leader as an optimist or pessimist is a useful first distinction in delineating character. The term "character" in the sense used here does not refer to a moral dimension. Whether a person is good or bad, moral or immoral is a judgment based upon observing that individual's actions.

Diagnostic categories used in psychiatry and psychoanalysis are meant to describe and not to judge. Certain categories are delineated by symptoms that individuals experience, such as depressive reactions, or obsessional neuroses characterized by ritualistic behavior. Other categories refer to dysfunctions such as sexual impotence in males. And still other classifications refer to manifestations in obsessional character traits, such as the classic triad of parsimony, orderliness, and obstinacy. It is often difficult to draw a line between character traits that are disabling and those traits an individual puts to good use in daily living.

For example, an accountant may find obsessional character traits useful in his or her profession. The same traits that can be useful might make the individual difficult to live with and might make her or his life miserable. They might become a cause for seeking treatment when the person's lifestyle produces dissatisfaction in intimate relations and a growing sense of how much he or she is missing out on the pleasures of life.

Healthy-mindedness and optimism are usually visible character traits. But at what point are these traits fostered at a cost of one's attachment to reality? Clearly, when these traits border on mania, when, for example, the person is unable to control spending, or becomes addicted to gambling, the traits others may find pleasing are in fact disabling in the person's life.

Character traits that appear negative to an outside observer are easily sustained in the individual's lifestyle because they can be rationalized. A reckless driver perversely gets pleasure when stopped by a policeman. The pleasure is in arguing with the cop, sometimes enjoying a victory in not getting a traffic ticket, but more often causing trouble for himself. The ability to rationalize, to see virtue in one's character traits that are costly in relationships with others, is endless—which testifies to the stubborn hold these traits have on the person. What will propel a person to seek treatment? When the character traits become submerged in the appearance of sexual dysfunctions, which cannot be rationalized. At that point, the individual begins to take himself seriously.

What to some, such as newspaper editorial writers, appear to be the character traits of a sociopath, may have a different and somewhat more sympathetic underlying cause. Ambition for power and actually achieving an office with considerable power can be lonely and stressful. Do actions that appear habitual, and even perverse, function to control anxiety? A young man markedly successful in his career risks losing all his power and achievements by periodically engaging in a homosexual act with a total stranger, a pickup in a restroom in some public place like a railroad station. The perversion is an alien experience, but compulsive in its drive to regulate a more fundamental sense of anxiety. From the outside, it appears reckless to risk one's public standing in this way, as in the case of an aide to President Lyndon Johnson, who was apprehended by police while soliciting strangers for homosexual acts.

The lack of access to a power-holder's inner life limits what one can know and explain about the person. The healthy-minded pose special problems. For one thing, the healthy-minded, such as President Eisenhower, appear to be truly once-born personalities. Such personalities live in, and are of, a social structure. The military was Eisenhower's life. He grew up as an optimist and found his place in the military. Even in times of disappointment, such as sustaining an injury that prevented him from playing football, seeing only staff service during World War I, or, more devastating, losing his son during the influenza epidemic of 1918, he never lost his faith in and attachment to the military. While there were many sides to the presidency that he truly abhorred, his sense of duty, inherent in his career as a military officer, led him to accept the nomination in the first place and sustained him in a political career in civilian life about which he had reservations. He was a man accustomed to living in an environment he knew and trusted, which in turn displayed confidence in him. Apparently he had little need for introspection. The lack of introspection is the mark of an optimist and once-born personality.

Reagan's optimism and ostensible healthy-mindedness is more difficult to fathom. Only Nancy Reagan is said to have been his confidante as well as his soul mate. While Reagan enjoyed immense popularity, he was adept at keeping his inner life to himself. Yet he managed to reveal some of his history when it suited his purpose, as with *Where's the Rest of Me*. Apart from his planned revelation, he was not prone to introspection, certainly not in public, but, questionably, not even in his solitary moments. He was a fatalist who believed that what would be would be—a later version of a deep belief in God's will.

Biographers seem to agree that the entry to understanding Reagan's life is his career as an actor. Lou Cannon's understanding that Reagan was forever a role player did not stop him from including in his biography shrewd speculations on the makeup of this optimist.

Relying on treatises on alcoholism and the effects of an alcoholic father on a son (in a footnote, Cannon reported that his father, too, was an Irish-Catholic alcoholic), Cannon states, "These adults keep feelings to themselves, lie when it would be as easy to tell the truth, frequently seek approval and affirmation, over-react to situations over which they have no control and have difficulty with intimate relationships."[21] The only aspect of this description of the characteristics of adults who grew up with an alcoholic father that would not necessarily apply to Reagan is lying. As Cannon points out, Reagan believed the stories he told. He was not aware of lying or stretching the truth. He fancied science fiction and he loved telling stories such as the story of the two boys and the roomful of manure.

An actor is supposed to be acutely sensitive to the audience, but Reagan was seemingly unaware of the effects of his storytelling on political insiders such as his cabinet officers and White House aides. They often reacted as they were supposed to react, while feeling frustrated at the repetitiveness of the stories, or the deflection the stories imposed on the subjects ostensibly under consideration.

With an acting career in films and television, and a largely unseen audience, Reagan's appeal as a great communicator relied on a remote response, and it seems highly probable that he was his own best audience. The initial response he sought and received was largely his own. The stories he told were an optimist's stories. But it would be difficult to conceive of his optimism as an outgrowth of the character of a once-born personality, a character with a secure position in a highly structured social system, with a fusion of his identity with his position in this social system. Once-born personalities are unaware of themselves. Their harmonious attachment to the reality they live in and accept without reservation matches the simple acceptance of who they are. An optimist can represent himself with all the positive connotations of a healthy-minded personality by the psychological defense of denial. Reagan could write about his father as an alcoholic, but with a political purpose in mind. Whether he genuinely felt the loss of his father that the alcoholism entailed, whether he genuinely felt the anger and betrayal and the sense of being a son abandoned by a father immersed in his addiction is questionable. All of the painful emotions in being without a father with whom one could identify, being a follower of a true leader, are buried in characteristic denial.

But the defense of denial runs deep. It not only wards off painful emotions connected with a figure from one's past, it also spreads into the inability to experience, genuinely, negative feelings that are a part of living with a deep appreciation of reality.

Ronald Reagan concluded his second term and left the presidency in 1988. He was 77 years old. He died in 1994 of Alzheimer's disease. During his second term in office he displayed a stubborn denial that his administration had been engaged in selling arms to Iran and sending the profits to the Contras in Nicaragua. Was his role in this scandal, at least in part, a result of the onset of a dementia that was to end with Alzheimer's? (He had reported memory lapses such as the inability to remember the names of cabinet officers.) Or, was the scandal the end point of a disengaged president subject to the whims and foibles of subordinates who took it upon themselves to fill in the blanks he left unattended?

Part 2

The Narcissists

To Be Single Minded: Admiral Hyman G. Rickover and the Nuclear Navy

Admiral Hyman George Rickover died on July 8, 1986, at the age of 86. He had served in the navy, starting as a midshipman in the naval academy in 1918 and retiring in 1982 as a full admiral. His 64-year span of active service, including the four years he spent as a midshipman, was a record defying all the rules of mandatory retirement. His retirement in 1982 was forced upon him when President Reagan, acting on behalf of John Lehman, secretary of the navy, refused to extend his active duty.

The Washington Post, announcing Rickover's death, called him "the irascible admiral who forced a revolution in thought and weaponry on the navies of the world." The obituary continued:

> In 63 years of Navy service, the Russian-born Rickover went from being a shunned Jewish midshipman at the U.S. Naval Academy to a flag officer with a vision that he forced into reality by being brilliant, indefatigable, unrelenting, bullying, heretical, and political. His dream was to free submarines and surface ships from the logistical tyranny of having to break off operations to refill their tanks with fuel oil. He would use the heat released from splitting atoms to make the steam needed for propulsion, giving warships below and above the surface limitless range. On January 17, 1955, the Rickover dream came true when the signal lamp on the submarine USS Nautilus, gliding down the Thames River in Connecticut blinked out the message, "Underway on nuclear power." The Nautilus would travel 62,500 miles on this first load of nuclear fuel, including a journey under the ice of the North Pole during a cruise from Hawaii to London. But many Navy leaders of the day saw the Nautilus and nuclear propulsion as no more than engineering experiments, not revolutionary developments that would change almost everything from naval tactics to the balance of power between the United States and the Soviet Union. Since the Nautilus' first trip, every President from John F. Kennedy to Ronald Reagan has wagered the security of the United States on the reliability of Rickover's nuclear powered submarines and the missiles they carry.[1]

Rickover's technical achievements in his appointments as head of nuclear propulsion both in the Navy Bureau of Ships and in the Atomic Energy Commission

(AEC) were profound. But his leadership style and modus operandi were unconventional by all standards of the navy and, indeed, by the standards commonly accepted in the theory and practice of organization, management, and leadership. How he could defy conventional wisdom, survive navy traditions, and produce monumental results challenges commonplace and well-accepted ideas about how to behave in positions of responsibility. An obvious shortfall in the lessons to be learned from the study of Rickover's life is the fact that it is nearly impossible to institutionalize and replicate what has become known as "the Rickover effect."

There is a deeper sense in which the "effect" might be instructive and might contribute to a discerning of the underlying psychology of the man. On the surface, it is clear that he was single-minded in his purpose, authoritarian in his behavior, and totally devoid of what writers on organization call "social skills." In the language of sociology, Rickover is the classic deviate. However, the task of this chapter is to go beyond description to inquire more deeply into the psychology of an "outsider," a committed leader who brooked no opposition to accomplishing his goal of making the dream of nuclear-powered submarines a reality.

Hyman George Rickover was born either in 1898 or in 1900 (the accepted date seems to be 1900) in Poland, and came to America in 1906 with his mother and an older sister. They joined his father, who had come over earlier to establish himself. The family settled in Chicago, where his father worked as a tailor.

Considering that Rickover was a famous man, the paucity of information on his early years is astonishing. He appears to have been bar mitzvahed at age 13, but not much more is known about his schooling, his religious upbringing, or his friendships. Part of the mystery is a result of Rickover's studied reluctance to reveal much about himself. He would tell his subordinates during the nuclear propulsion days that he would not inquire into their personal life and he expected them to keep away from inquiring into his personal life, past and present. Even his son, Robert Masters Rickover, seems to have known very little about his father's background and had no relationship with his paternal grandparents, aunt, or extended family. His first wife, Ruth Masters Rickover, died in 1972, and Hyman Rickover married Eleonore Bednowicz, a commander in the Navy Nurse Corps. The marriage ceremony took place in a Roman Catholic church, where Robert Rickover met for the first time cousins on his father's side.[2]

After his retirement from the navy, Hyman Rickover gave a speech describing his early years. The occasion for the speech is not recorded, but the taciturn Rickover uncharacteristically spoke about his past. What he said revealed a traditional Jewish orthodox background in Makow, Poland, with many hours spent, six days a week, in Hebrew school. He described how the drill of study and hard work early in his life marked his lifestyle throughout his adolescence. To help family finances, he delivered Western Union telegrams by bicycle after school, from late afternoon until midnight. This work brought him to the attention of Congressman Adolph Sabath, who knew Rickover's uncle, and resulted in his appointment to the Naval Academy. The appointment meant a college education, which would not have been affordable otherwise. A career in the navy was not uppermost in Rickover's mind when he entered the academy. A college education was the prize.

Fate seems to have conspired to ensure that Rickover would be a deviate in his naval career. He had to be quarantined in sick bay with suspected diphtheria, which meant he could not join his class upon entry into the academy. When he was released from sick bay, he was assigned to quarters outside of Bancroft Hall, the traditional residence for midshipmen, and lived apart from the bulk of the class. Rickover made clear his intent: to study hard and do well academically. To make up for missed classes and study, he habitually violated the rule about lights-out and studied after hours, garnering much criticism from classmates since competition for standing in class was intense. Rickover appeared uninterested in social acceptance and lived a spare, almost monastic, life in the academy. He achieved a decent, but not outstanding record, graduating 107th in a class of 540. He would have ranked higher in the class if academic performance had been the only criterion. Ranking also included evaluations of leadership and military bearing, aspects of performance that attracted him less than studies.

The pattern that characterized him during his shipboard years, following graduation, continued to be one of hard work, discipline, studies, and attention to detail. He performed well aboard ships, and seemed inclined toward engineering duties. He received good fitness reports and managed to take various correspondence courses on his own, including a course in naval strategy and tactics. After sea duty, he took postgraduate courses at the Naval Academy and earned a master's degree at Columbia University, extending his engineering and technical knowledge. While at Columbia, he met Ruth Masters, whom he later married (1932)—abandoning the religion of his parents and becoming an Episcopalian. (He wrote a letter to his parents announcing his decision to become an Episcopalian, and it took almost four years for a reconciliation to occur.)

Ruth Masters completed a graduate degree at Columbia and a doctor's degree at the Sorbonne in the field of international law. After their marriage, the Rickovers traveled to Asia and the Far East in conjunction with his navy assignments. Throughout their life they shared a wide range of intellectual interests that later included publication of books on education. These books were written by both of them but were published with his name as the sole author.

Given Rickover's assignments and the family separations these entailed, Ruth Masters Rickover became the main influence on their only child, Robert, although both parents thought as one when it came to the importance of academics and study.

When Robert was 14, his parents decided they needed more living space. At the time, they were living in a rented apartment in Washington, D.C. To solve the space problem, they rented another apartment in the same building and moved their son into the second apartment. After that, there were several moves within the same building until they found an apartment next door to the one Robert lived in and where they kept some of their belongings. The family took meals together, but the arrangement afforded Robert a degree of privacy few adolescents experience. At the time, Robert was involved in ham radio and electronics and, while characterizing the family's living arrangements as somewhat unorthodox, he thought they were fine.[3]

Hyman Rickover's dedication to his work in the navy entailed travel and absences from home. For a period of one year, beginning in July 1946, the Bureau of Ships named Rickover one of five naval officers and civilians assigned to study nuclear energy at Oak Ridge, Tennessee. He decided to leave his wife and son in Washington because of the heat in Oak Ridge and the difficulty in finding appropriate housing. The separation from his family enabled him to concentrate completely on learning about nuclear technology and its possible application to the propulsion of naval vessels. He was a man who thrived on concentration, and at Oak Ridge, he found his subject.

From his academy graduation in 1922 until he was promoted to lieutenant commander in 1937, Rickover had served on a number of ships ranging from battleships to submarines. His assignments were mainly on the engineering watch, although he also commanded the USS *Finch,* a broken down minesweeper in the China theater mainly used for towing targets in gunnery practice for large ships. Rickover was the third captain of the *Finch* in three months. The ship was in deplorable condition and its crew was demoralized. Rather than accepting the dreadful conditions as they were, Rickover decided to initiate a repair program to restore the ship to seaworthy condition. He worked the crew hard at scraping rust and painting. He was relieved of this command after four months, with the navy evidently continuing its practice of treating the *Finch* as a castoff.

Based on his 15 years of service, Rickover, then a lieutenant, was eligible for assignment to a new classification—"engineering duty only"—for officers who would become technical specialists but would be ineligible for assignment to command ships. He applied for this classification and was accepted, marking the start of unprecedented performance that lead ultimately to the successful development of nuclear propulsion for submarines and, later, surface ships.

The Japanese attack on Pearl Harbor found Rickover in Washington as head of the Electrical Section in the Bureau of Ships. During his tenure there, he had established a reputation for increasing the effectiveness of the electrical equipment aboard ships and, especially, assuring reliability under battle conditions. The Electrical Section not only created specifications for equipment, but it leaned hard on industrial contractors to meet the stringent specifications that reduced the bulk of the equipment and made sure the equipment was able to withstand vibrations during battle, and, wherever possible, was made from fireproof materials. Rickover and his group went beyond specified electrical equipment for ships. The Electrical Section undertook the design and manufacture of minesweeping equipment based on secret British plans. Without formal authorization, Rickover enlisted GE to provide diesels to power underwater cable used to detonate mines. Despite the violation of procedure for letting contracts, the Bureau of Ships affirmed the arrangement in recognition of the fact that Rickover's unorthodox work saved the navy considerable time in expediting an important technical advance that would save lives and ships at sea.

The journalist Clay Blair evaluates Captain Rickover's work as head of the Electrical Section of the Bureau of Ships.

> Many people disliked the Captain because of the way he did business: out of channels, minus the usual red tape and "formalization." He stepped on toes, went over people's heads, arrogantly criticized delays that were sometimes unavoidable. But the Captain had one great talent which endeared him to the Navy brass: *he got things*

done. Soon all sorts of odd jobs were tossed to him. Most of them he accomplished swiftly and efficiently, leaving a wide wake of disgruntled people. But the Captain was not concerned, because slowly and surely the task of providing naval vessels with revamped and battle-proof electrical equipment was being accomplished.[4]

Rickover, as head of the Electrical Section of the Bureau of Ships, worked directly with large corporations that produced equipment under contract with the bureau. Later, as an admiral and head of nuclear propulsion, he would use this experience in his dealings with large corporations such as GE, Westinghouse, and the Electric Boat Division of General Dynamics. Rickover approached these relationships with some skepticism about the motivation of businesses in relation to the navy. His last act, when he received the announcement that he would be retired from the navy, was to warn President Reagan that Electric Boat, in its claim for reimbursement for cost overruns, had cheated the U.S. government.

Originally, Rickover was not slated for the Oak Ridge assignment that was to launch him on his trajectory to the admiralty. Captain Albert G. Mumma, of the Bureau of Ships, was responsible for recommending the officers and civilians to the Oak Ridge nuclear study project, and Mumma omitted Rickover—largely because of Rickover's reputation for close attention to detail and centralization of control. Admiral Mills, under whom Rickover had worked as head of the Electrical Section, recognized these qualities in Rickover as the drive and determination necessary to succeed in developing nuclear propulsion plants. Mills overrode Mumma's recommendation but, undoubtedly as a compromise, did not name Rickover as officer in charge of the study group.

The five naval officers assigned to Oak Ridge for study officially reported to the senior army officer in charge of Oak Ridge. Captain Rickover was the senior naval officer in the group. Without formal designation, he managed to secure from the senior army officer at Oak Ridge authority to prepare the fitness reports of other naval officers in the group. When he informed those officers of this authority, what had started as a leaderless group transformed itself into a cohesive unit under his leadership. He immediately arranged to have the group billeted together and organized a formal study program, including the preparation of reports on the various topics under study. These reports were forwarded to the Bureau of Ships and formed a permanent record of the results of the study program under Rickover at Oak Ridge.

Captain Rickover's tactic of assuming command of the naval group at Oak Ridge demonstrates a number of characteristics of the man that went beyond his well-displayed capacity for hard work, attention to detail, and determination to accomplish important goals. He was sensitive to power and the art of bureaucratic infighting, and proved himself adept at playing what the political analyst Hedrick Smith called "the power game" in Washington.[5]

When the Oak Ridge naval group completed its mission, Captain Rickover expected his group to form the nucleus of an expanding effort to create nuclear-powered submarines. He soon learned that, instead, the group was to be disbanded, with members assigned to other duties in nuclear-related work and his own participation ambiguous and in doubt. Officers in the Bureau of Ships wanted

Rickover assigned back to Oak Ridge with the job of reviewing classification of documents, which would have sidelined him from any responsibility for developing nuclear propulsion for the navy. This assignment would also have represented a startling denial of Rickover's talent by placing him in a meaningless and trivial job.

The decision to break up the Rickover group came from a recommendation of Admiral Albert G. Mumma, the newly appointed coordinator for nuclear matters in the Bureau of Ships—a position for which Rickover would have been the likely candidate. Even Admiral Mills at first supported Mumma's recommendation to disband the group and leave Rickover in limbo. It appeared that Rickover was to be excluded from the navy's effort to create nuclear propelled ships.

Rickover was deeply committed to the importance of the nuclear submarine. And he had the scientific support of Dr. Edward Teller, who met with him and his group to discuss nuclear reactors. Dr. Teller believed that a reactor could be built within two years, provided the right talent and concentrated effort were applied. Teller wrote a letter to his friend Dr. Lawrence R. Hafstad, of the Department of Defense Research and Development Committee, supporting Rickover's ideas for nuclear-powered submarines and urging the Department of Defense to back him. He wrote in part:

> Captain Rickover and four of his friends were up here [the Los Alamos Laboratory]. I am sure you know of their interest. I was very much impressed by their enthusiasm and enterprise and also by their detailed knowledge which they picked up during their stay at Oak Ridge. I have the feeling that such people as these should thoroughly be made use of and that they should be encouraged to go ahead with an extensive program working toward tangible results within a short time. I do not know whether they can get a first model in working order in two years' time, but I think they should be encouraged to try. I think what they are trying to do has a very good chance of being feasible. It need not be in competition with other enterprises because their skills are different from the skills of physicists. For instance, they are more familiar with the use of high-pressure steam than most of the physicists working on similar problems. . . . One of our greatest shortages is that of capable men, and I don't think we can afford not to encourage a group of people like Captain Rickover and his friends.

Nothing came immediately as a result of Teller's letter, but, characteristically, Rickover was not dissuaded from the importance of building a nuclear reactor for submarines, nor did he intend to accept the imminent decision to bypass him in its development.

Once again, Admiral Mills rescued Rickover from the backwaters of navy assignments. Instead of sending him back to Oak Ridge as a declassification officer, Mills assigned him to the Bureau of Ships, where he would be reporting to Mills on nuclear activities. However, Admiral Mumma's formal title seemed to supersede Rickover's responsibility. For Rickover, the assignment, as he defined it, gave him responsibility without authority.

Again, Rickover was undeterred. He decided once again to reach beyond his authority, repeating the pattern he had established in his days as head of the Electrical Section of the Bureau of Ships. As luck would have it, the Oak Ridge group, while dispersed organizationally, worked near Rickover's office in the Bureau of Ships. Rickover had an idea. Why not prepare for the chief of naval operations, Admiral Chester Nimitz (the World War II hero of the naval battles in the Pacific and a former submariner), a letter strongly endorsing the navy's need for a nuclear-powered submarine? The logic for such a program was clear, at least in the mind of Rickover, Admiral Mills, and a few pioneers who had had visions as early as 1939 of the importance of nuclear fission.

Instead of relying solely on contractors to accomplish the task, Rickover used people in his nuclear propulsion organization to find solutions. Consistent with his experience at Oak Ridge, he insisted that the technical work on zirconium and other rare metals be fully described in handbooks that were published and widely disseminated. The end result of the work on zirconium led to commercial contracts for the production of ample quantities of this material. Commercial plants to produce the metal began operations in 1952 and reached full production in 1954, resolving the supply bottleneck. That year production reached 200,000 pounds at a price just over $13 per pound.

Unlike the traditional navy methods, in which the Bureau of Ships used its resources in an administrative process of contract management, Rickover's nuclear propulsion group applied a direct approach to resolving technical problems. It had technical experts on its staff with the ability to solve engineering problems, often working in close cooperation with government research facilities. These same technical people worked directly with contractors to identify and solve problems. The rule was to minimize, if not eliminate, formal lines of authority. Rickover demanded direct communication. He was the center of control over all aspects of the work in the navy's nuclear reactor group. He instituted a practice of having all correspondence prepared with an extra copy, which notoriously became known as a "pink" (the color of the extra copy). His secretary delivered the pinks at the end of each day and he reviewed them all. He insisted on being kept informed, especially when problems arose, and he expected his staff to know in detail progress being made in solving problems. Harry Mandil, who had worked with Rickover since the early days in the Electrical Section of the Bureau of Ships, had secretaries prepare yellow carbon copies for him. When Rickover called about a problem he had discovered while reading the pinks, not infrequently in the middle of the night, Mandil would know what Rickover was talking about having read his yellows. While Rickover had formal training in engineering, his technical talents derived from intuition. Mandil says of Rickover: "From an engineering standpoint, he could look at something and not know much about it but could tell if it would work or not work and his thing would be 'will it work?' Will this be practical? Can it be maintained? Some very simple questions."

A mystique grew among the people who worked for Rickover that produced a sense of awe about the man, especially his "sixth sense" about technical problems.

Theodore Rockwell describes this talent of Rickover as insight. "He had a lot of insight and nobody can really explain insight, but he had a feeling that certain things, certain aspects of nature, had to be treated with great reverence and awe, and other things you could work around." Rockwell adds:

> The standard experience we had with him, we'd come in and say we want to do such and such. And he'd say no that's not good, we're not going to do that, we're going to do so and so. And you would throw up your hands and say my God what are you thinking about? Why in the world do you want to do that? And so he'd start giving you the rationale, and the rationale was completely off the wall. His facts were wrong, his rationale was irrational, and you'd wander around in this swamp and finally when it became clear he was not going to be swayed, then he says, look, I'll tell you what. You'd say to him, Admiral, before we proceed we're going to have to make these calculations and make these experiments because we've got to know where we're going with this thing and give us three weeks to get it done. And he'd say O. K. and we would be confident that this was going to show that what he had in mind was really stupid. And then we'd come back all sheepish and say, well you know, it isn't really what you said, it's really quite different, but in fact it looks like the way we ought to go and he'd grin and say, why am I always right for the wrong reasons.[6]

Rickover's legendary technical competence, his sixth-sense intuition and insight grew out of his long-honed habits of work and problem solving. Admiral Mills of the Bureau of Ships came to respect early on Rickover's technical competence and his relentless search for solutions to problems encountered in shipboard electrical equipment. Early in his naval career, when Rickover was serving aboard ships in an engineering capacity, his first approach upon reporting to a new ship was to observe directly the ship's engine room and electrical systems until he had thorough knowledge of all the equipment. When he was serving aboard the battleship *New Mexico* as assistant engineering officer, he took charge of improving oil consumption. He managed to improve the ship's record from eighth place out of 15 to first place in the competition for the navy's "E for efficiency" award. He studied every aspect of fuel consumption, including the use of hot water for showers. He reduced hot water consumption by changing shower heads and limiting shower time. His stringent approach made him unpopular aboard ship but established his reputation for relentless attention to the tasks and goals at hand. For commanding officers who saw directly the benefits of Rickover's talents and conscientious attention, his indifference to, and often violation of, naval customs and norms were of little significance compared with the results of his performance.

Later, as head of the Electrical Equipment Section in the Bureau of Ships during World War II, Rickover's technical leadership and work ethic made certain that circuit breakers would no longer fly open when a ship's guns were fired because his unit redesigned the circuit breakers. Ship captains came to respect Rickover when they realized that water would no longer flow through electric cables into closed compartments because cables had been redesigned to seal off water flow.

Rickover was obsessed with getting a job done and done properly, regardless of naval protocols. If he observed an equipment problem aboard ship that was not strictly within his purview, such as a faulty water cooler, much to the irritation of the authority responsible, he would report the faulty equipment in writing. If he had been in industry, he would have been called a rate-buster. The operative norm "Never make your fellow worker or colleague look bad" held little meaning for him compared with the objective of getting the job done properly.

On June 5, 1953, Rickover, then a captain, submitted an editorial to a technical journal on the differences between a "paper reactor" and a "practical reactor." This editorial appeared about the time that the prototype reactor for the *Nautilus* reached criticality in its test runs. The *Nautilus* was a little less than two years away from its first cruise under nuclear power, a voyage in which it would be submerged from New London, Connecticut, to San Juan, Puerto Rico. To reach this stage of the nuclear submarine program, many technical problems had to be resolved, including the method of transferring heat from the reactor to the turbines without corrosion of metals. Two approaches had been tested on two different prototypes. One prototype under Westinghouse Electric's development at its Bettis laboratories utilized high-pressure water as the heat transfer agent. An alternate approach under research and development at GE's Knolls laboratories used liquid sodium for heat transfer. In early studies at Oak Ridge, the high-pressure water reactor design appeared favorable. While Rickover favored this design, the decision to go forward with Westinghouse's Mark I prototype and to build a land-based submarine mockup with the Mark I as the propulsion device grew out of the urgency to complete the *Nautilus* before the mid-1950s. In Rickover's eyes, no matter how well GE's prototype reactor turned out, it would not be completed on time. When GE completed its design for the liquid-sodium reactor, it became the power plant of the second nuclear submarine, the *Seawolf*. But there were operational problems with it, and Rickover ended up substituting the pressurized water reactor of the *Nautilus* type—which once again proved his intuitive technical competence superior to theoretical conclusions. Rickover preferred Westinghouse's style of management over GE's.

Science dominated GE's Knolls Laboratory, and for Rickover progress depended on engineering—a view acceptable to Westinghouse and its president, Gwilym A. Price, who had became interested in nuclear power in 1946 after conversations with Rickover. GE and its chief, Ralph Cordiner, on the other hand, were focused on the civilian uses of nuclear power for generating electricity. GE treated the navy as just another customer and its needs as being subordinate to the research interests of the Knolls. For Rickover, GE's attitude promised little in meeting his goals for the nuclear submarine. Furthermore, he intended to be involved directly in developing nuclear propulsion rather than using the indirect approach of administrator to contractor. Westinghouse accepted his direct approach—his close supervision of technical development and his focus on the high-pressure water reactor.

In his editorial, perhaps tongue in cheek, Rickover contrasts academic and practical nuclear plants.

Each of these two types of plants has eight characteristics. The academic plant is simple, small, cheap, light, and it can be built very quickly. The academic plant is also very flexible in purpose (an "omnibus reactor"), requires very little development using mostly "off the shelf" components, and is not being built now because it remains in the study phase. A practical reactor is being built now, is behind schedule, requires an immense amount of development on apparently trivial items ("corrosion in particular is a problem"), is very expensive, takes a long time to build because of engineering development problems. In addition, the practical reactor is large, heavy, and complicated.[7]

At the time of writing this editorial, the *Nautilus* was no longer a dream in a visionary's eye, but was soon to become the revolutionary weapon in naval readiness for warfare. The editorial intended to dramatize the differences between science and engineering. Scientists searched for elegant solutions while engineers were intent on the search for workable and practical solutions. Scientists could be dreamers while engineers had to keep reality constantly in front of them. Scientists were essentially conservative while engineers were risk takers willing to commit themselves to decisions before all the facts were on the table and evaluated. While both scientists and engineers respected the laws of nature, engineers were willing to look for solutions to deal with them even before theoretical issues had been resolved.

There is more than a hint of oversimplification in this distinction between an academic and a practical reactor, perhaps even to the point of sarcasm—a quality not likely to endear Rickover to his intended audience. But there appeared to be another audience for this editorial beside the scientist and engineer. Many intelligent people involved in making policy and decisions on nuclear matters had a limited technical background. Gwilym Price of Westinghouse was a lawyer and banker, yet he had to make a bet on behalf of his corporation concerning its strategy in the nuclear field. He relied on Rickover at least for Westinghouse's commitment to the nuclear submarine program. The commissioners of the AEC had a grave responsibility for national nuclear policies. They had to rely on scientists—such as Robert Oppenheimer, who led in the development of the atomic bomb; James Conant, president of Harvard University, an advisor on the Manhattan Project while on leave from Harvard; and Vannevar Bush of the Massachusetts Institute of Technology—for advice and direction in their policy decisions. Members of Congress, notably on the Joint Committee on Atomic Energy (JCAE), had to evaluate and recommend legislation and budget allocations to support the development of atomic energy programs, including the decisions affecting the navy's atomic submarine program. Rickover's editorial, and his way of doing his work, was well known to the above-mentioned groups and individuals and had a great influence in decisions that were made both for and against his ongoing career.

One of the most important decisions members of Congress undertook was to protect Hyman Rickover from the navy's attempt to retire him and exclude him from further work on the atomic submarine.

Rickover's name came before a naval selection board for promotion to rear admiral in July 1951. The navy, through the leadership, technical acumen, and single-minded determination of Rickover and his nuclear reactors group, had a nuclear submarine authorized and a prototype under construction in Idaho.

The selection board passed over Rickover for promotion. Under the navy's promotion rules, a captain passed over once could have his name on the list for promotion a year later. Just a week before the 1952 list of promotions was submitted to the president, the secretary of the navy awarded a medal to Rickover in recognition of his distinguished service. That same month, President Truman laid the keel for the *Nautilus*. But even so, the promotion board decided for a second time to omit Rickover from the list.

The contracts for the *Nautilus* had been approved, granting to Westinghouse the authority to construct the nuclear power plant and to Electric Boat to build the submarine. The decision to bypass Rickover meant that, at age 52, he would be forced to retire and could no longer head the navy's nuclear program.

Key members of Rickover's reactor group were enraged over the selection board's failure to promote the captain. They took it upon themselves, at risk of their navy careers, to appeal to the Congress over this injustice and over their concern that, without Rickover, the nuclear submarine was in jeopardy. Many members of the House and Senate knew Rickover as a result of his appearances before committees to explain the nuclear submarine program and to support appropriations. He had established a reputation for honesty and performance, for accomplishing goals he had set forth to the committees. He had proved himself a reliable advocate of the submarine program.

(A good example of the way Rickover's reputation was established and enlarged with the Congress can be seen in the following account: The then secretary of the navy, Dan Kimball, appearing before the JCAE, testified that he had asked the Westinghouse people how they had managed to solve in 12 months the intricate problems of producing zirconium in quantities necessary for cladding the nuclear fuel. The Westinghouse people replied, "Rickover made us get it.")

The entire promotion episode made it abundantly clear that Rickover was anathema to the navy. If there had been any doubt about how the traditional navy felt about him, the promotion episode made the navy's position clear. With the exception of the naval group and selected officers who felt grateful to Rickover for his ability to get things done, he was an outsider, a deviate, and even an enemy of the navy.

The epithet "enemy of the Navy" to describe Rickover came from Admiral Elmo R. Zumwalt, Jr., chief of naval operations from 1970 to 1974. Zumwalt wrote a book after he retired as chief of naval operations. He devoted a chapter (37 pages) to a detailed summary of his complaints about Rickover. The chapter is entitled "The Rickover Complication" and begins as follows:

> The fact that from the start of my watch to the end of it, Vice Admiral, and then Admiral, Hyman G. Rickover was a persistent and formidable obstacle to my plans for modernizing the Navy did not at all surprise me. I had expected him to be. Over the course of my service I had encountered Admiral Rickover a number of times. I knew that he would stop at nothing, bureaucratically speaking, to ensure that nuclear-powered ships received priority over vessels of any other kind. I knew that he had enormous influence on Capitol Hill, far greater than that of any other military man, so great that one student of the scene remarked to me, "Congress doesn't

really think of Rick as an admiral at all, but kind of as a Senator." I knew that his Division of Nuclear Propulsion was a totalitarian mini-state whose citizens—and that included not just his headquarters staff but anybody engaged in building, maintaining, or manning nuclear vessels—did what the Leader told them to, Navy Regulations notwithstanding, or suffered condign punishment. In sum, I knew as soon as I was designated CNO that developing a productive working relationship with Rickover was among the toughest nuts I had been called upon to crack. In my exuberance over being chosen to head the Navy, I believed I could do it. I was wrong.[8]

Rickover's heretical style of leadership was not the only thing about him that offended Zumwalt and other regular navy officers. There were major differences between the two men. As chief of naval operations, Admiral Zumwalt strongly favored a balanced navy made up of a combination of vessels capable of covering the vast seas with many ships and not just nuclear vessels. He was a proponent of what he called the "high-low" strategy of equipping the navy with its fleet vessels. The "high" part of this strategy described high-performance and high-cost ships. The "low" were moderate-performance ships relatively moderate in cost. If the Congress allocated defense funds heavily weighted toward high-performance ships, which included nuclear submarines and surface vessels, while keeping the overall funds for the navy within budgetary constraints, it would be difficult, if not impossible, to meet the balanced fleet objective.

Rickover advocated high-performance ships that included nuclear submarines as well as surface vessels. Nuclear submarines cost a great deal of money as their technical equipment and ordnance increased in sophistication. Zumwalt realized that, with Rickover's influence in the Congress, it would be difficult for him to block Rickover, so he attempted to strike a bargain with him. He would support *SSN 688*, Rickover's attack submarine (at a cost of $300 million per vessel), in the early years of his balanced fleet program, and, in exchange, Rickover would go along with emphasis on the low-cost ships in the later years. While it appeared that an agreement had been reached, Zumwalt remained skeptical that Rickover would temper his enthusiasm for emphasizing nuclear vessels at high costs. In fact, Rickover remained an antagonist of the program Zumwalt tried to implement.

Rickover locked horns with other government officials, including various secretaries of the navy and of defense. He was especially suspicious of systems analysis, advocated by Secretary of Defense Robert S. McNamara.

As Rickover grew older and past retirement age, regulations required that in order for him to continue on active duty he had to be granted an extension every two years. Paul Nitze, secretary of the navy during President Johnson's administration, proposed that Johnson force Rickover's retirement. Congressional pressure prevented this action. As the time approached for renewal of his extension, according to his son, Rickover experienced some anxiety about the prospects for renewal of active-duty status. But with each succeeding renewal, the admiral's power seemed enhanced. He seemed more willing to fight for what he believed in and defy navy norms and conventions. For example, he often appeared in civilian clothes where convention indicated that he should dress in uniform, as he did when he received the medal from the secretary of the navy. Earlier, naval officers were offended and horrified when he appeared in civilian clothes for President Truman's keel laying ceremony of the *Nautilus*. Rickover felt free to violate the navy's norms, the expectations of the way a naval officer should behave. Offending the sensibilities of the navy community meant nothing to him and may indeed have given him some pleasure in the recognition that he was beyond the control of what he considered meaningless codes of conduct.

Among his practices that offended the regular navy was his unusual way of interviewing candidates for the nuclear navy. Wearing his AEC hat, he controlled the selection of officers and enlisted men for the submarine service. Because of the expansion of the submarine fleet, promotion opportunities appeared greatest in the submarine service. Midshipmen at Annapolis applied in large numbers, as did officers in the conventional fleet. An appointment to the submarine service meant an intensive training program and enhanced opportunity for promotion.

The selection procedure started in a conventional manner. Rickover's senior staff reviewed the files of applicants and made note of class standings and other indications of academic ability, particularly in the sciences and engineering. They subjected the candidates to thorough and conventional selection interviews, and then Rickover himself conducted the final and decisive interviews. The candidates were usually kept waiting and, given the notorious reputation of the stress interviews Rickover conducted, were well along on the anxiety scale when they were ushered in to meet the admiral. As it turned out, Elmo Zumwalt, later chief of naval operations, was one of these candidates. He was selected as a candidate for two senior billets on nuclear surface ships. He wrote an account of his interview with Rickover, later published as part of the book he wrote after he retired. At the time when the interview took place, he was an aide to the assistant secretary of the navy. He showed the account to his boss, who passed it on to the secretary of the navy who in turn passed it to the secretary of defense.[9]

Judging from this written account, Rickover felt only contempt for Zumwalt's position as aide, which he made clear at every opportunity he had during the interview. He interrupted the interview three times, expressing anger over Zumwalt's responses. Zumwalt would be left cooling his heels in a room called "the tank," and when the interview resumed, the harangue would continue with Rickover accusing Zumwalt of trying to control the interview and acting as an aide, this said with a sneer and punctuated with a number of "goddamns" and shouts.

One might be tempted to conclude that Rickover seemed to gain sadistic pleasure in dominating and humiliating applicants who wanted to join the nuclear navy. Theodore Rockwell and Harry Mandil, who worked closely with Rickover and knew him well, discounted this speculation, pointing to instances in which Rickover had been caring and gentle with subordinates. When he first met Mandil, an officer newly recruited to join the Electrical Section early in World War II, Rickover made sure Mandil had a place to sleep his first night in Washington, offering him a cot in the Bureau of Ships' office.[10] While he often shouted and screamed in frustration, especially with representatives of shipbuilders and other contractors, he was characteristically patient when his group faced a substantive problem for which solutions seemed difficult to find. He respected the laws of nature, and he adopted an objective stance in the face of formidable problems.

On infrequent occasions, such as once on a picnic for members of the reactors group and their families, Rickover would show a side of himself rarely seen. He was gentle and humorous with families. He arranged to have the young son of a member of the reactors group represent him at a launching. As part of this assignment, the youngster was required to submit a report to the admiral on the proceedings.

Another possibly unknown aspect of his character was that his sense of humor. His office telephone rang one day, interrupting a meeting with his staff. He answered, and his staff heard him say angrily, "I'm too busy to get angry now—call me later." He hung up as the group howled with laughter. In another instance, he had a verbal battle with an admiral in the Bureau of Personnel. The bureau admiral soon called him and said that the two of them should not leave matters at such an unpleasant impasse and that he would come to Rickover's office to have a cup of coffee and talk things over. When he arrived, Rickover shouted to his secretary, "Coffee for the Admiral and hold the hemlock."

This gentler side of his nature was rarely evident. Characteristically, the anger and shouting dominated. What motivated him to engage in behavior that would only create further enmity for him in the regular navy? He had an uncanny sense of power. He learned how to consolidate and amplify his power base. When a member of his staff questioned him about his willingness to engage in conflict when the issue appeared unimportant or the gains questionable, Rickover responded that he did not go looking for conflict, but once involved, he would not back down until he won. He once said to Milton Shaw, a nuclear reactor staff member,

> Shaw, you still don't get it, do you? You keep urging me to get into fights I'd rather avoid. But when you get me into one, by God I'm going to win it. Each time you win a fight, you're that much stronger. People are more leery of taking you on. And each time you lose one, people start thinking, *He isn't invincible. He can be beaten. Maybe I've been too scared of him.* No sir, I'm never going to give an inch on any fight I get into. People know that, and that's why I'm generally able to win them.[11]

This tactical use of power applied to the personnel selection interviews. Rickover sensed intuitively how to secure the loyalty he needed from the nuclear program people. The stress interviews provided him with information on how candidates reacted to stress, and, at the same time, they also helped insure the loyalty of the people he hired. If an authority figure induces anxiety in a subordinate and then becomes the agent for allaying this anxiety, paradoxically, the subordinate feels grateful to the authority figure and tends to repress the memory of who induced the debilitating emotions in the first place. Rickover induced a state of anxiety arising from the humiliating experience of being shouted at and demeaned by him. A psychological double bind ensues with this type of manipulation of anxiety reactions. The experience evokes anger. But the anger has to be suppressed for the candidate to get through the interview with minimal damage to the evaluation that is taking place. Bottling up the anger produces the effect of helplessness, with diminished self-esteem and limited resources in dealing with the threat directly related to the interviewing experience. The only apparent solution, short of walking out of the interview, is to give in and try to play the game exactly how the interviewer wants, which means giving short and direct answers to questions. In learning after the interview that he has been selected for the program, paradoxically, the candidate feels gratitude and relief, which replaces the anxiety, anger, humiliation, and loss of self-esteem. The favorable outcome restores, and even enhances, self-esteem. The candidate feels part of a select group and has a sense of gratitude to the leader coupled with awe surrounding that leader's persona.

In the case of Rickover's handpicked staff, these regressive emotions came to be replaced over time by the more mature reactions of respect for him as he displayed his intuition and competence in technical matters and his concern for effective training and enhanced performance. Over time, people he had hired also came to respect his talents in the purposive playing of the power game. The cost to Rickover of this unorthodox behavior was to solidify the image of him as a deviate and outsider to the regular, or, what came to be called, the "real" navy.

But to imply a cost for deviant behavior, one would have to believe that there was painful retaliation. The only pain or anxiety for Rickover lay in the possibility that he would be forced to retire because the various secretaries of the navy would not extend his active duty. The secretary who finally succeeded in forcing Rickover's retirement, early in the Reagan administration, became a controversial figure in the highly visible dispute between private contractors and the government over cost overruns.

John F. Lehman, Jr., became secretary of the navy during Reagan's administration. He took on the objective of building the navy under Reagan's expanded defense budget. He wanted a 600-ship navy and was determined to meet this objective as he launched a huge shipbuilding program. Lehman reacted to David Lewis's threat to close down Electric Boat, recognizing that his 600-ship navy was in jeopardy. His subordinates in the secretary's office arranged a settlement with Lewis to the tune of $700 million.

When Lehman took over as secretary, he fervently wanted Rickover retired from the navy and to no longer be a force in shipbuilding and strategic planning. He engineered an agreement with Defense Secretary Casper Weinberger to convince President Reagan not to renew Rickover's active-duty status. Reagan agreed, though it seems unlikely that he knew much about the admiral's controversial background or the disputes with Electric Boat.

One day Rickover got a call from his wife telling him she had heard a report on the radio that Reagan was going to retire him. The next thing he knew, he received an order to report to President Reagan's office. He reported. Lehman and Weinberger were present along with James Baker, the president's chief of staff. According to Lehman's description of what transpired, Rickover immediately verbally attacked Lehman.

> "Mr. President, that pissant knows nothing about the navy." The Admiral turned toward me and raised his voice to a fearsome shout. "You just want to get rid of me, you want me out of the program because you want to dismantle the program." Shifting now toward President Reagan, he roared on: "He's a goddam liar, he knows he's just doing the work of the contractors. The contractors want me fired because of the claims and because I am the only one in the government who keeps them from robbing the taxpayers."[12]

Rickover insisted on meeting with Reagan privately. Reagan agreed and Lehman, Weinberger, and the others left the office. During this private meeting, Rickover continued his attack, and Reagan reportedly mumbled some words of praise for his defense and navy secretaries, complimented Rickover on his accomplishments and years of service, and then escorted the admiral out of the office. An act of Congress provided Rickover with permanent office space in the Navy Yard, secretarial help, and a car and driver. From his office, Rickover continued his campaign to call a halt to cost overrun compensation for Electric Boat. He was officially retired on January 31, 1982.

When Rickover died, the navy held a memorial service at the Washington Cathedral, officiated by a Catholic priest, an Episcopal priest, and a Rabbi. Admiral Watkins and others delivered eulogies to the 1,200 people assembled in the cathedral, including former President Carter and Secretary of State Schultz. Secretary of the Navy Lehman also attended. Rockwell, in *The Rickover Effect*, found that the noted social philosopher Max Lerner had captured the underlying cause of the fear and hatred of Rickover that seemed prevalent among highly placed figures such as Admiral Zumwalt and Secretary of the Navy Lehman. Max Lerner wrote, "The real hate and fear are not of *him,* but of their own weakness and bewilderment in the face of new forces they cannot understand. Rickover is the breed of men in our time who confront them."[13]

Among the books written about Admiral Rickover and the nuclear navy, a thread persists of a complex man, an outsider, an intuitive and gifted engineer, a dedicated hard worker, a politically astute manager, and perhaps above all, a man difficult to fathom.

The honors Rickover received included two congressional gold medals and the Fermi Award for contributions to nuclear technology. Zuckerman believed that these awards, which came to Rickover later in life, compensated for the hurts he had felt as an outsider earlier in his naval career. There is reason to doubt that any honor or award would have modified Rickover's aggression and his image as a deviate in the naval service. As Edward L. Beach, retired captain of the U.S. Navy, an early and loyal member of Rickover's nuclear propulsion group, wrote: "It has been said somewhere that 'you always have to take the whole man. You can't take only part of him. He comes as he is with all his faults and warts'. In Rickover's case, even his warts, like them or not, somehow contributed to the extraordinary success of what he accomplished."[14]

6

A Change Agent: Florence Nightingale and Medical Reform

In June 1849 Florence Nightingale, then age 29, refused a proposal of marriage. Richard Monckton Milnes had been persistent in his courtship. For the last time, he insisted that Nightingale make up her mind. This she did.

The refusal came at the end of tortured self-reflection, doubt, and a pervasive sense of guilt. Nightingale was deeply attached to Milnes. She had previously refused a marriage proposal from a cousin but felt no remorse as she did with Milnes. Milnes was the object of many of her reveries, including a deep "passional" attraction. These reveries, in a state familiar and deeply troublesome to her, consisted of what she called dreams—daytime reveries in which she seemed lost and detached from conscious awareness of her surroundings.

In Sir Edward Cook's biography of Florence Nightingale, much referred to in Cecil Woodham-Smith's later biography, the author quotes from her autobiographical writings about this marriage proposal and refusal.

> I have an intellectual nature which requires satisfaction, and that would find it in him. I have a passional nature which requires satisfaction, and that would find it in him. I have a moral, an active nature which requires satisfaction, and that would not find it in his life. I could hardly find satisfaction for any of my natures. Sometimes I think that I will satisfy my passional nature at all events, because that will secure me from the evil of dreaming. But would it? I could be satisfied spending a life with him combining our different powers in some great object. I could not satisfy this nature by spending a life with him in making society and arranging domestic things. . . . To be nailed to a continuation and exaggeration of my present life, without hope of another, would be intolerable to me. Voluntarily to put it out of my power ever to be able to seize the chance of forming for myself a true and rich life would seem to me like suicide.[1]

Nightingale's survival depended on finding a vocation. In 1837, when she was 17 years old, she heard God speaking to her. She heard this voice (which was to be repeated several times during the years before she found her vocation) commanding her to dedicate her life to a calling, but not specifying what this calling was to be. She spent the next 16 years in anguish, in conflict with her mother and sister, and in periods of illness, until she overcame doubts and family resistance to her increasing awareness that her calling was to be nursing.

But to simply identify her vocation in nursing fails to describe her extraordinary talents in administration; her leadership in reforming medical and hospital practice in the British military; her acuity in mobilizing and using power to carry out reform against notable resistance in government, military, and medical bureaucracies; and the achievement for which she is most famous, her creation of nursing training and practice that thrives to this day as a profession.

Nightingale refused to accept the identity her sex and station in life held in store for her. She was expected to marry, to have children, to conform to the image she had of her mother and sister who arranged parties and managed servants while they idled their time from one residence in the country to another and from "the season" in London to travel and periodic residence in Paris and Rome—all of which defined their role in life. Work and vocation had no precedent in this identity. Her life, as she actually defined and lived it, resulted from the imperatives of talent, a demand from within her ego that she responded to—although not without internal psychological conflict, and actual conflict, especially with her mother and sister.

To students of power, leadership, and command, Nightingale presents a challenge: how does one explain how she came to understand, hone, and use her talent? She benefited uniquely from the education her father provided by in tutoring her and her sister. She embraced this education and recognized that this honing of talent made a demand on her psyche. A significant portion of her life and work was carried out while she was ill in bed, or lying on her couch suffering from fatigue, weakness, and heart palpitations. She was exhorted by doctors and family to rest and give up the burdens of her work. She often expected to die and at times even longed for death. However, she persisted with the assistance of a few men of considerable prestige and accomplishment, who became her means of exerting power and leading change, while she lay ill and avoided a public presence.

Whatever its nature, the illness appears to have been an integral aspect of her character and a force deeply connected to her work. Besides the charisma attached to her person and reputation as "The Lady with the Lamp" that enabled her to force change, Nightingale was a prolific writer who prepared drafts for government documents on sanitation in the military, in hospitals, and in barracks at home and in India (where she had never traveled). The men who acted as her agents were devoted to her mission and person, but were often exasperated at her demands and her inaccessibility.

Despite her illness and the fact that she spent much of her life as an invalid, Nightingale lived to age 90, thus adding to the mystery with which her image was imbued.

Explanations of her illness eventually pass from fact to hypothesis and speculation. A surer formulation of her total personality and character will emerge if we shift our efforts of explanation from strict causality, which must remain speculative even if plausible, to the ways the illness played into her talents and her goal-driven behavior.

Nightingale's achievements were substantive, but also power related in that she could not bring about change without a shrewd and purposeful use of power.

She defied the common stereotypes of feminine passivity of her culture and upbringing and effectively entered the masculine world of power as an agent of change, but with a subtle use of indirection related to the passivity associated with her illness. There appears to be a startling role reversal in the coterie of men who formed her "cabinet" and became the instruments for effecting change under her leadership. She directed this cabinet and displayed a penchant for command that would brook no resistance to movement in the direction she visualized.

"In the course of a life's experience such as scarcely any one has ever had, I have always found that no one ever deserves his or her character. Be it better or worse than the real one, it is always unlike the real one" (Florence Nightingale in a letter to Madame Mohl, December 13, 1871.)[2]

After their marriage in 1818, William Edward (WEN) and Frances (Fanny) Nightingale traveled and lived on the Continent, returning periodically to England. Nightingale was born on May 12, 1820, in Florence. Her parents named both daughters after their places of birth. (Parthenope, Nightingale's older sister, was given the Greek name for Naples.) Fanny was six years older than WEN and stronger of mind. WEN tended toward reflection, aesthetics, and scholarship, which he put to good use in educating his daughters. When they returned from the Continent to live a more settled life in England, they returned to two properties. Lea Hurst, in Derbyshire, they used as a summer residence. Embley, in Hampshire, became the main family residence after WEN had it enlarged, according to his own design, to make it fit for Fanny's desire to become a noted hostess.

Florence Nightingale, of the two sisters the more able student of their father, recognized that she could not be content to live an indolent life arranging flowers, entertaining, and, with marriage, accepting the role of the woman with status and wealth. She would escape from the family to nurse sick women in the village. She was easily bored. Her father would insist that she and her sister listen as he read aloud from *The Times,* interspersing his reading with commentary. For Parthenope (Parthe), this activity of their father's was not burdensome. She could continue with her drawing as she listened. For Florence it was excruciatingly painful, "boring to desperation."

> To be read aloud to is the most miserable experience of the human intellect. Or rather, is it any exercise at all? It is like lying on one's back, with one's hands tied, and having liquid poured down one's throat. Worse than that, because suffocation would immediately ensue, and put a stop to this operation. But no suffocation would stop the other."[3]

When God spoke to her on February 7, 1837, and "called me to His service,"[4] the voice seemed real and not a dream. When she heard the voice, she was accustomed to what Cecil Woodham-Smith describes as living in a dream world. What was different in this experience was the seeming reality of the voice coming from outside herself. While she accepted this voice as a call to His service, what the service should be was unknown to her.

Gradually she came to the realization that perhaps her vocation lay in caring for the sick. She had nursed sick people near Embley and Lea Hurst. When her grandmother became ill, she nursed her. She nursed her governess during her last illness. But the realities of hospitals, the filth surrounding the sick, the complete lack of sanitation, as well as the deplorable reputations of the women who acted as nurses presented obstacles to accepting fully the vocation that presented itself to her. Her compassion for the poor, the sick, and the suffering were real and became focused during the famine of 1842. Two years later, she could no longer doubt that she was destined to a life of nursing and care for the sick and the unfortunate.

In June 1844, Dr. Samuel Gridley Howe and his wife, Julia, came to Embley as guests of the Nightingales. Dr. Howe was a noted American philanthropist, later well known as an abolitionist, whose medical work was with the blind. (Julia Ward Howe later became famous as the author of the "Battle Hymn of the Republic.") As Woodham-Smith reports it, one day Florence asked Dr. Howe to meet her before breakfast in the library. During this meeting, she asked, "Dr. Howe, do you think it would be unsuitable and unbecoming for a young Englishwoman to devote herself to works of charity in hospitals and elsewhere as Catholic sisters do? Do you think it would be a dreadful thing to do?" Dr. Howe replied, "My dear Florence, it would be unusual, and in England whatever is unusual is thought to be unsuitable; but I say to you 'go forward,' if you have a vocation for that way of life, act up to your inspiration and you will find there is never anything unbecoming or unladylike in doing your duty for the good of others. Choose, go on with it, wherever it may lead you and God be with you."[5]

Having realized that her vocation followed from her deep interest in hospital nursing, how was she to translate this interest into training? How was she to use this training, once achieved, to work at her vocation? The most formidable barrier she had to overcome was the hysteria and panic of her mother and sister over her desire to train as a nurse. The reputation of nurses, for the most part blackened by drunkenness and prostitution, made the profession unsuitable for a woman of Florence's background.

Unbeknownst to her mother and sister, Florence would awaken early and, before the day began, would read blue books on medical care, hospital function, and home care for the elderly and the sick. She had heard and read about the Institution for Deaconesses in the town of Kaiserswerth, Germany, founded in 1833 by Pastor Theodor Fliedner and his wife, Friederike Munster. The institute originated in a summer house in the pastor's garden as a refuge for discharged prisoners and, three years later, expanded to include an infant school and a hospital. It had by now become a worldwide charitable organization that trained probationers, who became deaconesses, to take care of infants, the sick, and prisoners. Florence admired the lack of pretense in this famous institution. She contrasted the common practice of using well-known names as founders and the high-sounding promises of prospectuses with the enduring and modest practicality of Pastor Fliedner and Friederike Munster.

> Eschew Prospectuses; they're the devil and make one sick. It is like making out a bill of fare when you have not a single pound of meat. . . . At Kaiserswerth, a clergyman and his wife have begun, not with a Prospectus, but with a couple of hospital beds,

and have offered not an advertisement, but a home to young women willing to come. At Berne, a Mdlle. Wurstenberger, a woman of rank and education, goes to Kaiserswerth to learn, and her friend to Strassburg. They return and open a hospital with two rooms, increase their funds, others join them and are taught by them. . . . To publish first is as bad a practical bull as is the name of the *Prospective Review*.[6]

Florence found in the image of Kaiserswerth a practical solution to the problem of finding her vocation. She desperately wanted to train there but had to overcome the protests of her mother and sister as they became aware of her determination to train in nursing. They tried to thwart her aim by hysterical outbursts of screaming, fainting, and tears. WEN grew weary of these outbursts and quarrels to the point that he would leave home to find peace and quiet elsewhere. The women also tried diverting Florence's attention through travel, which she actually enjoyed.

Florence met Selina Bracebridge, who, with her husband, Charles, was a friend of her parents. The Bracebridges respected her. She felt that Selina instinctively understood her deep desire for vocation. Selina appealed to her because she was not judgmental. Selina provided relief from the conflicts that were centered around Florence's mother and sister. Florence once wrote of Selina:

She never told me life was fair and my share of its blessings great and that I *ought* to be happy. She did not know that I was miserable but she felt it; and to me, young, strong and blooming as I then was, the idol of the man I adored, the spoilt child of fortune, she had the heart and the instinct to say—"Earth, my child, has a grave and in heaven there is rest."[7]

In 1847 Florence feared for her sanity—oppressed as she was by her reveries, her inability to forge ahead with her vocation, and the continuing intense conflict with her mother and sister. The Bracebridges came to her rescue. They were planning to spend the winter in Rome and invited her to join them. Under the beneficent care and attention of these loving friends, particularly Selina, she recovered and enjoyed her stay in Rome. She was particularly entranced with the Sistine Chapel and became engrossed in Michelangelo's ceiling. "Think of a day alone in the Sistine Chapel with [Greek Sigma for Selina Bracebridge], quite alone, without custode, without visitors, looking up into that heaven of angels and prophets."[8] This letter to Parthe is lyrical and displays Florence's talent for observation and description. It provided reassurance to the family that the winter in Rome with the Bracebridges was having its magical effect of curing her and, perhaps in the wishes of Fanny and Parthe, that it would permanently divert her from her determination to follow the vocation of nursing the sick in hospitals. But the apparent diversion was temporary.

When Florence returned to England, she renewed her concerns for the poor and made opportunities to visit hospitals while in London. Her moral nature found the life of the wealthy, with their homes in the country, a total avoidance of the cruel realities of poverty readily seen on the streets of London. This disparity weighed heavily on her conscience, and once again she was overcome with guilt and restlessness in being unable to follow her vocation. She thought, in the fall of

1848, that she would realize her wish to visit Kaiserswerth while her mother and sister took the cure at Carlsbad, but because of disturbances in Frankfurt, the trip was canceled. She was bitterly disappointed.

Once again, the Bracebridges, sensing her despair, proposed that she join them on a trip—this time to Egypt and Greece. Fanny and Parthe hoped this trip would change her so that she would be able to live a comfortable life suitable to the family's station. But the trip did no such thing. On the contrary, toward the end of this trip (on July 31, 1850), she arrived in Kaiserswerth for a two-week stay with the pastor, his wife, and the deaconesses. Following this stay, she wrote a description of the work at Kaiserswerth, which was published anonymously in England as a pamphlet. She was more firmly resolved than ever and rejected suggestions, following this article, that she follow a literary career. Marriage, too, was not to be for her. She had rejected it in refusing Milnes's final proposal even though she was strongly attracted to him and had moments doubting her decision.

As she continued determined, her mother and sister steeled their minds in opposition to her chosen path. The conflict in the family intensified, as Parthe, who was hysterical about Florence's determination to follow her own course in life, demanded her sister's complete devotion to her care. According to Cook, her first biographer, Parthe was jealous of Florence, who was the more attractive of the two sisters and who easily captivated friends such as the Bracebridges and Sidney and Elizabeth Herbert, prominent figures in British social life and politics.

Parthe demanded that her sister devote six months to attending completely to her wishes. Florence complied at considerable cost to her own state of mind. But in the end, she gained her wish to spend three months at Kaiserswerth. Accompanying her mother and sister to Carlsbad, she left them there, following a hysterical scene with her sister, and traveled on, on her own. "My sister threw my bracelets which I offered her to wear, in my face and the scene which followed was so violent that I fainted."[9] Although each step Florence took to liberate herself from her mother and sister appeared climactic, conflict always reappeared, centering on both Fanny and Parthe. Parthe's increasing hysterics forced Florence, once and for all, to settle for herself which course in life she would follow: either acquiesce to the conventional or stay true to her innermost desire for a life of independence and vocation.

The climax occurred in late 1852 and early 1853. Parthe had placed herself for treatment in the hands of Sir James Clarke, the Queen's personal physician and a friend of the family. Sir James told the family that Parthe, who was suffering from delirium and chronic irritability, must distance herself from Florence and the family. While Fanny made light of this recommendation, WEN acted decisively. He gave Florence an annual allowance of £500 and, thereby, financial independence.; he gave her financial independence.

Florence's stormy relationship with her mother and sister would appear to suggest that she would have difficulty in gaining sympathy and support from women. But, in fact, she had the deep admiration and help of a number of women throughout her life. At this time there was "Sigma" (Selina Bracebridge) and also Elizabeth Herbert, the wife of Sidney Herbert, who was to play a decisive part in Florence's future. Elizabeth admired her and became instrumental in having her appointed superintendent of an "Establishment for Gentlewomen during Illness." Aunt Mai, Mrs. Samuel Smith, WEN's sister, became devoted to Florence, even to the sacrifice of her own family, and provided enormous support and help over the years until family obligations forced her to leave Florence's side. Nightingale maintained deep friendships with other women and engaged in lively correspondence with them. And even with her mother and sister, despite the independent path she finally established for herself, and despite their adamant and emotional opposition to the one thing that meant the world to her, her love for them remained true and in place all her life.

In 1853 the committee in charge of "The Establishment for Gentlewomen" interviewed Florence and were impressed with her manner, but they were hesitant to take her on because of her social position and her youthful appearance. They finally settled on appointing her superintendent, acquiescing in certain conditions she had laid down as being contingent on her accepting the position. The conditions were that she would be in complete charge of the establishment including its finances, although she would receive no remuneration for her services. She would engage a matron—whose salary she would pay—as a means of overcoming the disadvantage of her youthful appearance. Along with Aunt Mai, she first supervised the renovations to the new establishment at 1 Harley Street in London, and at age 33, 16 years after she had first heard the voice of God, Florence Nightingale became head of The Establishment for Gentlewomen.

Florence displayed in her first post a flair for administration. She understood intuitively the logic of efficiency that was to become the hallmark of scientific management more than half a century later. She instituted programs to leverage the time and energy of nurses. For example, instead of nurses running up and down stairs to carry food to patients, she installed windlasses, mechanical devices for hauling food from kitchens to upper floors where nurses worked taking care of patients. She designed and installed devices for patients to signal nurses when they needed attention. She insisted on cleanliness, with laundered bedding and fresh linen. She understood the importance of financial management and cost control. She instituted purchasing procedures such as letting out contracts for food to be delivered in large enough quantities to assure wholesale prices. Above all, she understood the importance of maintaining power in her role and not permitting rivalries on the committee and among surgeons to affect efficiency of service. She controlled the various committees, rather than allowing the committees to determine how she should perform her job. She was in charge and made it clear to all that she was running the establishment.

There were two sides to Florence's nature. For patients and others who were powerless and impoverished she was extraordinarily kind, even at times helping them financially. She received many letters of thanks and the blessings of those who had benefited from her kindness. "My dearest kind Miss Nightingale. I send you a few lines of love." "I felt so lonely when I saw you going away from me." "All your affectionate kindness to me comes before me now and causes me many tears." "I am your affectionate, attached, and grateful." "Thank you, thank you darling Miss Nightingale." "You are our sunshine . . . were you to give up, all would soon fade away and the whole thing would cease to be."[10]

The other side of her nature was steel-like, purposeful, determined, and shrewd. She likened herself to someone who had become accustomed to intrigue and who had learned to manipulate. Intrigue and manipulation were the skills she learned in dealing with the two committees of Gentlemen and Gentlewomen in the oversight of the establishment as well as the committee of surgeons.

Having gained control of all aspects of the establishment, having brought order out of incipient chaos to the management of its affairs, Florence Nightingale became bored in the absence of new challenges. She entertained the idea of becoming the superintendent of nurses at King's College Hospital, with the support of the chief surgeon, Dr. William Bowman. Besides the hospital's large size compared with the Establishment for Gentlewomen, the position of superintendent of nurses would enable her to develop a program for training nurses—which would have the advantage of overcoming the severe shortage as well as creating a new standard for hospital nursing.

While contemplating a new challenge, she visited hospitals to gather firsthand data on the practice of nursing in hospitals, always with the aim of promoting reform. Her friend Elizabeth Herbert wrote to her on behalf of her husband, who was concerned about conditions in hospitals and sought to promote reform, especially in the quality of nursing care. Sidney Herbert wanted information on the condition of nursing in hospitals. "Sidney says if he could get some authentic information on the subject of nurses, their bad pay and worse lodging he could get the evil more or less remedied and public attention at any rate turned that way."[11] Thus began the important collaboration between Florence Nightingale and Sidney Herbert that continued through the Crimean War and beyond and informed Florence's intellectual and practical leadership as she got the government to act in altering the abysmal practices in hospital care and nursing.

Florence Nightingale prepared reports for Herbert, who wrote directly to her requesting additional information. As she negotiated for a new position at King's College Hospital, she also volunteered to superintend the nursing during a cholera epidemic in London. But the outbreak of the Crimean War in the Spring of 1854 set the stage for the monumental changes she would bring about in the care of sick and wounded soldiers in military hospitals, barracks, and beyond, to the birth of nursing as a new profession.

> In future years, in distant climes,
> Should war's dread strife its victims claim,
> Should pestilence unchecked betimes,
> Strike more than sword, than cannon maim,
> He who then reads these truthful rhymes
> Will trace her progress to undying fame.[12]

Florence Nightingale's "progress to undying fame," which she did not seek, and even avoided, began when England joined France in declaring war against Russia on March 28, 1854. Thus began the Crimean War. The Turks were already at war with Russia, but when the Russians attempted to control how the Ottoman Turks dealt with the Orthodox faithful, and other religious issues affecting important sites in Palestine came into conflict, France and England felt compelled to go to war.

The battles of Alma and Balaklava proved decisive in the siege of Sevastopol, which lasted for a year. The war ended with the Russian acceptance of peace terms definitively reached in the Treaty of Paris signed on March 30, 1856. Thus ended a bloody war with numerous casualties on both sides. But out of the war was produced an important side effect that altered public consciousness of the care of the wounded and the sick.

The Crimean War produced the first war correspondent in history. William Howard Russell of *The Times* traveled to the battlefields and hospitals to report on the condition of the soldiers. In his dispatches to *The Times,* he reported on the horrifying conditions in which the wounded and sick were treated. The British were proud of the courage and resourcefulness of their soldiers in battle. To learn that these brave soldiers had to endure terrible conditions aroused public opinion that turned against the government. In one report, Russell wrote:

> It is with feelings of surprise and anger that the public will learn that no sufficient preparations have been made for the proper care of the wounded. Not only are there not sufficient surgeons—that, it might be urged, was unavoidable; not only are there no dressers and nurses—that might be a defect of system for which no one is to blame; but what will be said when it is known that there is not even linen to make bandages for the wounded? The greatest commiseration prevails for the sufferings of the unhappy inmates of Scutari, and every family is giving sheets and old garments to supply their wants. But why could not this clearly foreseen want have been supplied? Can it be said that the Battle of Alma has been an event to take the world by surprise? Has not the expedition to the Crimea been the talk of the last four months? And when the Turks gave up to our use the vast barracks to form a hospital and depot, was it not on the ground that the loss of the English troops was sure to be considerable when engaged in so dangerous an enterprise? And yet, after the troops have been six months in the country, there is no preparation for the commonest surgical operations! Not only are the men kept, in some cases, for a week without the hand of a medical man coming near their wounds; not only are they left to expire in agony, unheeded and shaken off, though catching desperately at the surgeon whenever he makes his rounds through the fetid ship; but now, when they are placed in the spacious building, where we were led to believe that everything was ready which could ease their pain or facilitate their recovery, it is found that the commonest appliances of a workhouse sick-ward are wanting, and that the men must die through the medical staff of the British army having forgotten that old rags are necessary for the dressing of wounds. If Parliament were sitting, some notice would probably be taken of these facts, which are notorious and have excited much concern; as it is, it rests with the Government to make inquiries into the conduct of those who have so greatly neglected their duty.[13]

The Government did take notice of the aroused public anger. One official who took special notice was Sidney Herbert, the secretary at war in the British cabinet. Florence Nightingale also took notice. She wrote to Elizabeth Herbert outlining a plan to go to Scutari along with several nurses at no expense to the government and with official sanction to volunteer in the hospital. She appealed to Elizabeth

Herbert to be granted relief from her duties at the establishment. She also indicated that her uncle had already gotten her parents' permission to go to Scutari. It so happened that Sidney Herbert, without knowledge of Florence's letter, wrote to her outlining his plan to enlist her services in recruiting a group of nurses to work at the hospital in Scutari and to place her in complete charge of the group. Herbert and Florence Nightingale were of one mind.

They met in London and settled the arrangement, which was then sanctioned by the government and officially communicated to Nightingale. The official appointment as "Superintendent of the female nursing establishment in the English General Military Hospitals in Turkey" directed her to report to the chief army medical officer at Scutari "under whose orders and direction" she was to carry out her duties. While she was to be in charge of the nurses, the performance of her duties as superintendent was "subject . . . to the sanction and approval of the Chief Medical Officer."

The fact that a course of action had been reached in response to the public outrage following the special correspondent's reports in *The Times* reflects Herbert's ability to transcend the limits of his authority as secretary at war in the British cabinet. It also reflects Florence Nightingale's grasp of the opportunity presented to her to be of service and assume a larger responsibility than she currently held.

Florence embraced the challenge. She began immediately to interview and recruit women who would travel with her to Scutari and take up hospital nursing duties under her charge. The selection was difficult. Surprisingly few applicants appeared, and fewer still seemed qualified for the duties and hardships expected in the Turkish hospital. In the end, 38 women traveled with Florence and the Bracebridges, who elected to help her, to Marseilles and from there set sail for Scutari expecting to take up nursing duties.

But upon arrival, the party encountered poor preparation for their work and living arrangements. Supplies for the wounded and sick soldiers were substandard and severely limited, and they were no better for the party of nurses. Fortunately, Florence had had the foresight to collect a fund of about £30,000 under her direct control, over and above the special fund raised by *The Times* and administered by John Macdonald (an engineer and later editor of *The Times,* who was traveling with the party). Fortunately, too, she had had the foresight to buy supplies while awaiting the ship at Marseilles.

When she arrived with her party in Scutari, she faced obstacles resulting from incompetence in the military organization and the hospital administration, and from resistance and callousness to suffering on the part of the medical department. In particular, the medical department and doctors had neither asked for nor welcomed the help of the nursing contingent. Added to all these obstacles was the unwillingness of the purveyors to find supplies. The living arrangements for the nurses were cramped and dirty. Any person without the determination and resourcefulness of Florence Nightingale would have turned back in the face of the disastrous situation in Scutari.

The terms of her appointment and the degree of authority vested in her proved of little help in carrying out her mission. She had to rely on her talents, including her acuity in the practical aspects of power in a bureaucratic environment, to do what she had set out to do. For example, to avoid conflict with the head of the medical staff, she let it be known that the nurses would not appear on the wards until the doctors requested their help. The nurses occupied themselves with preparing bedding for patients and providing clean linen. But gradually Florence's tact, her deference to the status of the surgeons, and, especially, her competence in nursing—including her attendance at amputations—won the day in increasing requests for the services of the nurses.

What helped her in overcoming the resistance was the strict discipline she applied to the nursing corps. She demanded competence and circumspect behavior. She did not hesitate to send home nurses who were incompetent or unwilling to observe her rules of conduct.

Unlike her behavior before the medical staff, where she awaited requests for nursing to avoid the appearance of disregard for status, Florence acted autonomously in overcoming the bureaucratic caution of the purveyor and his staff. She had money at hand and used it to overcome the shortages of supply. She arranged to have a washhouse equipped to ensure clean bedding and shirts for the patients. She provided utensils for the patients to eat the improved food they were served. Her initiatives on behalf of the patients, and the care she and her nursing staff provided, enhanced her standing among the medical staff and increased the call for nursing on the wards. Her reputation grew, based on the quality of care she gave the appreciative patients in the barracks hospital. While she forbade her nurses to appear on the wards after early evening, she herself would make the rounds at night carrying a lamp. The grateful patients would await her evening rounds and would "kiss her shadow as she passed." Thus Florence Nightingale became "The Lady with the Lamp," a legendary figure in the hospital and at home in England.

Florence's tough-minded approach to overcoming administrative barriers led her to write stinging reports on conditions she sought to change. These reports, written typically in the late hours of the night, when she probably should have been sleeping, were addressed to Sidney Herbert. The two had a good relationship, disturbed only when Herbert acted contrary to the agreement that she would be in charge of all nursing services and would control the selection and deployment of the nurses. A crisis in their relationship occurred when Herbert, without her advance knowledge and in violation of his written directive to her, agreed to send to Scutari a group of 47 women under the charge of Mary Stanley, the sister of the dean of Westminster. In effect, Herbert's action, if left to stand, would have created a competitive structure and would have resulted in diminishing Florence's authority and dividing responsibility, violating her sense of organizational coherence.

Herbert's action infuriated her and she wrote him a stinging rebuke.

You have sacrificed the cause so near my heart, you have sacrificed me, a matter of small importance now; you have sacrificed your own written word to a popular cry. You must feel that I ought to resign, where conditions are imposed upon me which render the object for which I am employed unattainable, and I only remain at my post till I have provided in some measure for these poor wanderers.[14]

She did not resign, because of the moral responsibility she felt to her work. Nor did she send back the nurses.—Herbert recognized that he had neglected his own word that she had sole responsibility for the nursing service. The additional nurses were initially a burden since there was no room for housing them or otherwise attending to their needs. However, she overcame these problems, taking on the added work the new staff initially imposed upon her. Eventually, they were put to good use for the benefit of the patients.

Florence's seeming acquiescence to the presence of Mary Stanley's nurses represented a tactical retreat while maintaining her control over all the nurses in Scutari. Her rebuke of Sidney Herbert indicated that she would not be quick to accept Stanley in a cooperative venture, regardless of the fact that they had been friends while working together in the Establishment for Gentlewomen. In fact, she ended her friendship with Stanley and would not forgive Stanley's apparent attempt to establish herself in the power structure of the nursing services during the Crimean War.

One of the talents good administrators use in bureaucratic organizations is applying the art of circumvention. Strictly adhering to rules often sacrifices the real objectives of the organization. Florence became adept at circumvention, partially because she valued the real objectives of the hospital—the care and well-being of the patient—and had little regard for the rules and regulations that subordinated the real goals. But her ability at circumvention depended upon her control of resources, which she used to good advantage in overcoming the purveyor's insistence that he could not issue stores, vitally needed and in supply, without the authorization from a board. Bedding, shirts, and rugs to keep patients warm were paramount and the accounting needs of the purveyor of secondary consequence.

Cook discriminates between two sources of Nightingale's power during the Crimean War. The first was in "her masterful will and practical good sense," which he saw as inherent qualities of mind and personality. The second he calls "adventitious power" resulting from her position in the minds of government ministers and in the mind of Queen Victoria. This extrinsic power was based on the wave of adoration of Florence Nightingale on the part of the British public and the publicity that followed reports of her work in the care of the sick and wounded soldiers.

Florence regularly wrote reports to Herbert detailing the problems she encountered with the purveyor and other bureaucrats who seemed fearful of taking action lest they violate regular procedures. The purveyor would not issue stores without the advance approval of a board of survey. Approval required weeks of delay in the face of immediate need. Herbert, as secretary at war, supported her and joined her in lamenting the mentality that could not distinguish need from procedural correctness.

As Florence's reputation grew, she gained the support and admiration of Queen Victoria. A letter from the Queen, expressing to the sick and wounded at Scutari her heartfelt concern for their well-being, was posted in the wards and lifted the spirits of the patients. In a letter to Herbert, Queen Victoria asked to be kept informed through his wife of the condition of the soldiers in Scutari. The Queen also sent gifts:

> packages containing some comforts and useful articles which Her Majesty wishes to be placed in your hands for distribution, as you may think fit, amongst the wounded and sick at Scutari. . . . The Queen has directed me to ask you to undertake the distribution and application of these articles, partly because Her Majesty wished you to be made aware that your goodness and self-devotion in giving yourself up to the soothing attendance upon these wounded and sick soldiers had been observed by the Queen with sentiments of the highest approval and admiration.[15]

Thus grew the extrinsic source of the Nightingale power.

Florence's efforts to improve sanitation received considerable support with the appointment of a three-man Commission on Sanitation under the authorization of the government to inspect and alter sanitary practices in the barracks hospital at Scutari. The commission had authority not only to identify poor sanitary conditions but, more important, to oversee improvement. The commissioners brought about the improvements Florence had long identified and sought in her reports to Herbert, who, in turn, had brought them to the attention of government officials. The head of the commission, the physician Dr. John Sutherland, became an ally of Florence's and, after the Crimean War, a member of her informal cabinet devoted to hospital reform.

The work of the commission, coupled with Nightingale's efforts, was widely believed to have markedly lowered the death rate in the Scutari Hospital. By 1855, it had fallen from 40 percent to 22 percent per thousand patients.[16] With this improvement and the stabilizing of patient care, Florence decided to inspect the military hospitals in the Crimea and the nursing services there.

In a letter, she wrote, "[H]aving been at Scutari six months today, I am in sympathy with God, fulfilling the purpose I came into the world for."[17] Nightingale's purpose in the tour of the Crimean war zone was to inspect the various general and regimental hospitals. While there was some ambiguity concerning her authority over nurses in these hospitals, she assumed responsibility under her general mission to superintend nurses in both Turkey and the Crimea. She applied her same zeal and competence in the Crimea as in Scutari and brought about improvements in sanitation, in the comfort of the patients, and in their well-being through the comforts of clean bedding and wholesome food—much of which she supplied through the funds under her control. The travel from hospital to hospital (frequently on horseback), her tours of the front to inspect the conditions of the soldiers in the trenches, and her exposure to disease as she tended to soldiers ill with fever left her fatigued and vulnerable. She came down with Crimean fever and, for a time, appeared to be close to death. When she recovered, it was much to the relief of not only her family and friends, but also the multitude who admired her—including especially the soldiers and Queen Victoria. The prince consort, at the Queen's request, designed a brooch "the forms and emblems of which commemorate your great and blessed work, and which I hope, you will wear as a mark of the high approbation of your Sovereign!"[18]

By August 1855 Nightingale was back at work despite the doctors' urgent prescriptions that she rest. She had refused to return to England and insisted that her duty demanded she stay with the soldiers as long as the war continued. Indeed, she did not return home until four months after the war ended the following March.

The Crimean War ended officially on March 30, 1856. Nightingale delayed her return to England for four months to conclude her mission in the Crimea and Scutari. For her voyage home, she was offered passage on a British man-of-war. Preparations were being made for a tumultuous welcome home for the heroine of the Crimean War. But Nightingale wanted no public demonstrations of the nation's gratitude. Neither did she want special recognition. She declined the offer of the man-of-war and, keeping her plans secret, returned quietly and privately home to Lea Hurst. She carried with her a tuft of grass from the Crimea as her personal remembrance of the bravery of the British soldier. This tuft of grass memorialized for her the wasted lives, not just of soldiers slain in battle, but of the many who had died as a result of the inefficiency and lack of forethought of the establishment in dealing with the well-being of the British soldier. Nightingale returned from the Crimean War determined to fight the political battles necessary to lead a reform of sanitary conditions in the peacetime military and to imbue parliament, government, and the military with a new sense of responsibility for the well-being of the men who served the nation.

Her experience in Scutari and the Crimea of overcoming resistance to efficient hospital care and promoting the importance of sanitary conditions and a healthy diet for the sick and wounded prepared her for the battles she intended to fight for reform in the military. Uppermost in her self-defined mission was to establish nursing as a profession in hospital care. But instead of using the adoration of the nation as her main weapon in the battle for reform, she kept public esteem in the background in her political tactics. Her image in this idealization was a power source that propelled her substantive ideas to the attention of the establishment. She formed a cabinet of men who were dedicated to her mission and acted as her front line in influencing the British parliament and government in her reform movement.

Nightingale's cabinet included Sidney Herbert, who was an important political figure in British governing circles and who, besides having been secretary at war, had also been secretary of state. The cabinet also included Dr. John Sutherland, who had headed the Sanitary Commission sent to the Crimea and Scutari to report on the conditions affecting the health of the army and hospital sanitary practices. Sir John McNeill, who had served on a commission to inquire into commissariat performance in the army during the Crimean War, became a devoted collaborator and member of the informal cabinet.

Dr. William Farr, a leader in medical statistics, had a deep respect for Nightingale's sophistication and interest in using statistics to measure the incidence of illness and to assess the outcomes of surgery. With Dr. Farr's advice and support, Nightingale instituted standard statistical reports on mortality rates in hospitals. She designed the forms for these reports that became widely used in hospital statistics.

Nightingale remained in the background, expending great effort in the preparation of reports members of her cabinet used in influencing officials. One notable exception where her influence was direct occurred shortly after she returned from Turkey. Queen Victoria summoned her to Balmoral Castle, where Nightingale presented her views directly to the Queen and Prince Albert concerning the need for a commission to study sanitary and health practices in the military and to recommend reforms. The Queen and the prince consort were impressed with her knowledge as well as her personality. They supported her recommendations for reform but recognized the limits of their power. Critical to moving reform from words to practical initiative was the formation of the Royal Commission on the Health of the Army.

Herbert and other members of Nightingale's cabinet were pleased with her apparent success in her meetings with the Queen, the prince consort, and, in particular, with Panmure. As Nightingale discovered, a gap existed between Panmure's expressions of support and implementation due to his tendency to procrastinate. But ultimately, the royal commission was formed with its membership largely made up of the men she had proposed.

Thus began Florence Nightingale's political influence following her return from the Crimean War. Not only did she, with her cabinet, favorably affect the living conditions in military barracks, she also affected sanitary conditions in military hospitals. And she succeeded in implementing plans for an army medical school and for construction of a new military hospital. As time went on, she was called upon to review plans for the construction of hospitals, and she gave interviews to European princesses who advanced her cause in improving hospital care and the training of nurses. She wrote her book *Notes on Nursing: What it is and What it is Not*, which appeared in 1859 to much acclaim since it offered practical advice on nursing the sick at home. And she established the Nightingale Training School of Nurses at St. Thomas Hospital in London in 1860.

What drove Nightingale after her experience in the Crimean War was a powerful attachment to the ordinary soldier. She was obsessed with the need to improve the conditions of the living soldiers in memory of those who had died—especially the victims of poor sanitary conditions and medical practice, which she had observed firsthand.

She had a profound faith in the good sense of the ordinary soldier. Unlike the common conception among government officials and high-ranking military officers that seemed to denigrate the character of the soldiers, she believed their apparent bad habits, such as excessive drinking and wasteful spending of their meager pay, reflected the beliefs about their character on the part of their commanders and the high-ranking officials in the military and the government. She set out to prove that her assumptions about the true character of the soldiers were more accurate than the views generally held by their superiors. During the Crimean War, she instituted a program that enabled soldiers to save money and send it home. Officialdom met this program with derision and disbelief. But the facts supported her. Many soldiers did save and send money home once the mechanism for doing so in her plan had been established. She also had another theory about the apparent bad habits soldiers displayed. She believed that many of these bad habits resulted from soldiers having few opportunities to use leisure time to their advantage. She recommended that military barracks be equipped with books and facilities for reading and other uses of leisure time. But beyond the practical implementation of her faith in the character of the soldier and the solicitude she displayed for the sick and the wounded, she held a mystical attachment to the soldier and a deep reverence for those who died as a result of battle and sickness. They became, in her own thoughts, her children and drove her relentlessly to overcome the barriers to her program for reform.

Along with her cabinet, Nightingale had to overcome tendencies to procrastinate in government ranks and parliamentary circles, and to push through bureaucratic resistance to change, particularly in the War Office. She led her cabinet and refused to accept any tendency on their part to slow down the drive for reform or to seek rest from the labors she enforced. She refused to recognize that fatigue and illness, from which she herself suffered, were legitimate reasons that prevented her and her cabinet from pressing forward in carrying out the parliamentary reforms.

After Herbert's death, Nightingale's life took a paradoxical turn. She took to her bed with the illness that had plagued her following her return from the Crimea. She appeared near death, yet the illness defied diagnosis and treatment. While in her bed and unable to leave her lodgings, she worked like a person possessed. Reform of the War Office and the conditions in military hospitals and barracks remained central to her work, which also included formulating plans for the care and feeding of soldiers who were expected to undertake an expedition to Canada as Britain planned to intervene in the civil war in America. Along with her influence on the sanitary conditions in the British Army in India, she pushed through sanitary reform for the civilian population there as well and advised the Viceroy in this regard.

After many years of illness, and as she grew older, Nightingale left her bed and joined members of her family in their homes. She cared for her mother and for her sister, and became a devoted aunt. She gained weight as she aged, and lost the angular look of her youth and middle years, the softening of her looks reflecting the softening of her personality. But she never lost her charismatic and legendary character in British society. Her reputation grew steadily, even during the years she secluded herself. Her illness was the explanation given for her lack of a public presence, but the truth seemed to lie elsewhere. As she returned from the Crimea without fanfare and avoided public displays of adoration throughout her life, she remained an enigma as well as an idol. How could she be so forceful and commanding in her work and yet so fragile in her flirtation with illness and death?

Sir George Pickering, a distinguished British physician, who was fascinated by the "secondary gain" of illness, wrote, "Of one thing I am quite sure. I should not have liked to be the doctor who tried to explain to Miss Nightingale the nature of her illness."[19] Secondary gain refers to a common observation that, frequently, people with illnesses are able to gain some advantage from the illness despite the suffering involved. One advantage, for example, might be to control the behavior of other people, usually people close to the patient. Pickering was not the first to focus on Florence Nightingale's illness and its relation to her work. Cook, Florence's original biographer, described in detail her illness and, indirectly, her propensity for illness in the anguish, self-doubt, and guilt she displayed before she set herself firmly on the path of her life's work in nursing.

With obvious reference to medical opinion, Cook presents a diagnosis of the illness that appeared upon her return from the Crimea. The diagnosis of neurasthenia was first reported in the psychiatric literature of the 1860s. It appeared to be a loosely grouped set of symptoms notable as fatigue, sleeplessness, heart palpitations, stomach distress, and nausea. Bed rest was the prescription for treatment, and physicians offered little beyond this. Neurasthenia seemed closely related to the illness called hysteria, and, over time, the vagueness surrounding it led to its disappearance as a diagnostic category for nervous diseases and mental illness.

Men were diagnosed with neurasthenia, although the illness appeared more prominent among women, and especially among women who sought through education and career to go beyond the stereotype of appropriate activity. Florence Nightingale certainly fit this characterization. But beyond the social and cultural attributes of neurasthenia, there seems to have been some suggestion that heredity played a part, along with disturbance in sexual function.

In his early work on mental illness, Freud distinguished between the actual neuroses and the psychoneuroses. He believed, and later abandoned, the hypothesis that the actual neuroses stemmed from the damming of libido as a result of sexual frustration, which created a noxious substance in the body that produced the symptoms associated with neurasthenia. The psychoneuroses resulted from unconscious conflict, the opposition of wishes deeply repressed. The symptoms of neuroses, such as hysteria, which included functional disturbances such as temporary paralysis or loss of speech, represented conversion of psychological conflict into loss of, or impairment of, functions. Freud believed, in these early formulations, that the actual neuroses were not amenable to treatment by psychoanalysis, whereas the treatment that came to be called "the talking cure" was ideally suited to bringing into consciousness the repressed conflict and thus to curing the illness.

Both Cook and Pickering conclude that Florence Nightingale's invalid state resulted from a psychoneurosis. A psychohistorical analysis by Donald R. Allen attempts to trace Nightingale's development through the psychosexual and psychosocial stages exemplified in the work of Erik H. Erikson.[20] Using Erikson's work as a template, Allen attempts to match the little that is known, with any degree of certainty, about Florence's unconscious mental life with the expected crises in development such as identity formation. In Allen's view, Florence's transition through the life cycle of early childhood and adolescent development was problematic and left a residue of guilt and shame, which was only partially resolved in the sublimation of sexual and aggressive energy through her work. Allen also suggests a masochistic trend in Nightingale's personality. He suggests that her aggressiveness in work found a balance in her need to suffer, as reflected in her lengthy illness and her expectation of death as a release. He concludes his essay with the following observation:

> Future research on a psychohistorical study of Florence Nightingale will have to include not only the best observations emanating from psychoanalysis but also new information on her pregenital and adolescent development, which has not yet come

to light either in the previously published biographies or in the main corpus of her own writings and papers. Only then will we be able to present a complete psychohistorical interpretation of this fascinating and captivating woman."[21]

In the culture in which Florence Nightingale lived during her formative years, her perception of marriage was that it would require her to give up what she called her moral and active nature—self-abnegation, which she likened to suicide. Her moral and active nature was a product of inherent talent, which, as with instinctual life, makes a demand on the ego. Work must be done to hone talent, activate it, and use it in fulfilling ways. Had she been limited in her talent simply to the education her father had provided in his tutorial, nothing would likely have come of a distinctive nature in her life. Her talent went well beyond the excellent education she received. She had intuitive gifts that enabled her to exceed, by far, the limits imposed by her culture and the bureaucratic organizations she encountered first in Scutari and later in achieving her program for reform.

Her intuitive gifts included an understanding of how to gain control of her environment through shrewd accumulation of and use of power. She converted ideas into power while deferentially avoiding self-aggrandizement in the worshipful adoration of public opinion.

The conflict between what she called her passional nature and her talent, both of which demanded ego work, led to compromise formations in which illness played a significant part. At times she begged for relief in the form of death, which she seemed to welcome. But this fantasy of masochistic surrender in illness and death wishes conflicted with her power interests in speeding reforms in hospital care.

Positing talent as an integral aspect of Florence Nightingale's neurosis brings into focus the culture in which her illness maintained itself as the result of the compromises her ego sustained. In another time, a person with her talents would have had ample opportunity for education, work, and self-development. The Victorian era imposed limitations on what a woman could do to express her talents. To argue as some have that a masculine identification led the way in Florence Nightingale's self-expression misses the point. Identity as a woman, in the terms her mother and sister fostered, excluded ego interests resulting from talent. Florence accepted illness as a consequence of her desperate need to find her vocation. The voice of God was necessary to propel her forward as though she were passive to the demands of her ego. Passivity was a form of self-deception for her that, along with her illness, provided the best answer she could find to the many conflicting trends in her personality. Florence Nightingale had good cause to wonder: what is the true nature of one's character?

7

The Uses of Aggression in Overcoming Bureaucracy

Hyman Rickover and Florence Nightingale had one trait in common: they were totally uninhibited in using aggression to further their aims and in overcoming bureaucratic tendencies that elevate form over substance and procedure over purpose. Their aims in their respective organizations were directly related to talents honed over many years, talents that were the source of their distinctive competencies and that gave rise to narcissism.

In Freud's view, leaders tend to be narcissistic. In an exaggerated and often misunderstood formula, leaders are the object of admiration for others but in the end love no one but themselves. It is not simply the attractiveness of the person that supports identification with the leader; the talent of the person also attracts followers. If the leader's talents become amplified in group work that achieves purposes, material rewards flow to group members, solidifying identification with the leader.

In *Group Psychology and the Analysis of the Ego,* Freud proposes an explanation for group cohesion. His interest in group psychology intersects nicely with his development of the theory of the ego. His theory, in brief, states that individuals identify with objects that become consolidated into their ego. If members of a group identify with the same object, in the representation of the group's leader, then the basis for group cohesion has been established.

Identification is not a one-time psychic event. It is strengthened or weakened with the ebb and flow of success or failure in achieving results that produce concrete rewards for group members. Thus, if a leader continually proves his or her competence, the strength of the identification grows and group morale flourishes. And just as success in achieving objectives of common purpose enhances the probability of future success, failure has the reverse effect and ultimately diminishes morale and the probability of future success in whatever goals are common to a group's purpose. Failure has harmful effects on the group members' egos.

At the time of writing *Group Psychology,* Freud was engaged in a major revision of psychoanalytic theory, not in the least diminishing the central place of unconscious mental life and conflict in this theoretical structure, but instead positing a more sophisticated representation of how the mind works. This revision opened up psychoanalysis to the possibility of being applied generally rather than being limited to neuroses and other mental impairments.

In the midst of these important modifications of psychoanalytic theory, including other attempts at broadening its reach into history and society, Freud remained committed to a parsimonious use of concepts. For example, he avoided making lists of human motives. He did not deal with needs, but remained committed to instincts. Sex and aggression, more abstractly the life-and-death instincts, were the bases of instinctual life. This speculation created controversy concerning the place of the death or destructive instincts in the foundations of human motivation. The controversy centered on whether or not there was a need for an abstraction called "the death instinct" as part of the recognition of the importance of human aggression, for better or for worse, in the foundation of human motivation.

Freud was aware of the effects of real or felt deprivations in the formation of character and the propensity for action. As Alfred Adler had put it, one strives for power to compensate for a sense of injury or deprivation. In a brief essay, "Some Character-Types Met With in Psychoanalytic Work," Freud describes a type he calls "the exception." These are individuals who seek revenge for suffering endured or felt in their history. Freud's example of an exception is the duke of Gloucester, in Shakespeare's *Richard III*, who, because of a deformity, will not enjoy the common pleasures of love and companionship. He therefore seeks revenge, becoming himself a villain.

> But I that am not shaped for sportive tricks,
> Nor made to court an amorous looking-glass;
> I, that am rudely stamp'd, and want love's majesty
> To strut before a wanton ambling nymph;
> I, that am curtail'd of this fair proportion,
> Cheated of feature by dissembling Nature,
> Deform'd unfinish'd, sent before my time
> Into this breathing world, scarce half made up,
> And that so lamely and unfashionable,
> That dogs bark at me as I halt by them;
>
> * * * * *
>
> And therefore, since I cannot prove a lover,
> To entertain these fair well-spoken days,
> I am determined to prove a villain,
> And hate the idle pleasure of these days.[1]

This speech is from the opening soliloquy. Gloucester subsequently becomes king.

Freud acknowledges in Nietzsche's "pale criminal" one of the type he calls the exceptions. The pale criminal murders out of a preexisting sense of guilt. The guilt is not a consequence of the criminal act. The act itself is a means of expressing, perhaps expiating, the sense of guilt by objectification. The criminal act is an expression, however pathological, of the criminal willing himself to power.[2]

The problem with treating power as a compensatory motive is that it gives short shrift to the complexity of power in the life of the individual as well as in the collective experience of bureaucracy and society. In *Group Psychology* Freud is proposing that a member of the group tends to subordinate his or her need for power to the needs of the group and from attachment to the leader or the representation of the leader in the group's psychology. There is compensation for this subordination of the individual's willing himself or herself to power in the alternate sources of self-esteem available from the group. For most individuals, the largest component of self-esteem derives from a sense of belonging. Membership is rewarding, not the least in representing who one is to oneself and to others. To the extent that a cohesive sense of identity is important to an individual, membership provides the foundation for this cohesion. A silent trade-off occurs. The individual, perhaps unwittingly, will substitute accepted opinion for individual thinking. For some, the love of self, or narcissism, will give way to the esteem derived from membership.

All individuals are influenced by the identifications they make with the various groups of which they are members, beginning with the family. Freud recognizes this influence, but he also reserves for the individual the possibility of thinking and acting beyond group influence:

> Each individual is a component part of numerous groups, he is bound by ties of identification in many directions, and he has built up his ego ideal upon the various models. Each individual therefore has a share in numerous group minds—those of his race, of his class, of his creed, of his nationality, etc.—and he can also raise himself above them to the extent of having a scrap of independence and originality.[3]

If one is to achieve this "scrap of independence," one is required to detach himself or herself from the psychology of the group, substituting a degree of narcissism for identity through belonging. Narcissism is the turning of the libido from objects in the external world to the internal world of the ego. In the extreme, it can be pathological—that is, if the turn inward substitutes self-love for interest in, and action on, the outside world and on other people, or if there is a complete investment in objects, depleting the ego and diminishing capacities. Just as the presence of objects in a person's life is no guarantee of healthy narcissism, so a dependency on groups or individuals may indicate depletion in a person's sense of self-worth. This depletion may come from undue attachment to others, whether through group memberships or love relationships, which can impoverish the ego. In this form, dependency appears as strict conformity to group norms and a consequent lack of independence in judgment. Dependency may be marked in love relationships, resulting in feelings of uncertainty when a severe imbalance exists between getting and giving in the distribution of satisfaction. The object on whom a person's wishes become exaggerated or dependent often feels depleted by the incessant demands he or she is expected to fulfill in order to gratify the other. A similar effect occurs when the object is used as a reflection of the self. Narcissus fell in love with his own reflection in the pool, but he could just as easily have fallen in love with a person who reflected an inner image of himself. The relationship created by narcissistic choice is an unreliable and ultimately depriving one. Human relationships thrive when people enter each as a separate person, rather than as mirror images. Mirror images tend to be archaic relics of the past, and carriers of the seeds of disappointment and anger.

Becoming a member of a bureaucracy and being fully invested in its process entail the risk of subordinating one's talents in the interests of conformity to accepted ways of thinking and acting. In the spring of 2002, a public debate ensued over the failure in 2001 of government agencies and the White House to acknowledge and act on information of impending aircraft hijackings and possible terrorist attacks. An FBI agent in Phoenix, Arizona, had reported suspicious activity on the part of a few Middle Eastern residents in the United States who were entering flight schools seeking training in flying large planes but bypassing training in takeoffs and landings. The FBI hierarchy failed to acknowledge and act on this warning. An official in the Minneapolis office of the FBI released a letter sent to a congressional committee investigating the failure in intelligence leading up to the attacks on September 11, 2001. The letter accused officials at FBI headquarters of thwarting an investigation into the actions of a suspected terrorist who had been reported by a flight school because he wanted only flight-simulator training and had a large amount of cash. This man was arrested in August 2001, and the agents in the Minneapolis office wanted headquarters' permission legally to search his living quarters and computer. This permission was not granted. It later turned out that Zacarias Moussaouis was probably training to be the twentieth hijacker in the September 11 terrorist attacks. The Minneapolis agents, in 2002, accused Robert S. Meuller III, head of the FBI, of misrepresenting the FBI's actions three weeks before the attack.[4]

The allegations concerning the failure of intelligence and high-level officials to interpret and act on the various warnings that Osama bin Laden's organization was planning a major terrorist assault on the United States squarely raise questions about dysfunction in bureaucratic organizations. The same questions came up shortly before the 2002 reports of the FBI's alleged failure. The Immigration and Naturalization Service issued visas in the names of two terrorists who died during suicide missions on September 11. The probable explanation of this highly embarrassing action on the part of lower-level INS officials is the tendency in bureaucracy for officials to follow rules of procedure slavishly. The primacy of rules in the mentality of bureaucracy is the victory of process over substance.

The German sociologist Max Weber described bureaucracy as an ideal type of organization because it stressed rationality as its dominant principle. Bureaucratic organizations are hierarchical in structure with clearly delineated authority at each level. As an ideal type of organization, bureaucracies are supposed to operate dispassionately and without bias either in the uses of authority or in the personal characteristics of those granted authority. Prejudices and favoritism have no place either on the part of its members or in their relation to clients.

Since Weber's time, a cottage industry has emerged among students of organizations to show that bureaucracies seldom function at the ideal level. They produce a level of incompetence that results directly from three sources: narrow rationality, power, and identification.

Workers in bureaucracies become so fixated on following rules and adhering to procedures that they lose their perspective and displace the purpose of the organizational procedures. "Trained incompetence" describes the tunnel vision that life in a bureaucracy seems to promote. When INS officials issue visas to dead terrorists, they are simply following the rules of the organization. The context of action may not enter consciousness as individuals continue to follow the set procedures. Adherence to routines may not easily permit independence of thought.

Trained incompetence goes hand in hand with bureaucratic dysfunction that results from the displacement of goals. The sociologist Robert Merton provides an example: Admiral Byrd's pilot in the expedition to the South Pole applied for U.S. citizenship some time after the expedition. The requirement for an application to be accepted was five years' continuous residence in the United States. The immigration service refused to accept the pilot's application, ruling that service with Admiral Byrd had meant leaving residence in the United States. In other words, the INS refused to accept the applicant's time with Admiral Byrd in Little America as residence in the United States.[5]

Power in bureaucracy flows directly from the authority allocated to a position. Thus, the initiatives one takes, as an official, are supposed to follow the prescribed order of actions permitted in the hierarchy. When in doubt, one should act only in the spheres assigned to one's position. Conversely, one should resist encroachments on one's power base. This principle of power does not easily encourage collaboration or even spontaneous sharing of information and ideas. Power is not supposed to become personal at the risk of distorting the bureaucratic ideal of rationality, but it does.

When power conflicts occur, the cause is most often the encroachment of one bureaucracy on the perceived rights and responsibilities of another. The national security advisor to the president of the United States is supposed to limit his or her function to organizing for the president the materials related to issues of foreign policy. The advisor is supposed to be neutral to the issues under consideration. But, as in most cases of the gap between the real and the ideal, there is reluctance on the part of advisors to limit their role to consolidating information for the president. As national security advisor to President Nixon, Henry Kissinger competed with the secretary of state in foreign policy, usually emerging as the dominant figure as a result of his assertiveness and cleverness in expanding his range of activity well beyond the limits of neutrality in supposedly preparing materials for the president's consideration. When he succeeded to the position of secretary of state, Kissinger made sure that power remained in his new office and not in the old office of the national security advisor.

Playing the power game without a clearly defined substantive talent tends simply to reinforce the bureaucratic malaise of subordinating process at the expense of substance.

Admiral Hyman Rickover and Florence Nightingale were adept at playing the power game. These two creative types fused power with talent. In fact, one could easily conclude that power for them was a means of exploiting a passion that went well beyond individual interests and lay at the heart of a grand mission. In Rickover's case, the mission was to provide a new and deadly weapon to the U.S. Navy's arsenal. For Nightingale, the mission was to reform medical practice in the military while establishing a new profession called nursing.

Rickover identified himself as an engineer. It is not clear how his education fostered his talent. He was not a product of book learning, although he was well educated and had graduate training in engineering. He was the kind of engineer who fit the description of the *bricoleur,* or handyman, who learns how things work and how to fix them by applying intuition. He learned the hard way.

Rickover was an ambitious man who intuitively grasped the notion that to succeed in a bureaucracy, one followed a simple rule: make oneself useful. Defying group norms and the desire to be accepted by the group, he proved his proficiency and imagination in all his assignments. This resulted in promotions and excellent fitness reports. The key event in his campaign for usefulness occurred in his assignment to the Bureau of Ships Electrical Section, which brought his self-assertion and initiative to the attention of the bureau's head and led ultimately to his being named the head of the bureau's nuclear propulsion division.

His shrewdness in the game of power led to his gaining appointment to the AE. The dual appointment enabled him effectively to bypass control over his activities by the navy hierarchy. Further, his sense that to be effective he had to consolidate in his hand all the sources of authority in the nuclear program led him to foster relationships with the Congress and the press based on his ability to deliver, time and again, what he promised. As we have seen, this last source of his power effectively saved his career in the navy when the hierarchy decided to punish him for flouting the "real navy" as he ran his job to bring nuclear power into the submarine and other surface navy vessels.

While attending to his power, relative to the various sources of authority that lay outside his immediate control, he assured his position through centralization of his organization with the "pinks." This degree of involvement required hard work on his part, a pattern learned early and followed throughout his life.

His intuitiveness as an engineer and his simple but shrewd decisions at crucial points in the nuclear propulsion program, also accrued power to him. The decision, for example, to build a prototype propulsion plant on land, and to build it in complete detail, was decisive in the nuclear program. Building it piecemeal on board a vessel under construction would have entailed huge risks. Instead, the prototype replicating all the restrictions of space found in the real plant saved valuable time in avoiding costly errors. The successful runs of the *Nautilus* proved to the various constituencies that the navy had a truly invaluable asset in Hyman Rickover. Rickover's power rendered him untouchable and impervious to the reasonable arguments of the chief of naval operations to limit the number of nuclear ships to be built in order to control the costs of construction of new vessels.

The one area where his control was in doubt was in his relation to the outside contractors, notably Electric Boat. His attempts at control through intimidation and the use of his inspectors were tenuous, largely because of Electric Boat's sources of power. The navy needed its suppliers, and its suppliers could translate this need to gain the edge in bargaining over responsibility for cost overruns. Veliotis, as head of Electric Boat, was almost as shrewd as Rickover in his capacity to engage in power struggles. Veliotis's scheme of charging the government for cost overruns resulting from Boat's quality failures succeeded because the navy needed Boat's work in the program to build a 600-ship navy and because, by this time, Rickover's influence with the Congress had waned as a result of retirement issues and reappointment problems.

Florence Nightingale's experience with power would appear at first blush to bear little resemblance to Admiral Rickover's. This woman, who achieved prominence in the mid- and late-nineteenth century and who fought the medical hierarchy, the prime minister, and the various officials in the British government in the interests of reform, applied power by indirection. The sources of her power lay in her charisma as the Lady with the Lamp and in her extraordinary intellect. She understood the importance of maintaining control over the activities in her scope of responsibility.

By her own choice, she was a deviate in her culture. The battle with her mother and sister strengthened her ego, but also left her with a residue of neurotic conflict that resulted in debilitating illness for most of her adult life.

Nightingale, despite her illness, was sure of herself, and this certainty perhaps resulted in a disdain of medical knowledge. She was late in accepting the work of the germ theorists, but before criticizing her for this oversight, one must recognize that medical practitioners were also latecomers to germ theory. A painting by Thomas Eakins (1844–1916) entitled *The Gross Clinic* and dated 1875, depicts the operating room at the University of Pennsylvania hospital under the supervision of Dr. Gross, a noted surgeon. All of the surgeons, assistants, nurses, and spectators in the gallery observing the procedure are without gloves, masks, or the other protections against sepsis readily accepted in hospital operating rooms today. That Florence Nightingale was uninformed about, or unimpressed by, germs as the cause of infections seems characteristic of medical practice in the late nineteenth century.

There is an important distinction between the underlying deviance of Rickover and that of Nightingale. They were similar with respect to their shrewdness in understanding power, with enormous ego strength in sustaining their vision of social and technological change in the bureaucracy. But they were different in that Florence never abandoned her early background and identity. Rickover consciously turned away from his background, leaving the religion of his parents and abandoning any vestiges of his early childhood. He became the epitome of the self-made man, the person who gave birth to himself.

This denial of his past gave him extraordinary freedom. He was truly a narcissist, who could develop his capacities through hard work but did not need, nor look for, support from his peers or the institution of which he was a part. He could use his innate aggression freely without guilt because of his belief in his talent and his mission in the nuclear program for the navy. He received institutional support when his superior officer protected him from the apparent jealousy of his peers and made certain he would have a place in nuclear propulsion. He repaid the institution in his dedication to the mission of making real the dream of a vessel that would be able to function submerged almost indefinitely.

Rickover had support from other sources—his first wife, Ruth Masters, and after she died, Eleonore Bednowicz. He was the dominant person in these two relationships. One gets the impression that the relationship of husband and wife, centered as it was on Rickover, left no room for the son. Robert Masters Rickover comes across during an interview as a somewhat detached, compliant, and well-meaning individual. The twists and turns in his career could hardly have pleased his father and probably reflected a troubled attempt to find himself after a number of false starts.

Rickover made it no secret that he wanted no one to inquire into his inner thoughts or probe his psyche. He was not psychologically minded, and lived externally in two worlds. One world was centered on engineering, in which he was intuitively gifted. The other centered on power. In this second world, he was self-taught. As far as the record shows, he was not schooled in Machiavelli's *The Prince*. Yet he seemed intuitively attuned to at least some of the lessons contained in this sixteenth-century classic: "[A] prince should show that he is an admirer of talent by giving recognition to talented men, and honoring those who excel in a particular art."[6] "[F]or a man who wishes to express goodness at all times must fall to ruin among so many who are not good. Whereby it is necessary for a prince who wishes to maintain his position to learn how not to be good, and to use it or not according to necessity" (p. 127). "[B]ecause friendships that are acquired with a price and not with excellence and nobility of character are bought, but they are not owned, and at the right time they cannot be spent. And men are less concerned with hurting someone who makes himself loved than one who makes himself feared, because love is held by a link of obligation, which since men are wretched creatures, is broken every time their own interests are involved; but fear is held by a dread of punishment which will never leave you" (p. 139) "Nothing makes a prince more esteemed than evidence of great enterprises and evidence of his unusual abilities" (p. 185). "Since a prince must know how to make good use of the beast, he should choose then the fox and the lion; for the lion has no protection against the traps and the fox is defenseless against the wolves. It is necessary, therefore, to be a fox in order to know the traps, and a lion to frighten the wolves" (p. 145).

However he may have learned his lessons on the accumulation and uses of power, Rickover applied them with great skill. In the end his power failed him and he was forced to retire. His lack of psychological sensitivity created a blind spot: he could not recognize that the limits of his power, because of advanced age, would catch up with him. He would have been the wiser person to plan his own retirement, to move on in life beyond his devotion to the navy and nuclear propulsion of vessels. But it was against his nature to accept limits on his power. The lesson in life is "don't linger."

Both Rickover and Nightingale sought an identity that was apart from the social structure in which they lived and worked. Their ego identity was built on the confidence they displayed in their talent. A formula seems to apply: the greater an individual's belief in his or her own talent, the less the need for approval from the social structure. This confidence may not result in successful change, particularly as the resistance to innovators heightens in bureaucratic structures, but if the identity is built on distinctive talents that become crucial to the aims of the bureaucracy, the chances for successful innovation increase. A second formula seems to apply: the less an individual is a product of his or her social structure, or the higher the degree of narcissistic investment in his or her own thoughts, the greater the probability that he or she will display a "scrap of independence and originality."

Part 3

The Managers

The Education of Robert S. McNamara: Secretary of Defense, 1961–1968

Robert S. McNamara published an extraordinary book in 1995, a quarter of a century after his departure from the Johnson administration as secretary of defense. *In Retrospect: The Tragedy and Lessons of Vietnam* was clearly a painful exercise in retrospection. Few executives like reviewing the past and pointing to errors of judgment, individual and collective, that determined bad policy and faulty implementation. Fewer still are engaged in measuring failure in terms of human lives lost and in terms of suffering. But McNamara had a noble purpose: to learn from experience and, possibly, to prevent the recurrence of tragedy in human affairs. He might have been excessively optimistic about what his treatise would accomplish. He was probably surprised, and undoubtedly saddened, that his book received the scorn and criticism it encountered from reviewers and editorial writers.

In *The New York Times* of April 17, 1995, Anthony Lewis wrote:

On March 9, 1969, James Reston wrote in his *New York Times* column: "The art of resigning on principle from positions close to the top of the American Government has almost disappeared. Nobody quits now as Anthony Eden and Duff Cooper left Neville Chamberlain's Cabinet with a clear and detailed explanation of why they couldn't be identified with the policy any longer. . . . Most, at the critical period of escalation [in Vietnam], gave to the President the loyalty they owed to the country." In that prescient comment Reston identified the real issue raised now by McNamara's book on his role in the Vietnam War. The book is a *mea culpa* for his policy, which says he was "wrong, terribly wrong." But Mr. McNamara expresses no regret for his greater wrong: failing to speak the truth then, when it mattered most.

Frank Rich wrote in *The New York Times* of Sunday, April 16, 1995:

Robert McNamara says that he published his book now to combat the "cynicism" threatening the relationship between Americans and their leaders. . . . But far from ending such cynicism, his disingenuous memoir will compound it. Even as the man quotes Aeschylus and appears as a teary tragic figure in prime time, his words tell us that the contrition is a pose and that he has learned nothing.

In an editorial that appeared on Wednesday, April 12, 1995, *The New York Times* stated:

Comes now Robert McNamara with the announcement that he has in the fullness of time grasped the realities that seemed apparent to millions of Americans throughout the Vietnam War. At the time, he appeared to be helping an obsessed President prosecute a war of no real consequence to the security of the United States. Millions of loyal citizens concluded that the war was a militarily unnecessary and politically futile effort to prop up a corrupt Government that could neither reform nor defend itself.

Throughout all the bloody years, those were the facts as they appeared on the surface. Therefore, only one argument to be advanced to clear President Johnson and Mr. McNamara, his Secretary of Defense, of the charge of wasting lives atrociously. That was the theory that they possessed superior knowledge, not available to the public, that the collapse of South Vietnam would lead to regional and perhaps world domination by the Communists; and moreover, that their superior knowledge was so compelling it rendered unreliable and untrue the apparent fact available to even the most expert opponents of the war. With a few throwaway lines in his new book, *In Retrospect,* Mr. McNamara admits such knowledge never existed. Indeed, as they made the fateful first steps toward heavier fighting in late 1963 and 1964, Mr. Johnson and his Cabinet "had not truly investigated what was essentially at stake and important to us." As for testing their public position that only a wider war would avail in the circumstances, "We never stopped to explore fully whether there were other routes to our destination."

Such sentences break the heart while making clear that Mr. McNamara must not escape the lasting moral condemnation of his countrymen. . . . It is important to remember how fate dispensed rewards and punishment for Mr. McNamara's thousands of days of error. Three million Vietnamese died. Fifty-eight thousand Americans got to come home in body bags. Mr. McNamara, while tormented by his role in the war, got a sinecure at the World Bank and summers at the Vineyard. . . . His regret cannot be huge enough to balance the books for our dead soldiers. The ghosts of those unlived lives circle close around Mr. McNamara. Surely he must in every quiet and prosperous moment hear the ceaseless whispers of those poor boys in the infantry dying in the tall grass, platoon by platoon, for no purpose. What he took from them cannot be repaid by prime-time apologies and stale tears, three decades later.

Mr. McNamara says he weeps easily and has strong feelings when he visits the Vietnam Memorial. But he says he will not speak of these feelings. Yet someone must, for that black wall is wide with the names of people who died in a war that he did not, at first, carefully research or, in the end, believe to be necessary.

McNamara justified his silence from the time he left the post of secretary of defense to the time he published his book over two decades later on the grounds of loyalty to the president and constitutional obligations as a member of the cabinet. MacGeorge Bundy, who was national security advisor, likened the position of a cabinet officer to a person having been given the trust of the president but also a pistol. For a cabinet officer to speak out, according to Bundy, is to violate the trust, but also to use the pistol to shoot the president. Evidently, Mr. McNamara subscribed to this view as a defense for his protracted silence following his departure from the cabinet. Columnists and editorial writers came down hard on this defense on the grounds that officials have a higher duty and obligation to the American people.

For the cynic, the explanation for McNamara's silence, even though he doubted the rationale behind American action in Vietnam, was his desire to hold power and status as a cabinet officer. One might observe that even when he left the cabinet, it was not to a post of obscurity. He left to head the World Bank.

There is still another frame of reference for narrating and analyzing McNamara's involvement in the Vietnam War, and that is that by virtue of his background, experience, and intellect, he was unprepared for the demands of the cabinet post he assumed. An unquestionably bright and talented man, he was forced into a position requiring on-the-job education in areas where he was unprepared intellectually and, perhaps more serious, emotionally. By disposition, prior training, and as a result of his desire for power, he was ill-equipped for the learning this new job required.

"President Kennedy knew that I would bring to the military techniques of management from the business world, much as my colleagues and I had done as statistical control officers in the war. I was thrilled to be called again to work for my country."[1]

There are two observations to be made about how McNamara tells his readers about himself in his book on Vietnam. First, he is exceedingly sparing in describing his early years and later development. He displays great reticence in telling his readers anything about his parents, his relations with them, and his early years growing up in San Francisco. He does not mention them, his sibling, or the influence his family had on his development other than to record that his parents were ambitious for his education. Second, while he probably intended to establish a sense of privacy, it also becomes clear that he is unaccustomed to, or very uncomfortable with, emotions or introspection. He writes about his reactions to a horrible event. On November 2, 1965:

> A Quaker named Norman R. Morrison, father of three . . . burned himself to death within forty feet of my Pentagon window. He doused himself with fuel from a gallon jug. When he set himself on fire, he was holding his one-year old daughter in his arms. Bystanders screamed, "Save the child!" and he flung her out of his arms. . . . Morrison's death was a tragedy not only for his family, but also for me and our country. . . . I reacted to the horror of his action by bottling up my emotions and avoided talking about them with anyone—even my family. . . . There was much Marg and I and the children should have talked about, yet at moments like this I often turn inward instead—it is a grave weakness.[2]

Deborah Shapley interviewed McNamara 20 times for her biography, published two years before *In Retrospect*. Evidently he revealed more about himself during these interviews for her book than he cared to reflect in his own memoir. Shapley provides the following information. Robert McNamara was born on June 30, 1916, the firstborn of Claranell and Robert James McNamara, who were a little more than 20 years apart in age. He was Roman Catholic and she Presbyterian, and she insisted that their children be raised as Protestants. According to Shapley, Claranell believed raising her children as Protestants would elevate them in social status, as compared to Catholics. Robert James did not protest this decision, which suggests that although he was the breadwinner of the family, he assumed a relatively passive position regarding the upbringing of Robert and his sister, Peg (born in 1919). The parents, besides their age difference, were markedly different in personality and in their respective roles in the family. Claranell was the dominant figure, particularly with respect to her son's upbringing. She was openly ambitious for him, stressing education and grades.

While Claranell doted on her son and instilled in him the expectation of education and achievement, Robert James worked hard to support his family in a job he had in the shoe business. Although both parents were very frugal and even conveyed a sense of living on the edge of poverty, Robert James rose in the shoe business to regional manager and succeeded in supporting his family. He had nothing to be ashamed about in his role as a provider. He moved the family to a section of Oakland that bordered on a wealthy neighborhood, and that enabled Robert to enroll in a prestigious high school of a higher status children than his family represented.

Robert James was a withdrawn, taciturn individual, somewhat severe in the persona he presented to his children and their friends. Never having gone beyond the eighth grade, and not immersed in books, he nevertheless went along with his wife in stressing the importance of formal education. In a rare moment of self-revelation, McNamara told Deborah Shapley, "The pressure on me was unbelievable. If I got an A minus, the question was, 'Why didn't you get an A?' It was like growing up in a Jewish home."[3] McNamara did well in high school. Besides his studies, he joined the Boy Scouts and rose to Eagle Scout. He was also a member of the high school Honor Society.

In 1933, McNamara enrolled in the University of California at Berkeley and plunged right into student activities. He lived at home to save money, commuting daily to the campus with a fellow student. He became friendly with the university president and enjoyed a rich academic and social experience, graduating with honors and having been elected to Phi Beta Kappa. His decision to enroll at Harvard followed his disappointment in not being elected a Rhodes Scholar.[4] But if ever a person and a school came together in a fateful encounter, that encounter was McNamara and the Harvard Business School. They were the perfect match.

The Harvard Business School was founded in 1908 as a venture to bring a high degree of substance and vitality to "the oldest of the arts and the newest of the professions," as presidents of Harvard University proclaim in granting the degree of master of business administration to its graduates. In the school's earliest conception, professors Frank Taussig and A. Lawrence Lowell had a vision that set the stage for a new branch of professional education.

In 1919 Wallace Brett Donham became dean of the school, and eight years later the new campus was dedicated on what was called, sometimes affectionately but other times derisively, "the other side of the river."

The school's pioneering work with the case method set the stage for a new approach to business education. Scores of research assistants under the supervision of professors went into the field interviewing executives on current problems to be presented to students in the various courses in the curriculum. This approach made the student an active participant in the situation, faced with problems that required, at the outset, definition and analysis, along with recommendations for a course of action to solve the problem. Much to the frustration of first-year students, professors refrained from taking a didactic role, but instead promoted student-centered learning. There were no right answers to the case, and students gradually experienced what it was like to assume an active role in the business situation.

Without necessarily recognizing during the early years just what the new method of instruction entailed in the psychology of the student and pedagogy, the business school experience for the student (and the faculty as well) could be likened to a conversion experience—a major experiment in socialization. While for most of the students, whose main experience in education had placed them in a relatively passive position of listening to lectures and acquiring knowledge often external to their own identities, the case method required a transformation from passivity to activity. To shore up this work of transformation, there was little reliance on authority. The student had to find authority in his own grasp of the situation and his active position regarding the problem at hand.

For example, the economic theory of marginal utility puts forth the principle that the peak of efficiency will have been reached when the cost of the last unit of production equals exactly the price received for the sale of this last unit. This principle can be expounded, traced to its origins in economic theory, and even illustrated by various examples. But suppose a student is presented with a case study in which a manager has to price a product. The student begins to puzzle out the relationship between sales volume, unit prices, cost of production at differing levels of output, and unit and aggregate profits. In reality the student is engaged in the application of marginal utility theory, but without the reliance on the authority of the theory. He or she is engaged in discovery though problem solving. The psychological effects of this discovery, repeated countless times in a myriad of circumstances through the case method, is to create enormous self-esteem and confidence in one's ability to master complicated problems.

It is not at all evident whether or how the interest in the human aspects of business affected McNamara in his studies. He clearly favored the quantitative fields of accounting and control and the seemingly rational aspects of business administration. The "softer" fields of human relations probably held little interest for him, and the presence of this field in the curriculum at the time he was a student was limited. It was not until post–World War II that the human aspects of administration became integrated into the curriculum.

But McNamara was fully prepared to engage the active role propounded in the business school curriculum. The subject matter of control drew his attention under the influence of the kindly but persuasive Professor Ross Walker, who was a subtle practitioner of transforming the mentality of students from the passive to the active frame of mind. The subject of control emphasized organizing and using information to make rational decisions. In McNamara's time, students took accounting courses, but the subject of control shifted the emphasis from the standards of the accounting profession to the needs of the manager for information necessary to foster rational behavior.

The focus of control found validity in the changes that occurred in business practice, following the leadership of Pierre du Pont in the resurrection of the General Motors Corporation (GM) under Alfred Sloan in the late 1930s. GM pioneered decentralized management with centralized financial and operating controls. The key to this organizational structure was the accuracy of information and its general availability to top management and divisional management. In effect, the entire management hierarchy was reading off the same page, facilitating the setting of goals and the appraisal of results against the goals.

The logic of control introduced another subtlety into authority relations. In its earlier versions, authority relations were often dictatorial and even abusive, and they were personalized in the relations of superior and subordinate. Under control, there is no room, at least in theory, for the authoritarian boss since all levels are constrained by the same logic of control, an impersonal and highly rationalized system for viewing the performance of all divisions and levels of the organization.

While control was an influential discipline at the school in McNamara's time, courses in marketing also affected students' outlook on business. Marketing shaped students' thinking to orient their perspective toward the customer. What are the needs of the customer and how does one more efficiently meet these needs in a competitive environment? McNamara became one of the prime students of Professor Edmund P. Learned, a leading figure in the field of marketing and, later, business policy. Learned was a key figure in the wartime program at the school— a program that trained air corps officers as statistical-control specialists to aid line officers in making rational decisions in managing the air force.

The two years at the Harvard Business School were formative years in the thinking and socialization of Robert McNamara. He had only one setback during this time. In order to receive honors upon graduating, candidates had to appear for an oral exam. At his oral, McNamara evidently failed to impress Professor Deane Malott, a senior faculty member (who later became president of Cornell University). Professor Learned, who was also a member of the examining committee, appealed to Professor Malott to award honors to McNamara on humanitarian grounds. McNamara's father had died during the second academic year of the program, and Professor Learned felt that under the circumstances, McNamara had not been able to perform at his best. Malott refused to back down, and McNamara received a grade of High Pass for the oral exam—which fell short of the level required for honors.

McNamara returned to San Francisco upon graduation and accepted a job with Price Waterhouse, a leading public accounting firm. But auditing held little attraction for him, and he gratefully accepted an offer from Dean Donham to join the Harvard Business School faculty to teach accounting. He and his new wife, Margaret (Margy) McKinstry Craig, moved to Cambridge and a new life together in 1940. As junior members of the Harvard Business School faculty community, they joined a tightly knit group propelled by its pioneering spirit in business education, and its sense of isolation from the larger academic spirit of Harvard University. More than the width of the Charles River and the short distance from Harvard Yard separated the business school from the college and university. Unlike the faculty of arts and sciences, the faculty of the business school disdained reflection and intellectual pursuits as self-contained aims. The business school appealed to the instincts for action, for problem solving, and for a rational approach to business administration.

World War II created a great opportunity for Harvard Business School. Not only did the school assist in the war effort, but it had the chance to perfect the transition from passive accounting to active control. General H. H. Arnold, with the backing of Assistant Secretary of the Army for the Air Force Robert Lovett, proposed to the school that it undertake the training of newly commissioned air corps officers in the techniques of management controls. Dean Donham accepted this challenge readily and assigned Professor Edmund P. Learned to take a group of young faculty members, including Robert McNamara, to Washington to meet with Captain Charles B. Thornton. Thornton had a proposal for the joint Harvard Business School and air corps on statistical control.

Thornton was a charismatic figure who had a vision for the new program that appealed to the experience and aims of the Harvard group: statistical information for management decisions and the control of operations. The air corps was to expand rapidly. The information needed to manage this expansion had to be developed rapidly, not only for planning the expansion, but also for field operations. Data had to be developed to measure the requirements for spare parts, for aircraft replacement, for pilot and crew training, for supplying fuel and armaments, and to measure losses in aircraft and crew in order to project replacement needs.

Shortly after launching this program, the air corps asked McNamara and Myles Mace to work in England as consultants, a posting that was to be followed by a field commission as captains. McNamara rose in rank to lieutenant colonel and served in various overseas assignments in Asia as well as on bases in the United States. As one might expect, the introduction of statistical-control officers met with resistance, especially in cases where the results and recommendations of statistical analysis did not make intuitive sense to line officers. The program at Harvard Business School emphasized to officers the importance of tact as well as sophisticated analyses and presentations. But this caution did not always work as expected. One report sent to General Curtis LeMay recommended eliminating fighter escorts on bombing missions to Tokyo and other Japanese cities. General LeMay scrawled on the report, "BALLS." Morale would suffer if bombers flew unescorted, especially in view of the fact that bomber crews had to fly 25 missions before they were rotated. Despite statistical analysis showing an 80 percent chance of survival, crews believed they were at high risk to complete 25 missions. LeMay's dismissive reaction reflected the dismay of practical line officers to some of the work of the statistical group.

McNamara and his wife were both stricken with polio in 1945. His case was relatively mild, and he soon made a complete recovery. Margy, however, faced the prospect of prolonged and expensive treatment. This unfortunate set of circumstances forced McNamara to revise his plans. Instead of returning to Harvard

Business School to resume an academic career, he accepted an offer from Henry Ford II to join Tex Thornton and the "Whiz Kids" in bringing modern management to the Ford Motor Company. This decision eased McNamara's financial problems and shifted his career from teaching to managing and, finally, to the beginning of his tour of duty as secretary of defense.

The story of the Whiz Kids and the Ford Motor Company appears in David Halberstam's book on the rise of the Japanese automobile industry and the competitive pressures on the domestic industry.[5] Halberstam vividly presents the conflict between the traditional automobile people and the statistical-control group, who knew little about automobiles and the place of this product in the American psyche. The Whiz Kids, as he calls them, also seemed to show little interest in the manufacturing end of the business, but instead worked hard to overcome the absence of reliable information to control the management of the company. Finance and control became the favored route to advancement at Ford, displacing manufacturing in the power structure. Halberstam shows the methods the manufacturing people used to hide information from the statistical-control group. He concludes:

> Years later in Vietnam some American officers, knowing McNamara's love of numbers, cleverly juggled the numbers and played games with body counts in order to make a stalemated war look more successful than it was. They did this not because they were dishonest, but because they thought if Washington really wanted the truth it would have sought the truth in an honest way. In doing so they were the spiritual descendants of the Ford factory managers of the fifties.[6]

To offset the power of the Whiz Kids and their statistical-control techniques, Ford brought in, as head of the company in the mid-1950s, Ernest Breech, a more traditional automobile executive from GM. But over the years, the statistical-control group ascended in power, and, finally, with the appointment of McNamara as president of Ford in 1960, the new group dominated the power structure of the company.

During McNamara's tenure at Ford, he honed his talents as a manager fully expert in statistical analysis and control. He advanced from the position of corporate controller to become deputy to Lewis D. Crusoe, head of the Ford division. When Crusoe became a group vice president, McNamara moved up to head the Ford division.

In the politics and rivalries of the Ford Motor Company, McNamara had become an ally of Breech, who had an antagonistic relationship with Crusoe. As a Breech ally, McNamara challenged Crusoe first on the Thunderbird product line and second on the Edsel. When the Edsel failed badly as a new product, McNamara finally rose to the position of president of the corporation, reporting to Henry Ford II.

The lessons McNamara learned at Ford went well beyond gaining expertise in the application of managerial control techniques. According to the account in Deborah Shapley's biography, McNamara became expert at playing the power game in the rivalries openly at play at Ford, stimulated by Henry Ford himself.

According to Shapley, McNamara became abrupt with subordinates and displayed irritation with them and a tendency to tear down their presentations. He created an atmosphere in which subordinates feared coming to him with their reports and proposals. Apparently, he had few inhibitions in displaying aggression in his relations with subordinates.[7] But with his bosses, his demeanor was pleasing. He learned to tell them what they wanted to hear, employing his skills with quantitative analysis. It would be an error to view McNamara as a sycophant. He asserted his independence and nonconformity by living in Ann Arbor, enduring the inconvenience of a long commute to his office rather than choosing Bloomfield Hills (both localities near Detroit), the center of the automobile executive's lifestyle. (The academic community of Ann Arbor suited McNamara, but it was probably Margy who determined this choice.)

There is a paradox in McNamara's having been named president of the Ford Motor Company. He had little direct experience and few intuitive gifts in product design and development. Like most of the Whiz Kids, he seemed to have little patience with the mystique of the automobile and the American love affair with the internal combustion engine. He thought that the Americans' preference for powerful engines and large cars was irrational. Why take a huge car with a powerful engine on a short ride to go shopping? He favored a small, efficient car that used fuel sparingly. Despite the fact that he did not win out in this contest of preferences with the true automobile people at Ford, Henry Ford chose him to run the company—reflecting the importance Ford attached to changing the culture of the Ford Motor Company.

No sooner had McNamara reached this pinnacle of executive responsibility than he was faced with a new challenge. The newly elected president of the United States wanted Robert McNamara as his secretary of defense.

Robert Lovett had recommended McNamara for the job. When President Kennedy met with McNamara in Georgetown while awaiting inauguration, he offered him the job of secretary of the treasury, which McNamara declined, claiming he was not qualified. This disclaimer was probably realistic, given McNamara's inexperience in fiscal issues and his lack of background in economics or Wall Street affairs. When Kennedy offered him the job of secretary of defense, McNamara backed off again, claiming he was unqualified. This disclaimer was probably insincere since McNamara viewed himself as a professional manager expertly attuned to managing a complex organization. Kennedy charmed him, telling him that there was also no school for training a president.

In an article in *The New York Times Magazine* in 1964, McNamara writes, "President Kennedy's charge to me was a dual one—to determine what forces were required and to procure and support them as economically as possible."[8] In this article McNamara philosophically distinguishes two concepts a secretary of defense could adopt in determining his style of leading the defense establishment.[9] The first concept he calls judicial: a relatively passive approach defined as receiving and approving recommendations initiated by other officials. The second concept he calls active: an aggressive approach to defining issues, raising questions, suggesting alternatives, and finally, making decisions. Seeking consensus and acting as a mediator was a role foreign to McNamara's disposition, his training, and his experience.

Although he proclaimed an active approach to his role as secretary of defense, he did not necessarily choose among various potential elements in defining the job. There were dichotomies he did not address. For example, would he separate policy from implementation, leaving policy to political actors and reserving implementation for the Department of Defense? What was his preferred relation to the service secretaries? Were they to be advocates for their respective services or were they to go beyond an advocacy role and position themselves above seemingly parochial issues while acting for the good of the nation? Would he accept the separation of military premises and problems from a purely management position, maintaining the integrity of professionalism as the primary position of the military? Would he allow the Joint Chiefs of Staff independence in presenting their views to congressional committees on defense readiness and expenditures? How would he deal with the dual role of the secretary as advisor to the president on defense issues and as manager of the Department of Defense? How would he deal with the variety of ambiguities implicit in each of these questions and many others in defining himself as secretary of defense?

McNamara did not accept any of the dichotomies listed above in defining his job. He came to the job with little preparation for a high-level position in the president's cabinet. He characteristically assumed the position and the power it entailed as an activist secretary for whom policy and implementation were both within his scope of responsibility. His central focus was to create a rational basis for making decisions most of which were centralized in his office despite his espousal of favoring making decisions at the lowest level of the organizational pyramid based upon the availability of the information necessary to make rational decisions. And a rational decision, as he defined it, was the result of cost-efficiency analysis—to achieve the best decision at the least cost.

McNamara was not alone in his perspective on the role of the secretary in the Department of Defense. He staffed the various deputy and assistant secretary positions with people who were in complete sympathy with his philosophies. He named as comptroller Charles J. Hitch, who was a product of the Rand Corporation and an expert in budget management and cost-benefit analysis. Alain Enthoven, an expert in systems analysis, served as Hitch's deputy and later assistant secretary. Robert N. Anthony, a professor at the Harvard Business School and an expert in managerial control, served as comptroller after Hitch left. All of these men were like-minded in stressing objective and quantitative analyses in making decisions. While acknowledging the place of experience, intuition, and judgment, McNamara and his team believed that decision making had to be based on objective and quantitative analyses.

The practical effect of systems analysis in the Department of Defense was a five-year planning cycle—an innovation in the department's management—instead of one- or two-year cycles. The core of the five-year cycle was a methodology called the Planning-Programming-Budgeting System (PPBS). The PPBS established the assumptions about military strategy that determined force levels and deployments for the military as a whole, apart from the single services. The nuclear posture assumed that the United States would never employ a first strike. Instead, the country would have the forces capable of responding to destroy enemy nuclear capability and supporting military forces. This strategy of MAD would act as deterrence against first-strike nuclear attack. Beyond a nuclear strategy, military readiness would enable U.S. forces to fight limited wars using advanced, yet conventional, weaponry. The PPBS would provide the numbers for manpower, weapon systems, air, sea, and land forces needed to carry out the deterrence and responses envisioned as an outgrowth of the two assumptions of strategic planning.

McNamara introduced early on a cost-reduction program with three guiding principles. First, buy only what is needed to achieve balanced readiness. Second, buy at the lowest sound price. Third, reduce operating costs through integration and standardization. The cost-reduction program applied to all three services accustomed to autonomy in procurement.

In less than two months after his swearing in, McNamara assigned to various offices or special task forces in the department a list of 92 questions he wanted answered within 30 to 90 days. He established a Defense Supply Agency for procurement and storage of supplies used commonly by the three services. He created the Defense Intelligence Agency, centralizing intelligence in the department. The Five-Year Defense Plan mentioned earlier depended on quantification, which McNamara established as a main principle in decision making despite resistance to the idea. Cost-effectiveness analysis became the basis for evaluating military projects, which had to be beneficial to the entire military establishment and not just to one branch. He assigned Anthony the job of studying the balance-of-payments problem and how to reduce the outflow of foreign currency in military procurement. And he introduced a study to reduce dependence on cost, and a fixed fee in contracting for military equipment and supplies. Fixed-price contracts forced suppliers to control their costs.

In his programs for active management in the Department of Defense, McNamara displayed an unusual set of personal characteristics that left those associated with him in awe. For one, he had enormous energy and powers of concentration. He could testify before a congressional committee for seven hours with only a one-hour break for lunch. He was remarkably able to present facts without reference to documents or assistance from staff members present.

Anthony stated:

> I think it is reasonable to conclude that the Secretary of Defense and the President, who are both strong willed-individuals, did not always see eye to eye on every issue. But not once did I hear the Secretary criticize, or imply a criticism, of any decision the President made. And in this statement, I mean not only in staff meetings at which a number of persons were present, but in quite private conversations as well.[10]

McNamara evidently earned the loyalty of his subordinates. Of a total of twelve subordinates six remained with him in the department during his seven-year tenure as secretary.

McNamara's active style of management and the emphasis on quantitative analysis and rational decision making did not sit well with a number of his constituencies. The Joint Chiefs of Staff did not admire his approach. Even before the Vietnam War and the differences of opinion about troop levels and the bombing of North Vietnam, major conflicts erupted over weapons decisions the secretary fostered in opposition to the service chiefs. He opposed building a nuclear aircraft carrier, a decision he upheld for a time but finally let go of in the face of opposition from the navy and Admiral Rickover. He supported a plan for a fighter-bomber to be designed and built for the air force and the navy as a cost-effective solution to procuring new aircraft by establishing a design common to both services. When this single-design aircraft became the focus of conflict surrounding McNamara, he revealed a side of himself that ran counter to his professed rationality. He became known as a stubborn man to the service chiefs and members of congress. While sure of himself he was vulnerable to emotional outbursts, fits of anger, and even, on one occasion while testifying before a congressional committee, tears.[11]

In *In Retrospect*, McNamara says, "I always pressed our commanders very hard for estimates on progress—or lack of it. The monitoring of progress—which I still consider a bedrock principle of good management—was very poorly handled in Vietnam."[12] The role of manager seemed extraordinarily applicable to the side of the job that entailed control of expenditures. McNamara felt completely confident of his capacity to manage the Department of Defense. He believed that the principles of management he had learned at the Harvard Business School and later applied in the Air Force Statistical Program and the Ford Motor Company were universal and equally applicable to running a government department such the Department of Defense. Much to his sorrow, as expressed in *In Retrospect*, the logic of management did not apply to the job of advising the president on issues where military and foreign policy intersected.

Strategic planning faced an early test with the Cuban Missile Crisis, following on the heels of the ill-fated Bay of Pigs military adventure inherited from the Eisenhower administration. McNamara served as a member of the Executive Committee advising President Kennedy throughout the 13 days of the crisis that began with the discovery that the Soviet Union had delivered and was installing nuclear missiles in Cuba. The decisions to impose quarantine on Soviet shipments to Cuba along with diplomatic pressure to remove all the nuclear weapons on the island proved successful in averting war. Some advisors wanted to bomb the island immediately, but cooler heads prevailed and the Soviets backed off. McNamara played a significant role in the deliberations of the Executive Committee, advocating the naval blockade. He used a direct line of communication to the naval commanders in charge of the blockade, bypassing Admiral Anderson, chief of naval operations, and the Joint Chiefs of Staff. And he made sure the U.S. ships had Russian-speaking people on board. President Kennedy remained at the center of the Executive Committee and his brother Robert took an active part in making decisions, and in communicating directly with the Russian ambassador. Khruschev backed down and ordered the Soviet missiles removed, thereby averting a nuclear war, which some advocates on both sides seemed intent on starting.

Vietnam was another story. McNamara in 1960 attended a briefing with President Eisenhower and president-elect Kennedy on Southeast Asia. Eisenhower declared firmly that the United States had to defend Laos and Vietnam to avoid the domino effect and the loss to communism of all of Southeast Asia. No one, least of all McNamara, questioned Eisenhower's firm positing of the domino theory, and thus began the slide toward increased military involvement of U.S. forces, air bombardment of North Vietnam, and the loss of over fifty thousand Americans and three million Vietnamese.

Faced with reports of increased infiltration of South Vietnam from the North, President Kennedy decided to send General Maxwell Taylor and Walt Rostow of the NSC to assess the situation. Their report recommended increasing the support to the South Vietnamese government and military and adding combat forces to the American advisory group in Vietnam. McNamara endorsed these recommendations in a memorandum to the president. He soon regretted his endorsement and along with Dean Rusk, the secretary of state, sent the president another memorandum urging caution in sending combat troops. McNamara wrote in his book:

> The dilemma Dean and I defined was going to haunt us for years. Looking back at the record of those meetings [in 1961], it is clear our analysis was nowhere near adequate. We failed to ask the five most basic questions: Was it true that the fall of South Vietnam would trigger the fall of all of Southeast Asia? Would that constitute a grave threat to the West's security? What kind of war—conventional or guerrilla—might develop? Could we wing it with U.S. troops fighting alongside the South Vietnamese? Should we not know the answers to these questions before deciding whether to commit troops? It seems beyond understanding, incredible, that we did not force ourselves to confront such issues head-on. But then, it is very hard, today, to recapture the innocence and confidence with which we approached Vietnam in the early days of the Kennedy administration. We knew very little about the region. We lacked experience dealing with crises . . . finally and perhaps most important, we were confronting problems for which there were no ready or good answers. I fear that, in such circumstances, government—and indeed most people—tend to stick their heads in the sand. It may help to explain, but it certainly does not excuse our behavior.[13]

The answer to these questions would have required going outside the normal administration resources to enlist experts on Vietnam and Southeast Asia as well as the Soviet Union and China to engage in a discussion of the assumptions on which U.S. involvement in the Vietnamese conflict was based. The salient fact for the purposes of this study of McNamara is that he did not go outside to look for answers.

Despite McNamara's earlier optimistic assessment of the war, he issued a grave forecast following a trip to Vietnam that December. He supported increased U.S. forces and a combat role, but not at the levels General Westmoreland and the Joint Chiefs recommended. The rule seemed to be a compromise, giving the military part of what it wanted, but keeping short of the escalation the generals and the Joint Chiefs recommended. Meanwhile, dissent in the U.S. increased, both in the press and on college campuses.

Neither McNamara nor Johnson anticipated the popular uprising against the war.

Congress passed the Gulf of Tonkin Resolution on August 7, 1964, following an alleged attack on U.S. ships. As interpreted by the Johnson administration, in which McNamara was still secretary of defense, this resolution became the equivalent of a declaration of war and a legitimization of the entry of American troops into a direct combat role. Previously, the role had been advisory and also clandestine. The stage was now set for open warfare, bombardment of the North, and full involvement of the U.S. military. Later, the Johnson administration and Secretary McNamara were accused of falsifying information to create the Gulf of Tonkin Resolution. Congress and the press, and the American people, felt they had been misled, and this belief undermined the legitimacy of the involvement of U.S. troops in Vietnam.

In his memoir, McNamara says he was unsure whether he had resigned or been fired. He had become disillusioned by the war, having finally concluded that he could not rely on the generals in Vietnam and the Joint Chiefs for plans to win. In mid-1967, he had commissioned the preparation of the Pentagon Papers, a research project detailing the U.S. role in Vietnam, probably as a prelude to his effort to a way of reevaluating the failed American initiative in the war.

McNamara's disillusionment came late, perhaps without his understanding of the breakdown of morale on the part of the Americans serving in Vietnam. The ditty quoted above suggests that the servicemen knew well ahead of him the true state of the war. The reporters covering the war were well aware of the ineptitude of the South Vietnamese army and leadership.

In *In Retrospect* McNamara repeatedly makes the point that no one, including himself, stopped to question the basic assumptions underlying the U.S. involvement in Vietnam. To quote McNamara:

> A major cause of the debacle there lay in our failure to establish an organization of top civilian and military officials capable of directing the task. Over and over again, as my story of the decision-making process makes shockingly clear, we failed to address fundamental issues; our failure to identify them was not recognized; and deep-seated disagreements among the president's advisors about how to proceed were neither surfaced nor resolved.[14]

This mistaken conclusion is an indication of a sad gap in McNamara's educability. George Ball, undersecretary of state in the Kennedy and Johnson administrations, consistently and early on questioned the basic assumptions and patiently kept to his position only to find no support from McNamara, Dean Rusk, or McGeorge Bundy, the national security advisor.

In his book, Ball differentiates two roles for McNamara: secretary of defense and secretary of war. As secretary of defense, McNamara earned high ratings as a manager attempting to control expenditure and assuring that maximum value would be received for the funds expended on national defense. In this role, he displayed his facility for quantitative analysis and projection. But as secretary of war, a term Ball uses to differentiate internal defense management from advising on policies for conducting warfare and foreign policy, McNamara was outside his experience and competence.

> Though he tried at the outset in 1961 to be realistic about the inherent difficulty of the struggle and the risks of its enlargement, he could not help thinking that because the resources commanded by the United States were greater than those of North

Vietnam by a factor of X, we could inevitably prevail if only we applied those resources effectively—which is what our government frantically sought to do for the next ten years.[15]

Clark Clifford, in his memoir *Counsel to the President,* presents an appraisal of McNamara similar to that of George Ball.

> In reforming the Pentagon, his talents had served him well, but in the prosecution of the war, they sometimes failed him. Vietnam was not a management problem, it was a war, and war is about life and death, filled with intangibles that defy analysis. He had never been in a war, and perhaps he did not fully appreciate at first its stupid waste and its irrational emotions, and the elusiveness of facts and truth when men are dying. Nor did he fully understand the political roots of the conflict until it was too late. He had tried to master the war as he had everything else in his remarkable career, using pure intellect and his towering analytical skills—but Vietnam defied such analysis. In the end, this man, who was probably our greatest minister of defense, was not well suited to manage a war—yet this was precisely what was required by the circumstances.[16]

Before serious escalation had occurred, including bombing of the North, Ball completed (on October 5, 1964) a single-spaced 67-page memorandum that concluded with the recommendation of pursuing a negotiated settlement of the conflict and opposing escalation and bombing. Ball had the memorandum delivered to McNamara, Rusk, and McGeorge Bundy. "Bob McNamara in particular seemed shocked that anyone would challenge the verities in such an abrupt and unvarnished manner and implied that I had been imprudent in putting such doubts on paper."[17] The recipients of Ball's memorandum met on Saturday, November 7, 1964. Ball met only with negative reactions and disinterest in his analysis. He decided it was hopeless to pursue discussions further. In his book, McNamara pays Ball compliments on his sagacity, cultivated mind, and iconoclasm, but effectively minimizes Ball's contribution because Ball did not develop a plan to implement his recommendation for a negotiated settlement. McNamara admits that he and his colleagues seriously erred in their failure to explore further the views outlined in Ball's memorandum.

With McNamara treating Vietnam as a tactical problem, and advocating compromise between the demands of the Joint Chiefs and the demands of the field generals around—and with Lyndon Johnson's inexperience in foreign and military policy—American military and foreign policy in Vietnam came to a dead end during the Johnson administration. (The war itself was not to end until 1973, when Nixon and Kissinger negotiated the withdrawal and the victory of North Vietnam and the Viet Cong in unifying their country under the regime of Ho Chi Min.)

The theme running throughout McNamara's retrospective on Vietnam is the failure to question the basic assumptions propelling U.S. involvement in the internal struggle between the North and the South. It is as though individually bright officials lacked the intelligence and courage to stop and question, like the little boy in Ball's giraffe story (a little boy upon seeing a giraffe is told that it is a giraffe, to which the boy responds, "Why?"), the "why" of all the assumptions, starting with the domino theory. McNamara does not propose an answer to the question of how or why this happened, except to point out that the officials were all too busy with other affairs—no answer at all. It takes an independent intellect and perhaps an innocent state of mind to break out of the pressures of group conformity to ask fundamental questions concerning policy. McNamara's dismissive and insulting response to Ball's memorandum during the meeting of November 7, 1964, is indicative of the way group pressure works to force conformity to the acceptable and conventional wisdom.

On McNamara's last full day in office (February 29, 1968), he attended a meeting in Dean Rusk's dining room to consider General Westmoreland's request for two hundred and five thousand more troops. Rusk supported Westmoreland's request and in addition wanted to increase the bombing of the North, believing erroneously that the Tet Offensive represented a victory for the South and the United States. McNamara lost control of himself. "The goddamned Air Force, they're dropping more on North Vietnam than we dropped on Germany in the last year of World War II, and it's not doing anything! We simply have to end this thing. . . . It's out of control."[18] He was having difficulty speaking and suppressed sobs. He was overwrought and bereft of the convictions that had sustained him in his long career. He had come to the recognition that his belief in quantitative analysis and cost-benefit efficiency had been inadequate in dealing with the beliefs and assumptions that had propelled the United States into the Vietnam War. He had to struggle to control his emotions when President Johnson presented him with the Medal of Freedom to honor his service as secretary of defense.

From Monomania to Megalomania: Harold Geneen and ITT

When Harold Geneen, the former chairman and CEO of ITT, died, the obituaries invariably singled out the same large aspects of his public life: his unprecedented capacity for work, his relentless campaign to increase the size of ITT through acquisitions, his prominence as an advocate and practitioner of the corporate conglomerate, his overreaching in attempts to influence the Antitrust Division of the Department of Justice, and his offers of money to the CIA to overthrow the election of Salvador Allende as president of Chile. (When Allende was assassinated, Geneen and ITT were suspected of complicity.)

In the last five years of Geneen's tenure as CEO, according to *The Financial Times (London)*, the ITT stock had "underperformed the U.S. stock market by 30 percent. From there, it underperformed the market by another 40 percent."[1] Over the next several years, Geneen's successors, first Lyman Hamilton and then Rand Araskog, put in motion a plan to split the company. Araskog finally sold off the pieces, and in 1996 ITT ceased to exist.

While ITT under Geneen experienced spectacular expansion in sales and profits, its earnings per share merely kept pace with the growing economy. From a shareholder's perspective, which counts the most, this performance appeared mediocre or worse. Even Geneen, who masterminded the three-hundred-odd acquisitions from 1959 to 1977 that created a growth in sales from $765 million to $28 billion, realized comparatively meager profits on his stock and options. Araskog fared better as he divided the company and sold the pieces.

Geneen defended the conglomerate corporation despite the fact that the security analysts and the investing public had difficulty understanding this business form. There was no underlying rationale to his choice of the types of businesses toacquire. He seems to have bought whatever became available, often overpaying for the acquisition using ITT stock. Abetted in his obsession with growth through acquisition by Felix Rohatyn, an investment banker with the firm of Lazard Frères, Geneen seems to have felt little need to rationalize the businesses under his corporate umbrella. He bought Continental Baking, which made Wonder Bread and Twinkies, and Levitt, which built tract houses. He tried, but failed, to acquire the American Broadcasting Company (ABC) and succeeded in buying the Sheraton

Hotel chain. He bought Rayonier, a company, with forest lands in Quebec, that produced pulp for conversion to rayon; the Avis car rental company; and a number of auto parts manufacturers. All these diverse businesses became part of his conglomerate, which had begun with a base of companies in the telephone and switching equipment businesses in Latin America and Europe.

In his later years Geneen became a prophet extolling the virtues of the conglomerate. He wrote (with ghostwriters) two books that promote his business philosophy and disdain all theories of management besides his own. In *Managing*, published in 1984, years after he had left ITT, Geneen reveals himself to be a control freak, establishing roles and procedures for making certain he knew what was going on in the operating companies under the ITT banner. He had built a large corporate staff of troubleshooters who swarmed all over the operating companies that were on the verge of underperforming. He warned associates against surprises and believed in unalterable facts that had to be ferreted out and revealed to him. He read voluminous reports, working 70 to 80 hours a week. His management meetings were notorious. Every month he conducted two-day meetings in Brussels and New York attended by close to 200 executives and staff representing operating companies and ITT headquarters. His ability to absorb and remember details on operations, exceeding the grasp even of those responsible for preparing the reports, created an aura about him that left people in awe of this prodigious worker, this sponge for "facts."

Despite the many articles and books about him, one question persists: who was Harold Geneen?

> And to the memory of my mother, Aida Valentina DeCruciani, born in Plymouth, England, of Tuscan parents and schooled by Jesuits; she was a tower of unyielding principle and strength throughout her life. In a new world she raised her two children, followed her career, and remained throughout her life of eighty-one years a remarkably warm and youngish woman, and a role model of courage for me."[2]

This statement, from the dedication in *The Synergy Myth,* is typical of Geneen in its impassiveness. Like many chief executives sensitive to the workings of power, he displayed little inclination for introspection and less for telling others about himself. One might argue that his long hours of work and absorption of written reports loaded with numbers created self-imposed barriers to introspection.

The biographical facts are these: Harold Geneen was born in 1910 in Bournemouth, England. His mother, Aida, was a teenager when she married Samuel Geneen, a Russian born Jew who converted to Roman Catholicism in order to marry her. Harold was baptized and raised as a Catholic. The family emigrated to the United States in 1910 when Harold was 11 months old. Shortly thereafter a daughter, Eva, was born.

At the time of his marriage, Samuel Geneen was an agent who booked musical acts and concerts. Aida was a singer. Geneen, in *Managing*, provides some information about his background, but does not mention how his parents met. The link was probably the music business. Samuel came to the United States in 1910 to pursue work and, shortly after he arrived, brought Aida and their son to the country.

Geneen described his father as an entrepreneur. He says in *Managing* that over the years his father tried his hand at a variety of ventures. "He produced concerts, records, plays, and even one movie. He ran restaurants and he invested in real estate. Many of these had been highly successful; some were not, but he was always optimistic."[3] When Geneen's parents separated in 1915, his mother took the five-year-old boy to visit her family in Bournemouth. He recorded his memory of this visit. Notably, he describes climbing a steep cliff under the dare of an uncle. He succeeded in climbing this "awesomely high" cliff with "fear in my heart. But I did it."[4]

The parents' separation and later divorce posed a problem for Aida. She had to work to supplement the income received from Samuel. This work entailed travel and separation from her children. She sent the two children to a convent school that Geneen describes as loving but strictly disciplinary. He reflects that the discipline, meted out even for misspelling a word, instilled in him a deep sense of responsibility. He conscientiously completed his homework.

At the age of eight, Geneen transferred to Suffield Academy, a prep school at which he was a boarder. His statement about the continuing separation from his mother is that the experience was worthwhile, and he was grateful to his mother for her choice of school for him. When he was 14, his father lost his money and equity in a failed land deal in Florida—indicative of the kind of speculation that seems to have characterized his investments—and Geneen waited tables at Suffield to help pay for his last two years there. His diploma, which he received along with the rest of his class, remained unsigned until he could pay his overdue tuition and boarding bills.

Probably coinciding with his father's land speculation and failure, Geneen took a summer job lugging lithographic plates; he traveled on the subway and worked until late in the evening. Characteristically, he looks on the bright side of this effort, in his autobiographical accounting, recalling an incident in which a plate was misplaced or lost. His boss called him in, listened to his explanation, and agreed that he had done the right thing in coming forward. In recalling this incident, he wrote, "For many years, that man's polite and fair treatment remained in my mind as a lesson."[5] In writing of this incident, he was ambiguous in explaining his gratitude. Was it gratitude for the fair treatment, or for the relief from anxiety over the incident of the misplaced lithographic plate?

"But even at sixteen I had seen enough of booms and busts in my father's life and their effects upon my mother. I thought I wanted something more stable and secure. But college, even night school, would have to wait until I earned some money."[6]

He found a job as a page on the New York Stock Exchange through the help of a family friend. He worked there for six years, through the crash of 1929, but was laid off when his firm failed. He claims he learned a lot working on the exchange, but felt that the world of stock trading was irrational and would provide little security. Through another family friend he found a job selling classified advertising for the merged New York *Telegram* and the New York *World*. The job paid $15 a week plus commissions. By dint of hard work, long hours traveling on the subway to meet building managers and owners, and reading books on how to sell, he earned a steady $100 a week and succeeded in landing one of two permanent selling jobs out of the 200 people competing for permanent jobs.

Even though he was making a good income for those days of the depression, his mother urged him to go to night school and prepare himself for a career that would provide status as well as security. He entered New York University night school, studied accounting, and, a few jobs later, joined Lybrand Brothers public accounting firm, as a temporary auditor. Again, he worked long hours, and did well in the job, becoming a permanent auditor while preparing himself and eventually qualifying as a certified public accountant. But as an auditor he felt he was a bystander in the drama of business. He wanted more direct involvement, wanted to be at the heart of making and selling products. His opportunity for this kind of involvement came with World War II and Pearl Harbor. He could not qualify for the armed services because of poor eyesight but found a job with the American Can Company subsidiary Amertorp, which had contracts to make torpedoes in two new factories.

In charge of contracting and finance, and commuting between the factory in Chicago and the other in St. Louis, he was in an active role in business, contributing to the war effort, and no longer a bystander or observer. He was 32 when he joined Amertorp.

Geneen found a role model in C. G. Preiss, a senior vice president of American Can. Under the pressure of making a new factory perform, tensions would build up among the management and staff. Preiss would periodically appear to throw a party, get the employees to sing together and enjoy drinks and a meal, to rebuild morale and cohesiveness. Within a few weeks tensions would mount again, and Preiss would reappear to resume building cohesiveness. Geneen thought Preiss was a great leader, and part of his leadership was that he helped solve problems, and that he made people feel good about themselves and one another with his periodic parties.

When the war was over, Geneen spent some months attempting to convert the Amertorp plants into peacetime production, but soon found himself working in American Can's headquarters with the title of expense clerk. He realized he was living on promises of a more suitable job but there was little substance to fulfill these promises. Just as he had turned to books in trying to learn how to sell, when he was on the newspaper's ad-sales force, he now turned to books on how to find a job. A book called *Pick Your Job and Land It* impressed him with its practical advice on finding a job by mailing broadside resumes to companies that might interest him. He sent out over three hundred letters, landed seven interviews and four offers, and joined Bell & Howell in Chicago. He would begin as controller at a salary of $11,000 a year, which exceeded what he had been promised at American Can. Once he had accepted this job offer, he listened to a pep talk from the president of American Can on all the great opportunities in store for him at that company, then allowed himself the small pleasure of getting even by saying, "But you should give this talk to a man who is coming into the company, not to one who is leaving it."[7]

Geneen enjoyed his work as chief financial officer (CFO) of Bell and Howell. "I got into many things which had nothing to do with accounting. For instance, I thoroughly enjoyed working out several innovative changes in our costing and pricing approaches, which allowed us to take on contracts we might otherwise have turned down."[8] He was also successful in negotiating price concessions from the Office of Price Administration in Washington, enabling the company to raise its prices. Geneen had volunteered for this job rather than taking his boss' suggestion that he falsify records as a way of getting better prices.

When the head of Bell and Howell died, he left a last will and testament designating Charles Percy as the new chief while urging that Geneen continue as CFO. Geneen had recently married his secretary (this was his second marriage) and bought a new house, and he had become dissatisfied with his pay of $14,000 a year in comparison to Percy's $70,000. He resolved to find a new job.

The new job, with Jones and Laughlin Steel Company (J&L), paid $40,000, but despite this figure, Geneen left Bell and Howell uneasily. "Strong doubts and misgivings besieged me right up to the evening that I left the plant. It had been my first real postwar job, a happy, good place to work, with responsibilities that had challenged my abilities. Looking back from the parking lot to the light still burning in my office, I wondered whether or not I should turn back. But I could not turn back." Geneen draws a moral from this experience of misgiving. "No one can turn back, not successfully. One makes a decision to go forward, for better or worse, and you go forward with the feeling and faith that if you succeed at one task, you have every reason to believe you will succeed at your next, bigger one. There are no guarantees, of course, but the risk must be taken, if you are going to live with yourself thereafter."[9]

"Most of my work [at J&L] seemed to entail persuading foremen and supervisors to institute controls upon their work, so that they could check and control the costs of their particular operations. The point I would make over and over again would be that I was there, not to spy on them, but to help them in their jobs."[10]

As vice president and controller, Geneen fought to overcome the resistance to change that seemed to him endemic in the steel industry. He recognized early on that cost control was essential, given the fact that there was little choice over prices set for steel products. In search of new ideas for J&L, he spent six days at GM studying Alfred Sloan's system of decentralized operations and centralized financial controls. Back at J&L, he encountered resistance to the ideas he had acquired at GM. He found top management, which in his view was hierarchical and bureaucratic, suspicious of ideas foreign to the steel industry even though they were common management practices in modern industry.

He soon came to the conclusion that the future for J&L and the steel industry lay in diversification. He proposed, with no success, that the company convert coal-tar into chemicals and further diversify with new plants, which would lead to a competitive position in petrochemicals. He made presentations to top management but met with no success in convincing senior officials to invest outside the traditional steel operations.

A new opportunity came to Geneen's attention while he was attending the advanced management program at Harvard Business School under the sponsorship of J&L. He learned that the Boston-based Raytheon Corporation was looking for a CFO. He went to see Charles Francis Adams, the president of Raytheon, presenting himself as a manager with interests and abilities beyond number crunching. Adams hired him with the title of executive vice president, at a salary of $100,000 a year. "[The job at Raytheon] meant that for the first time in my career I would make the big leap from staff to line, responsible for production and all that it entailed."[11]

Charles Francis Adams, the Brahmin chief executive of Raytheon, seemed content to allow Geneen to manage the operations of the company. Geneen took advantage of the leeway Adams accorded him and began to develop the system of controls and organization that later became his trademark at ITT. He had all the divisional controllers report directly to the corporate controller, where formerly they had reported to the head of their division. Many viewed this change as a form of undercutting the operating head, but Geneen believed the new reporting arrangement ensured that top management would receive accurate information, which was necessary to oversee the operating units. He also instituted the large monthly meeting of operating heads and corporate staff for which he became famous at ITT. Geneen frequently acted aggressively during these meetings much to the discomfort of those witnessing the display—piercing questions and impatience with less than clear answers. During one of the rare meetings that Adams attended, Geneen began cross-examining an operating executive. As he persisted, Adams angrily interrupted and said to him, "Stop that," and later he warned him to stop badgering people in open meetings. The reprimand failed to cause Geneen to alter his behavior.[12]

Adams and Geneen were cut from different bolts of cloth. Adams, patrician in manner, cared a great deal for good manners. He hated humiliating people whether in private or in open meetings. Geneen lacked this sensitivity. One time when he had scheduled a meeting for a Sunday afternoon, one of his subordinates said he could not attend because of the christening of his child. Geneen went into a rage and shouted that the subordinate should have rescheduled the christening for Sunday morning.[13]

Restraints on his behavior unsettled Geneen. Adams was less than enthusiastic about venturing into acquisitions, a move that Geneen advocated, and Geneen felt Adams was restraining him in his program of business diversification and expansion. He realized it was time to look for another job, and when he was offered the chief executive position at ITT, he decided to accept the offer.

In all his moves—from Lybrand to Bell & Howell, to J&L, then to Raytheon, and finally to ITT—Geneen seems to have been reluctant to make the change. He says he was in tears when he left Bell & Howell and seems to have wanted Charles Percy to persuade him to stay. In leaving Raytheon, he appears to have been intent on convincing Adams that he was merely considering ITT's offer, as though expecting Adams to urge him to stay. Instead, Adams advised him to get a contract that assured him of the top executive position at ITT.

Geneen's hesitancy in leaving a job suggests that he had not mastered the insecurity of his childhood and youth despite his denial of loneliness and of anxieties about the future. He talked about his personal life with no one. His first marriage, in 1936, led to a separation soon afterward and ended in divorce ten years later. He married his Bell & Howell secretary in 1949 when he was 39 years old. By most standards, it was an odd marriage. His work habits often left his wife uncertain about their plans. He would work through plans for dinner and theater and, not infrequently, would fail to appear for dinner at home. At the Harvard Advanced Management Program farewell event, which was attended by wives, June Geneen did not appear. To Geneen's associates, his personal life and marriage remained a mystery. While June Geneen was well provided for financially, what emotional satisfaction she achieved from her marriage is unclear. She was the mystery person in Geneen's life. For him, work was all that mattered—besides his devotion to his mother.

Geneen would typically make a statement like "the fundamental and basic job of management in any company is to manage,"[14] oversimplifying what it takes to manage a company successfully in a competitive environment. Upon taking over as chief executive of ITT, he introduced two organizational innovations. First, he had divisional controllers report to the chief controller at headquarters. Second, he created a staff system at the very top level of the hierarchy reporting to him. He had introduced both innovations at Raytheon, but they had not been on the scale nor had they had the intensity of the changes in the ITT organization. The two innovations had a single purpose: to assure him that he would get the facts he felt he needed to manage the business. Divisional executives perceived the changes as a spy system; but he would not be persuaded that he was limiting the autonomy of his divisional heads.

Geneen had an overriding obsession: in order to manage, he needed facts. He fundamentally distrusted bureaucracy and believed that the layering effect of an organizational pyramid inevitably distorted information coming to the top level. His staff executives became the early warning agents who spotted brewing trouble, and he granted them the authority to go wherever they felt they needed to go to spot and fix the trouble.

The root cause of trouble, in his philosophy, was failure to gain facts—incontrovertible and unshakeable facts. As he put it, "[T]ime after time in those early ITT management meetings I would question a man about his facts. Where did he get them? (Usually from some other man.) How did he know they were correct? *Were* they facts? So I wrote a memo about 'unshakeable facts.'"[15]

This memo opened with the notion that an incontrovertible fact is final and reliable reality. Referring to a meeting the day before he wrote the memo, Geneen stressed that facts that had appeared at that meeting were "apparent, assumed, reported, hoped-for, and accepted." He wanted his people to become as dedicated to real facts as he was, and emphasized the necessity of being able to smell a real fact from an apparent fact. He implored his people to make sure they found and presented "unshakeable facts," and concluded with the advice, or warning, that they should try shaking the facts to be sure they were "unshakeable facts."[16]

Geneen was an honest man, but also somewhat naïve when it came to ferreting real from apparent facts. In *Managing*, he describes a major blunder on the part of ITT's subsidiary, Rayonier, in its decision to expand its operations by building a pulp-to-cellulose conversion plant in the province of Quebec. Once completed, this plant would make Rayonier the U.S.'s largest cellulose producer. The analysis of this project was produced on paper with projections and risk analysis, and Geneen gave it the go-ahead. Once the plant was built, it turned out that, because of the climate in Quebec, the trees were too small in diameter to produce cellulose economically. ITT eventually sold Rayonier to recoup some of its losses from the ill-fated project. Geneen writes of this failure as one of a lack of unshakeable facts, but without seeming to have drawn the real lesson from the debacle. The analysis of the project had failed to include direct observation. Unalterable facts do not necessarily reside only in the abstractions of numbers on paper, they often reside in observation as well.

As much as Geneen loved facts, he hated surprises. He warned ITT staff and operating executives against them. Surprises occurred when the entire system of information and controls failed. He believed that trouble issued warnings. Surprises occurred when warnings were ignored. Being alert to early warning signs of trouble should lead to action on the part of staff, as internal consultants, even if warning signs were ignored in the operating units. He claimed to be generous when people made mistakes. In fact, the only way to avoid mistakes in Geneen's theory of managing is to avoid risk. According to him, though, managers have to take risks, but they must be calculated. By being alert to early warnings, managers can take steps to correct mistakes. Surprises signify a breakdown in the control system that, for Geneen, was paramount in a well-managed company.

Geneen also took a dim view of long-range planning. ITT prepared projections three and five years in the future, but the basic facts had to be inherent in the quarterly projections. He believed that if a company had the discipline to meet each quarter's projection, the year would take care of itself and would probably offer some assurance that long-range plans would be achieved.

Perhaps the most widely known innovation to which he introduced ITT was the general-manager monthly meetings. Most companies have monthly meetings to review results and fine-tune projections for the quarter. But no company has conducted monthly reviews with the intensity and staging found at ITT under Geneen. There were two monthly general manager meetings. One meeting occurred in Brussels for the European management and the New York staff. The other took place in New York for the American management and the New York staff. The meetings lasted at least two days each, and approximately 200 people attended each of them. In Geneen's words, the "normal GMM meetings ran from ten in the morning to ten at night. In Europe, they often went past midnight because we could spend only a limited number of days there. Our budget and business plan meetings almost always ran past midnight. We did not watch the clock. We worked on and on until the task at hand was completed."[17]

Seated at the head of an oval shaped table with a microphone at the seat of each of the 200-odd participants, and equipped with a book of tables and charts, Geneen led the questioning and the discussion. He studied the tables and charts before the meetings and noted questions with red marks. He would press the questions until he had a satisfactory answer; or if there was no way to get a satisfactory answer, he would make sure the corporate staff pursued the issues beyond the meeting. By his account, about 39 weeks of the year were devoted to meetings—either meetings for preliminary planning or general-manager meetings in Europe and the United States. Allowing four weeks of vacation and holiday time left 13 weeks to run the business. "How did we do it? We did it in overtime at night and on weekends and whenever we could, for it was truly at our meetings, and the face-to-face meetings down the line in our subsidiaries, that we ran ITT."[18]

From the time he arrived at ITT, it took Geneen two or three years to establish his management system. Once it was in place, he began his acquisition program to expand sales and profits quarter by quarter. The conglomerate corporation was not his invention, but the scope and intensity with which diverse and unrelated business units came under the ITT tent under his leadership was unique to him. And although he professed to understand and control these vastly different businesses, security analysts, Wall Street, and the investment community at large had difficulty fathoming what kind of monster he was putting together through his program of acquisitions.

With his firm belief that "managerial ability is a readily translatable commodity from one responsibility to another. . . . [a] manager can manage anything,"[19] Geneen was uniquely prepared for a program of aggressive acquisition. Even though there was no apparent logic behind deciding what companies to acquire, there was a logic behind the decision to diversify. ITT was dependent on its telephone and switching businesses abroad for sales and earnings. For Geneen this was an imbalance, and it was unacceptable. If the Castro government in Cuba could expropriate ITT's telephone company without compensation, it could happen in other Latin American countries as well. Even without the threat of expropriation, the imbalance of foreign and domestic revenues and profits seemed a restraint on the ability of ITT to raise capital and gain wide acceptance from the investment community. Approximately 85 percent of ITT's earnings came from operations abroad, where American standing was not secure—particularly in left-leaning countries. The way Geneen saw it, the time had come to acquire businesses in the United States, but there was little opportunity in the telephone and switching fields, which AT&T dominated. Looking far afield from its traditional operations held no peril for him. He had cut his teeth at Raytheon, examining acquisitions, so he was fully prepared to forge ahead at ITT. He was CEO and, subject to board approval, he had free reign to buy companies using ITT common and preferred stock.

His first acquisition proposal to the ITT board was a small personal-loan company. The board viewed the proposal negatively since the personal-loan business seemed more akin to a pawnshop than to a large corporation. Geneen countered with a display of ads in magazines touting the presence of financial services subsidiaries in corporations such as GM and GE. The ITT board acquiesced, and Geneen acquired Aetna of St. Louis for ITT stock. He then turned to pump companies and valve manufacturers, which were typically small, family-owned enterprises. Then came auto parts and consumer products.

Describing his early approaches to acquisitions as opportunistic and devoid of systematic or overarching logic, he says he bought what became available and also bought on tips arising from some fortuitous meeting. At first glance this intuitive and opportunistic approach seems out of character for a man schooled in control, a builder of a management system. But there were two sides to Geneen's character. He was obsessed with the need for control on the one hand and, on the other hand, he was impulsive, impatient, and intolerant of delayed gratification.

In his writings after he had retired from ITT, he placed great stock in risk taking. If managers must manage, largely through the system of controls, then they must also take risks to foster business growth. As we shall see, the impulsive side of his nature got him into deep trouble in domestic and foreign politics.

Geneen formed an alliance with Lazard Frères, the New York investment bank. Andre Meyer and his protégé, Felix Rohatyn, of Lazard, proposed to him that ITT acquire Avis, the rental car company. Lazard owned about a third of Avis' shares and therefore acted as a principal rather than financial advisor. Lazard realized $20 million when ITT acquired Avis in 1965.

Avis was profitable and expanded its business by starting a European operation and a worldwide reservation system. Avis' advertising campaign, based on the slogan, "We are number 2—we try harder," had been very successful in promoting its image to the consumer. But its relation to ITT was stormy. It refused to change its name to ITT Avis. It also insisted on measuring its performance by return on equity rather than by return on assets, the standard used by ITT. Avis management argued that it financed its car inventory through a leveraged leasing program. As a highly leveraged operation, it enjoyed a high return on equity, even if it was below the standard set by ITT's return on assets.

ITT sold Avis along with other subsidiaries under a consent decree with the Antitrust Division of the Attorney General's Office. The decree enabled ITT to acquire the Hartford Insurance Company. Besides the divestiture, ITT agreed to limit future acquisitions. The theory behind the divestiture order was that the larger the corporation, the more its size restricted the competition. Geneen fought this theory, and he fought the restriction that the consent decree put on his acquisitions. He only gave way, finally, because he was anxious to own Hartford, given its large cash flows from premiums and investment gains.

Other divestitures occurred as a result of the failure to meet goals and expectations. Geneen acquired the Levitt home-building company in 1968. Despite his later disparagement of the notion of synergy, he saw in Levitt expanded revenues and profits made possible by Rayonier's acquisition of land and the construction of Levitt communities abroad. Later, he called the Levitt acquisition one of ITT's biggest mistakes. The housing business was cyclical, affected by the rise and fall of interest rates. In addition, his management system did not work in Levitt's case—which he called a failure in meshing the management philosophies of ITT and Levitt.

Also in 1968 he moved into consumer products, acquiring the Continental Baking Company. He saw the acquisition of the company, with its Wonder Bread brand, Twinkies, and Hostess cakes, as putting ITT products into every grocery store across America. Possibly he thought that the widespread distribution of the Continental brands would enhance ITT's public image and the visibility of its stock among investors.

The pace of acquisitions in 1968 of companies Felix Rohatyn brought to Geneen was extraordinary. In some cases, it took Geneen only about twenty minutes to examine one of Rohatyn's proposals and agree to make the acquisition. Payment in all cases was in ITT common and preferred shares, so limitations of cash posed no problem in buying a company. In 1971, for example, after 15 minutes spent examining the company books of O. M. Scott & Company, Geneen agreed to acquire the company. Scott's business was in lawn-care products and seed, areas Geneen knew nothing about. But a lack of familiarity with or prior experience in a business proved no deterrent to buying companies. The decision was based, rather, on finding that a company had a lower price-to-earnings ratio than ITT's ratio. By the late 1960s, Geneen dominated ITT's board, which did not attempt to restrain his impulse to buy and expand. The only restraint came from government agencies.

Geneen would not accept the legitimacy of government concerns about the size of corporations and potential restrictions on competition. In keeping with his philosophy that managers must manage, he viewed government intervention as a barrier to overcome. He held this view with respect to domestic companies as well as foreign ones. His only problem was to find ways to overcome these barriers to his program of expansion. Hence the psychological shift from monomania, or obsession with growth, to megalomania, or delusions of grandeur. This shift caused him and ITT serious trouble; they risked criminal and civil liability and were subject to damaging publicity arising from allegations of bribery, perjury, and illegal interference in the domestic affairs of a foreign country.

When the trouble came, it was over ITT's proposed merger with ABC. In 1965 Geneen and Leonard Goldenson of ABC struck an agreement for ITT to acquire ABC in a stock transaction. The business logic that Geneen promoted to justify the acquisition rested on ABC's need for capital to update its facilities. Geneen assured the Federal Communications Commission (FCC) that ABC would operate independently of ITT, while ITT provided the capital the network needed. The likelihood that Geneen would stay at arm's length in the oversight and management of the network seemed remote, given his past practices in controlling subsidiaries.

While the FCC continued its hearings on the proposed merger, ITT's Washington lobby and public relations group worked the media to gain a favorable opinion for the merger. Ned Gerrity, the head of ITT's public relations group in Washington, put pressure on Eileen Shanahan, a respected journalist for the *New York Times,* to write favorable columns on ITT and ABC. In a Justice Department action against the FCC, which had ruled in favor of the merger by a four-to-three vote, the Shanahan case became a public issue. Allegations surfaced in court hearings that one of Gerrity's subordinates had spied on Shanahan to uncover aspects of her private life that might discredit her. The Justice Department brief states that ITT's interfering in Shanahan's work and private life "can only be regarded as attempts to impose on the judgment of an independent news receiver."[20] The abortive public relations campaign discredited ITT because it tried to convince the FCC that ITT would not interfere with the news-gathering activities of the network. Evidence also emerged that ABC did not need a capital infusion from ITT, and the history of ITT contained evidence of foreign alliances that suggested ITT would try to use ABC news departments to influence foreign governments.

Geneen writes, in *Managing,* "American industries have operated over the past fifty years in a virtual adversary relationship with the American government."[21]

His hostility toward the American government stemmed from the actions of regulatory agencies in blocking various ITT-attempted acquisitions. The ABC spoiled acquisition infuriated him, but his ire and resolve to fight the government reached their peak in the Hartford insurance case.

Acquisition of the Hartford Insurance Company would offer Geneen the opportunity to use its free cash flow to expand other ITT subsidiaries. Richard McLaren, head of the Antitrust Division of the Department of Justice, opposed this merger on the grounds that the size of the corporation would result in lessened competition in American industry. Geneen had ample legal grounds to fight McLaren since the various antitrust laws did not identify size alone as a case for antitrust action. (Indeed, McLaren's predecessor, Donald Turner of the Harvard Law School, believed that Congress should enact further or clarifying legislation to establish corporate size as a criterion for antitrust action on the part of the government.)

Geneen and Rohatyn lobbied Congress, the Nixon administration, and McLaren to withdraw opposition to the Hartford merger. The early lobbying efforts were entirely legal, but as opposition continued, the attempts to foster its position led ITT, under Geneen's leadership, close to crossing the line that separates legal and illegal influence.

The journalist Jack Anderson, who took over Drew Pearson's syndicated column in the *Washington Post,* dropped a bombshell in his exposé of ITT's attempts to influence the Hartford decision in offering the Republican National Committee $400,000 to underwrite holding the 1972 Republican presidential convention in San Diego. The Anderson column published a confidential memorandum from Dita Beard, one of Geneen's main lobbyists in Washington, to her boss, W. R. Merriam, outlining the offer of money for influence. The personal and confidential memorandum, dated June 25, 1971, stated:

> I am sorry we got that call from the White House. I thought you and I had agreed very thoroughly that under no circumstances would anyone in this office discuss with any one our participation in the Convention, including me. Other than John Mitchell, Ed Reineke, Bob Haldeman, and Nixon (besides Wilson, of course) *no one* has known from whom that 400,000 commitment had come. . . . I hope dear Bill that . . . all of us in this office remain totally ignorant of any commitment ITT has made to anyone. If it gets too much publicity, you can believe our negotiations with Justice will wind up shot down. Mitchell is definitely helping us, but cannot let it be known. Please destroy this, huh?[22]

During her first interviews with Brit Hume, Anderson's assistant, Beard affirmed the authenticity of the memo. She later denied that she had written it, but there were too many contradictions in her attempts to defend herself. She had been caught in the act of conspiring to promote the payment of $400,000 in exchange for a favorable antitrust ruling on the merger with Hartford.

McLaren's settlement of the Hartford-ITT merger was announced on July 31, 1971. Under the terms finally negotiated, ITT agreed to divest parts of Grinnell, a company in the fire protection business, along with Avis, Levitt, and the food company Canteen.

When the Nixon tapes became public knowledge in 1973 as a result of the Watergate investigation, it became clear that the highest reaches of the administration, including Nixon, John Mitchell (who had resigned as attorney general to run Nixon's reelection campaign), and Richard Kleindienst (the deputy attorney general named to succeed Mitchell), had all been involved in the pressure placed on McLaren to settle the case and permit the merger to proceed. In one of the transcripts of the Nixon tapes, the following telephone conversation between Nixon and Kleindienst occurred: Nixon to Kleindienst, "You son of a bitch, don't you understand the English language? Drop the God damn thing. Is that clear?"[23]

When the Anderson column appeared, at the end of February, 1972, Kleindienst, who had already been approved by the Senate to succeed Mitchell as attorney general, requested and was granted a reopening of the hearings so he could clear his name from Anderson's charge that he had participated in the unsavory deal. The hearings were protracted, lasting close to two months and producing more than 1,700 pages of testimony and exhibits. Kleindienst eventually received approval and became attorney general. Later, however, Nixon tapes revealed that he had perjured himself in his committee testimony and eventually he was found guilty. He received a suspended sentence and a miniscule fine, but his reputation, along with Geneen's and ITT's, suffered immeasurable harm.

The notoriety received added momentum when Anderson revealed that Geneen and ITT had offered in excess of seven figures to the CIA to prevent Salvador Allende from gaining the presidency of Chile. ITT had a telephone company in Chile, and Geneen feared that Allende, with leftist leanings, would expropriate this property. If Allende were to expropriate, he would have to pay compensation under the provisions of the Hickenlooper Amendment to a 1962 foreign-aid bill. Geneen had written the amendment, aided by his lobbyists, and had forced it through the Senate despite the opposition of the Kennedy administration and Lincoln Gordon, then ambassador to Brazil. (This opposition infuriated Geneen and he vowed to have Gordon fired—a retaliation that proved unsuccessful.) Despite the protection of the Hickenlooper Amendment, Geneen was not satisfied to let Chilean electoral procedures run their course. He did everything he could to prevent Allende's succession to the presidency of Chile.

It was difficult to prove criminal action on the part of ITT in Allende's assassination. But Anderson and other investigative journalists and editorial writers kept alive the implication that the CIA and ITT were involved. Whether criminally involved or not, it was clear that Geneen would go to any length to protect ITT's interests. Hence the notion that for Geneen, ITT was a sovereign state beyond the control of the United States or the governments in countries where ITT operated. A book published in 1973 made the charge that ITT appeared to be beyond the restraints of governments.[24]

The scandals of the Hartford Insurance deal and Allende's assassination hastened the ITT Board to move forward on management succession. The statute of limitations expired on the investigations of perjury and conspiracy haunting Geneen, but charges against other ITT executives remained in force until the government decided to abandon trials on the grounds that information revealed in the courtroom would jeopardize security.[25]

On January 1, 1978, Lyman Hamilton succeeded Harold Geneen as CEO of ITT. Geneen remained chairman until the end of 1979, and remained on the board until March 1983. Lyman Hamilton was not his choice as successor to the CEO position. Hamilton made it clear that he was going to reorganize ITT to make it more comprehensible to the investment community but also internally to its management. He intended to divest various businesses, to merge operating divisions into five units, to have each unit operate under a senior executive, and to do away with the Geneen type management meetings. Each operating group would have more autonomy under Hamilton and would be subject to less control from the top. All these moves were intended to end the Geneen management style, and they succeeded in earning Geneen's anger.

Geneen still had influence on the board, and he convinced the outside directors to fire Hamilton, much to the strong opposition of the inside directors— ITT executives who supported Hamilton and his reorganization of ITT. The outside directors controlled the board, and the compensation committee informed Hamilton at a breakfast meeting on July 10, 1979, that he was out. The board affirmed his ouster that afternoon at its regularly scheduled board meeting.

While Geneen had prevailed in Hamilton's being fired, his actions diminished his influence both on the board and on Rand Araskog, who succeeded Hamilton as CEO. Geneen had been an enthusiastic supporter of Araskog. Consequently, he could not turn on him and oppose his program as CEO, which essentially followed Hamilton's plan for reorganization, rationalization, and divestiture. Geneen had demonstrably lost power when Araskog went to one of the outside directors and said, "I just can't live with this fellow. If you brought anybody from the outside to run the company and made him chief executive, he would not take the job with Geneen as chairman."[26] Araskog continued on his way without interference from Geneen. He split the company into five units and sold them off, proving contradictorily that the sum of the parts was greater than the value of the whole.

Harold Geneen was a one-of-a-kind manager. He ran the company as an extension of himself. He thought he was the creator of a management system that was easily replicable, as with Alfred Sloan, who had established a management structure at GM that was not only replicable but had become the standard in management structure and practice. But Geneen's style of management was not transferable, it was sui generis, with no likely successor. He defies categorization, but invites reasoned inquiry as to what manner of man he was.

Freud writes:

Individual psychology must . . . be just as old as group psychology, for from the first there were two kinds of psychologies, that of the individual members of the group and that of the father, chief, or leader. The members of the group were subject to ties, just as we see them today, but the father of the primal horde was free. His intellectual acts were strong and independent even in isolation, and his will needed no reinforcement from others. Consistency leads us to assume that his ego had few libidinal ties; he loved no one but himself, or other people only in so far as they served his needs. To objects his ego gave away no more than was barely necessary.[27]

Most psychoanalysts prefer to be conservative in interpreting the lives of others. Speculation is not the favored approach. Yet cases appear where reasoned speculation seems warranted, particularly when the subject is a public figure who reveals as little as possible of her or his inner world. As noted earlier, Harold Geneen avoided introspection and made it a point to disclose little about himself.

In the one instance where he wrote about his childhood in the convent school, he used the example of sitting alone in the classroom in a school whose pupils were home on holiday to assert that he needed no one. He was content to read a book and to refute the pity of the Mother Superior. From this fragment of childhood memory, he insisted that he was independent of the needs common to most human beings.

Here, in his denial of loneliness, he displays a propensity for playing mental tricks on himself. He failed to recognize, in the memoir in which this recollection of childhood appears, that as an adult he was seldom alone. He was surrounded by people, who for the most part were subordinate to his authority and power and at his beck and call. The mental trick he played on himself was to have people near him while denying that he needed them as objects. Without a shred of guilt, he could keep his wife waiting for him, and miss dinner and the theater, while he displayed his independence and assertiveness to his subordinates.

Another trick he played on himself was to believe that work could not proceed without him; that without him, those dependent upon his position would engage in self-delusion, ignoring facts and substituting supposed facts for unalterable, hard facts. But at the same time, he maintained the fiction in his own eyes that his power was not personal, but derived from a logical approach to solving problems. He believed he was not asserting himself over others, but instead leading them away from frivolous thinking to realistic thinking, which in the end would serve their purposes better than if they were left to their own mistaken devices.

In a poignant sense, Geneen grew up bereft of both his mother and father. He was a parentless child, even though he claimed an attachment to his mother in the dedication of his book. It does not take a psychoanalyst to wonder what became of the anger that belongs to a parentless child. He could rail against the government that sought to prevent him from gaining the ends he alone deserved. But he could not deal with—did not acknowledge—the anger and aggression toward his father who abandoned the family with two small children. His mother became heroic, but does a child comprehend the absence of a mother, regardless of the reason? Emotions are what they are despite the fact that as an adult one uses repression to buttress denial as a psychological defense against rage and anxiety. If emotions lived with and recognized become too painful, one can attempt to repress them by attention to the outside world, by hard work, by long hours at labor, and by focusing one's mental powers on the outside world to close off the inner world. Thus is born monomania, an obsessive attention to acquisition, to power, and to control.

The impulsive nature of the mania to acquire reflects a greediness and an inability to delay gratification as a derivative of an inner hunger that will not withstand the need to think and reason.

Did business interest Geneen? He was chiefly interested in it from the vantage point of abstract numbers and reports. The drama of business in the play of products and markets held no abiding appeal for him. Making the quarter became his benchmark. The fact that security analysts did not understand ITT or Geneen's hunger for acquisitions did not trouble him or cause him to evaluate his approach to management. The analysts suspected there was some fudging of numbers to secure the increased earnings he reported quarter by quarter. Nothing was uncovered regarding these suspicions, but if analysts do not understand the business, it is almost second nature to them to suspect some cooking of the books. Another aspect of Geneen's personality is that, despite his ambition and impatience with bosses who did not see the world as he did, he had a great deal of difficulty leaving a company to take a better job. Part of this reluctance can be attributed to insecurity, which he overcame with rationalizations that one must go forward and not retreat, or that it was necessary to take risks to advance one's position in life. These rationalizations appeared to be after-the-fact justifications as he wrote his books, following retirement, to present a picture of himself as a self-sufficient person.

The narrowness of Geneen's ego interests might be mistaken for focus, a desired attribute of an effective manager. Another way of looking at this narrowness of ego interests is that it was a constriction on how he functioned as an individual. He lacked education and the qualities of a fertile mind. His formal education had been limited by the circumstances of his relatively impoverished childhood, both financially and emotionally. Without the influence of parents or teachers, the practical education he sought in accounting and the career he pursued by applying to the limit the elements of this narrow education evidence an absence of intellectual curiosity. He took up the imperative of making a living following his mother's advice, but curiosity will not succumb to the restrictions of circumstance. People find many avenues for the expression of inquisitiveness. More impressive are the self-imposed limits one accepts on mental flexibility and curiosity.

The restrictions one imposes upon the ego in the service of defending oneself against impulses and anxiety-producing fantasy generally reflect a tendency toward overkill. The turning outward in interests and activity can easily be out of proportion to the perceived danger stemming from one's inner world. Geneen's religious upbringing, and the absence of parents who could help mediate against the self-imposed restrictions on the ego and the intellect, offered him little chance to experience the avenues of self-enhancement.

One could argue that Harold Geneen's career was an aberration. But one might also say that of the careers of other persons of accomplishment, who in exaggerating certain tendencies of personality become caricatures of what might be considered "normal" personalities. In most cases of caricatures, the influence of such personalities touch other people's lives only indirectly. In Geneen's case, as with management as a profession, the influence is more direct. Here, power, among other definitions, may be the potential one individual has to make other people's lives miserable.

The Myth and Reality of the Managerial Mystique

Robert McNamara and Harold Geneen both identified themselves with the practice of management. Their respective careers were on a trajectory of success, yet both were caught in the trap of mistaking the part for the whole, of believing that a technique of managment could substitute for imagination applied to situational thinking. For McNamara, the mantra was the methodology of cost-benefit analysis; for Geneen, it was acquisition as the instrument for corporate growth. As McNamara confesses in his book, he failed in his leadership by not examining the assumptions underlying the successive escalations of U.S. military presence in Vietnam and by not examining critically the reports from his commanders in the field and their recommendations for escalation. In the case of Geneen, his mania for growth led to a slavish reliance on the formula of the price-earnings gain through acquisitions without regard for the way the financial marketplace values conglomerates. ITT became incomprehensible to stock analysts and the broader financial community, which eventually led to its breakup and sale.

All organizations rely on routine: the day-in-day-out performance that ensures that their goals will be attained. The most imaginative strategies will be undermined by poor implementation. But when the unexpected occurs, the routine of an organization will seldom measure up to the challenges of crisis management, which require sophisticated thinking combined with the naïveté of imagination to discover solutions.

In 1962 the CIA reported to President Kennedy the sighting of Soviet missiles being put in place in Cuba. The U.S. government had to decide what steps to take in light of this imminent threat to American security. Should the United States bomb the sites immediately or, alternatively, should the government take a step-by-step approach to signal to the Soviet Union that its actions in Cuba would not be tolerated. American strategists needed insight into how the Soviet elite thought collectively and how it would respond to the signals, the end point of which would be bombardment of the missile sites unless the Soviets backed off. While the Soviets were inclined to provoke, were they also capable of withdrawal? Was there a degree of flexibility in the Soviets' provocative behavior? The special crisis group Kennedy convened planned a series of signals to test Soviet intentions and flexibility.

The U.S. task force imposed a naval quarantine to prevent Soviet vessels from completing the voyage to Cuba and the continuation of missile placements. Members of the Joint Chiefs of Staff proposed immediate bombardment of the missiles in place in Cuba; as it happened, though, the embargo worked and war was averted. Kennedy dealt with crises by using diplomacy. The averting of war when the Russians blockaded Berlin is another case in point. Dealing with the blockade diplomatically averted the crisis.

How do decision-makers think? A conceptual code for the analysis of this process was posited by Nathan Leites, a political scientist sophisticated in psycho-analytic theory. Leites, writing in the early 1950s for the Rand Corporation under contract with the Department of Defense, developed a treatise on what he called the operational code. Published in various forms and eventually under the title *A Study of Bolshevism* (1954), the treatise received the attention of political scientists, but perhaps because of its imprecise and discursive nature, Leites's work seemed to come to a dead end. In 1967 Alexander L. George, attempting to explicate the operational code in another Rand publication,[1] proposed an implicit vertical dimension in the examination of the way decision-makers think.

Before discussing the operational code, let us look at the way the perceptual apparatus of the mind works. Perception is oriented outward to the environment. The apparatus is part of the ego and is close to consciousness. To protect the ego from being flooded and overwhelmed with the sheer quantity of perceptions of the environment, a screening mechanism limits the extent to which the mind attends to perceptions. This mechanism is a function of the preconscious, a part of the mental apparatus that limits and sorts the quantity of impressions the mind must deal with. The preconscious is a level below conscious awareness, but is susceptible to conscious attention as the tasks at hand require. It helps focus conscious attention, with a minimum amount of energy. The unconscious operates at a deeper vertical level and is not directly or easily accessible either to preconscious or to conscious levels of the mind. Derivatives of the unconscious find their way into awareness, but in disguised or censored form. The ego utilizes defense mechanisms here, too, to protect the perceptual apparatus from being flooded with unconscious thoughts and imagery. Defense mechanisms are activated by anxiety, which provides a limited amount of unpleasant affect to call forth the protective functions of the ego.

The professional manager, as defined and formulated in the operational code, was the model for Robert McNamara and Harold Geneen, both of whom latched on to management without a sense of imagination about what they were pursuing in life. What was the nature of their talent? Instead of a talent built on the intrinsic demands made on the ego (as was the case with Rickover, for example), they adopted a logic external to themselves: that is, cost-benefit economics and the conglomerate as a business form.

In the structure of the operational code, the three levels of the vertical dimensions of mental activity are implicit. Also implicit is a sense of history and of culture. As a group, decision-makers are tied to a past, but in ways that are deeply embedded in the mental apparatus and beyond conscious awareness.

While Leites formulated the operational code as shared ideas and assumptions of a political elite, it was a study both in group and in individual psychology.

Members of the elite in any culture or occupational group develop these shared assumptions, beliefs, and defenses as a result of common features of upbringing and education.

It seems promising to extend the ideas and methodology of the operational code to professional and occupational groups. Managers make up a significant elite in the American culture and beyond, and offer a test case of the validity of the operational code in understanding decision-making in the routines of organizations as well as in crisis management.

While McNamara and Geneen differed in their upbringing and later career paths, both thought of themselves as managers. The differences in their career paths become superficial in relation to the commonly held assumptions that made up their operational code and that determined their actions. With the dominance of the master in business administration (MBA) today and the prominence of the business schools that grant this degree, the operational code of the manager has become internalized through the choice of career open to young men and women. For the successful manager, the rewards both monetary and psychic are huge relative to other career opportunities. Thus, reinforcement of the commitment to the operational code powerfully sustains its effects on the thinking and motivation of managers.

Organizations are instruments for achieving goals. In the operational code of the manager, organizations are the perfection of systems of cooperation. The code is premised on the axiom that the essence of organizations is to attain purposes that result in rewards for members, and that the organizational universe is essentially one of harmony. The ideal is cooperation. While conflict will appear, belief in the wisdom of organizational processes will assure its satisfactory resolution. Therefore, optimism will be the desired state of mind, since the organization is sustained by belief in the wisdom of process. Process will ensure that harmony and cooperation emerge from conflict in organizations. In directing process, the manager will accept as a goal the conversion of win-lose situations into win-win situations so that rivals or contenders can once again become agents of cooperation.

In the proper functioning of the operational code, win-lose conflict must be converted. Win-lose conflict is most likely to occur in the decisions allocating resources. Because resources are always limited, allocation must overcome the fear of scarcity, even though no participant will consistently get all that he or she wants. Therefore, to sustain harmony, process must be rational and impersonal. The bedrock of rationality in organizations is the consistent application of cost-benefit analysis in decisions about the allocation of resources. Linking process to the technique of cost-benefit economics creates a sustained belief that rationality will prevail.

A manager's fundamental values center on reward. Therefore, an organization is valued based on the prospects for reward in monetary terms and in career satisfaction. It will behoove this manager to identify with an organization, to work hard to achieve goals; but she or he must be prepared to leave an organization to further her or his own aspirations and desires. A career in management is not associated with one organization. Career advancement depends upon the ability to scan the environment and to leave one organization for another according to perceived opportunities.

While this attitude of mobility may seem to contradict the value of loyalty, it subscribes to a higher value of rationality. To the code manager, just as a house is not a home, neither is the organization a home; it is a place to work. He or she may subordinate self-interest to long-term gains in remaining in one organization, but this attitude must also be subject to constant appraisal and to rational decision-making.

The professional manager recognizes the importance of self-interest, but understands that selflessness is a reflection of an immature attitude. Therefore, organizations will be prepared to bargain. Monetary rewards will be put in place to ensure that talented managers stay with the organization, and various compensation practices are designed to assure a high incentive to do so. Compensation committees of the board of directors and specialists in human resource management will constantly appraise the competitive values in compensation plans—such plans having a variety of forms of compensation such as competitive salary levels, short-term bonuses, and long-term achievement rewards (including stock options and even grants of restricted stock).

A professional manager does not worry about the future. Confidence in oneself is the distinguishing feature of this manager. Worrying about the future is perceived as a form of mental masturbation. But to take seriously the assessment of risk is a necessary mental activity and is intrinsic to rational thought and behavior. The manager seeks guidance in formal cost-benefit economics in which high risk must forecast a proportionately high reward. On the other hand, he or she does not bet the ranch on a rash or risky venture no matter how high the potential reward.

While the manager does not concern himself or herself with predicting the future as a long-term exercise, prediction within shorter time frames is essential. Various constituencies depend on the accuracy of short-term predictions and will reward or punish an organization and its managerial elite depending on the accuracy of predictions. The time frame under consideration here is the quarter and the year. Three- and five-year planning cycles are tolerated but taken with a grain of salt as compared with the quarterly and annual time frames.

Control in the short term is a function of tactics. The manager expects the system of controls including budgeting, forecasting, and cost-benefit analysis in evaluating capital projects to exert pressure on an organization to meet goals and expectations. The more rigorous the control system, the more precise the goals and expectations are.

Organizations live in a competitive environment. The professional manager scans that environment to discern the strategies of competitors, and to keep herself or himself aware of technological changes that are impending and forecast the rate of change in the competitive environment.

Professional managers are oriented to reality. They abhor superstition, do not believe in chance, and they scorn all evidences of irrational thought and behavior. In the organizational code, opportunity is the gift of the prepared mind and does not flow as a result of good fortune or random events, and managers place their trust in acting rationally under all circumstances. While there are good and bad times, and cycles of favorable and unfavorable economic climates, managers of this type see these vicissitudes as expected rather than being a matter of chance or luck.

The practice that underlies the manager's day-to-day behavior is the studied use of power to deal with the instrumental and policy issues of the organization. Power, in this case, is the potential he or she has, by virtue of being in a position of authority, to alter or control the behavior of others. To realize this potential to its maximum degree, and avoid negative consequences, the manager over time will need to develop a set of rules on how to play the power game in day-to-day behavior. These rules serve to guide the manager's behavior in getting things done through his or her people.

The professional manager subscribes to the understanding that it is inefficient, and even awkward, to direct another person to take an action. Ultimately, that person will resent the order because he or she will feel reduced—in autonomy and self-esteem. Indoctrination into a methodology, on the other hand, will have the effect of getting things done, without the negative fallout, because the person will feel like a participant in an action based on rational considerations.

Frederick Winslow Taylor (1856–1915) was the methodologist who provided managers with the key to the impersonal uses of power. He invented scientific management and provided tools and roles for using his system in factories to get the work done without one person inflicting his or her will on another. By observation, measurement, and standardization of steps in the tasks performed, the one best way to do a job could be established. While this system could easily be seen as a method of coercion and control, as a limit to individual autonomy, the overriding principle of efficiency was to yield higher monetary reward than the use of idiosyncratic methods. Taylor believed that his system eliminated arbitrary and authoritarian behavior.

In such a system of managerial control, both the boss and his subordinate exist outside of a personal relationship where one person tells another what to do. Both individuals in this relationship of authority are subordinate to the system, and if both internalize the system, there is no issue of will being exercised or limited in an authority relationship. The systematized ideal is to eliminate conflict and substitute instead spontaneous cooperation.

Extend the reach of Taylor's concept beyond the factory to the executive suite and the same principle of impersonal power residing in a logic or a system holds sway. Thus, McNamara could tell Admiral Rickover that he was not limiting the number and type of nuclear submarines for the fleet. Instead, the number and type was set by the logic of cost-benefit analysis. Similarly, Geneen sincerely believed his management system would produce optimal results as compared with having each individual manager determining his objectives independently. With the idea of monitoring the behavior of managers through decentralized operations and centralized controls—the innovation of Alfred Sloan of GM—Geneen designed the innovation of centralized staff consultants and controllers reporting to headquarters rather than to divisional general managers to spot and cure trouble in the field before, rather than after, the fact. These methodologies can be sold to employees as tools that will help individuals improve their performance rather than as tools of power to limit autonomy and control behavior.

Developmentally, the training a person receives as an adult—through education, and through the observation of and subtle hints from others—tends to solidify his or her defensive structure, which is inherent in defined character traits (that which is recognizable to others). Character is the constant that maintains one's image, assuring identity to oneself and to others.

The tool for power, no matter how impersonal or muted, is the manipulation of people. In the organizational structure, as in any context, the ways of manipulation should not become overt or obvious. Machiavelli's advice to princes carries forward to this day in the way managers learn to use power. One tactic is to deflect attention from the object of manipulation. An example is in Alfred Sloan's placating of Charles Kettering, the gifted inventor who advocated an innovation in the copper-cooled engine; Sloan set up a separate organization to develop the innovative engine with Kettering in charge while proceeding, himself, with standardizing product design in the interests of factory efficiency. Sloan knew nothing would come of this arrangement since Kettering was unskilled in running an organization. But Kettering and his admirers on GM's board went along with the contrivance and it soon disappeared while product standardization ruled factory organization.[2]

In the organizational system there is a danger inherent in manipulation. Once started, it may not be limited in its application. Other managers will respond in kind and before long, interest politics take over and communication becomes flawed. To overcome interest politics, strategic decisions will have to be centralized at the top levels of the hierarchy—even though centralized decisions run the risk of leaving individuals at lower levels feeling disenfranchised. Ideally, direct communication without a trace of manipulation permits individuals to evaluate proposed courses of action and to respond directly and honestly to them. Centralization must be selective and clearly differentiated from operating decisions. This differentiation will be rationalized and accepted as long as a wide enough area of discretion is maintained at operating levels of an organization.

Chester Barnard named the area between involvement and noninvolvement the zone of indifference. Barnard, the head of the New Jersey telephone company and a thoughtful student of organizations, in a treatise on the job of the chief executive,[3] noted that individuals have a selective range of involvement. They care deeply about certain issues affecting their lives and self-esteem and are prepared to act, even aggressively, to preserve their interests. But the psyche cannot function with the same intensity regarding all the decisions made by others that may affect an individual's self-esteem. Where the individual is indifferent regarding the options available for selective decisions, she or he is prepared to accept whatever choice a legitimate authority figure makes. By expanding the zone of indifference, the decision-maker will expand his or her autonomy and power. The most common way a manager can expand a subordinate's zone of indifference is to build trust in process. Trust comes from confidence that the organization's authority structure, and the processes for decision-making, will result in the greatest good for the greatest number. Performance that repeatedly demonstrates the fairness of decision-making and the result of rational choices will enhance trust and secure the widening of the zone of indifference.

Another way to widen this zone is to become seductive by manifesting concern for the legitimate interests of others and subtly to encourage identification with authority. This tactic seemingly contradicts the notion of rationality as the guiding principle in organizations. But seduction and its companion, dependency, need not overflow into areas where important decisions are made and objectivity is at a premium.

It is seductive when an authority figure shares confidences with a subordinate. This sharing may appear to be a prelude to asking for advice. The real intent is to solidify the bond between superior and subordinate to the point where the authority figure has increased freedom of action. Sometimes the sharing of confidences is nothing more than gossiping, telling stories about other people or situations that evoke interest and the feeling that the listener is an insider in the power game. The line between shared confidences and gossip is hard to draw, but the effect may be the same in enhancing the feeling of self-importance on the part of the listener.

A power figure who is seductive is inclined to use flattery to draw individuals into his or her web of influence. While in affairs of the heart, flattery will work its wonders, in the building of confidence in a relationship where power is the medium of exchange, to become known as a flatterer is to cause doubt about one's sincerity. Either the object of flattery will take this ploy with a grain of salt and keep an eye on the real issues in the relationship or he or she will become disenchanted. Trust then evaporates, to be replaced by guardedness and a focus on what is really at stake in decisions. The end result is a narrowing of the zone of indifference.

For the professional manager to lose his or her equanimity is to be known as a person of questionable reliability. Managers must seek to become experts in control, and this includes self-control—being consistent in the eyes of others and recognizable in their own eyes. They give up a great deal in depth and richness of character to achieve the ideal of presenting a face to the world. People associated with a manager share the complaint that they know very little about who he or she really is. Part of the mystery is deliberate. The manager will withhold his or her past in the interests of maintaining a high degree of anonymity. But the larger part of the mystery is the result of the mechanisms of defense employed to protect the ego from painful memories and emotions. While the protective armor of character and the mechanisms of defense may be readily tolerated by those who work with the manager, the price paid in family and intimate relationships may be very high.

The psyche of the manager poses an interesting challenge to psychoanalysts. Managers seldom appear for intensive therapy, and those who choose to be psychoanalyzed rarely display symptoms characteristic of their neuroses. They appear to be highly adaptive individuals, free of conflict. What will bring them to seek psychoanalysis is an impasse or disappointment in the progress of their career. This disappointment then reveals a deeper dissatisfaction in their intimate relationships with their spouse and children. In the course of their treatment, there may be revealed symptoms of sexual dysfunction and, occasionally, an isolated and well-hidden perversion, which seems to be encapsulated in the functioning of an apparently "normal" personality.

The late psychoanalyst Helen Tartakoff of the Boston Psychoanalytic Institute described this syndrome of "normality" in a paper entitled "The Normal Personality in Our Culture and the Nobel Prize Co."[4] The term "Nobel Prize Complex" in the title applies specifically to gifted men in the sciences for whom the prize is a hidden ambition. But if the prize is taken to represent outstanding achievement in any field, including management, the syndrome can be understood as a cultural phenomenon that masks more traditional neurotic symptoms.

The so-called Normal Personality, as presented by Tartakoff, is usually a gifted individual who is likely to shine in college and graduate school, holding high promise for the future, and gaining great reward in the approval of professors. As rewards flow toward him (Tartakoff studied only males), his expectations heighten, especially in the goals he sets for himself. He is highly adaptive, having learned to scan the environment and to accept the criteria for success, and having dedicated his efforts to achieving the pinnacle of reward and recognition. Nothing less than the Nobel or its equivalent will satisfy this deep longing for success in his career.

Personal histories of men who are in Tartakoff's category of normal personality reveal a close attachment to the mother. This is the case with both Robert McNamara and Harold Geneen. Being a first-born or an only child, both these men internalized their mothers' ambition that they achieve great works. Tartakoff reports, regarding the normal personality, that "the accomplishment of their goals, whatever direction or configuration they took, . . . [became] essential to the maintenance of their psychic harmony."[5] Besides being talented, a child who fits the profile of the normal personality shows a sense of optimism early in his development. Supported by his doting mother, he believes that steps taken toward goals will be the result of hard work and dedication to the tasks and that he will be appropriately rewarded. Relationships with the father tend to be distant. Not uncommonly, the son's achievements will be expected to outpace those of his father and be integral to the relationship with the mother. With some residual problems of repression, the son takes the place closest to the mother, leaving the father outside the relationship. The failure in the father-son relationship is contained in the detachment of the father, his inability to separate mother and son, and his willingness to allow the mother to remain secure in the attachment to her son.

The vulnerability, in the normal personality, to impasses in career and the consequent feelings of depression tend to force him to become aware of dissatisfaction in his marriage and his family to the point where he seeks therapy. Once in therapy, he gradually recognizes that he lives with an inner sense of emptiness. Memories of the past and the intensive tie to his mother reappear in the present in his transference to the analyst. The repetition of the past occurs in his seeking approval of the analyst, his desire to be the special one. He strives to be a very good patient, is eager to display psychological knowledge, and precociously attempts to outpace the analyst in achieving a cure. He may produce lurid dreams in the attempt to keep the analyst's interest, and will seek approval in arriving first at interpretations of the dream. Resistance will appear when the analyst's approval is not forthcoming, rekindling his fear of distance from his admiring and supportive mother.

It is interesting to observe in the early stages of the career of the manager the repetition of earlier patterns of intimacy in the service of securing the necessary maternal support. A very bright MBA candidate, facing the competitive atmosphere of the MBA program, will form an attachment with a female student who becomes an admirer as well as a lover with the promise, often implicit, that after completing the program the two will marry. Almost at the very end of the program, with the MBA assured, the man announces the end of the relationship, leaving his erstwhile partner heartbroken and disillusioned. Having attained the "prize," with the former insecurity now buried deep in the psyche, the normal personality is ready to move on, seeking new prizes and new conquests in the name of achievement. He does not easily make commitments and often lives life out of a suitcase, unburdened by obligation but still deeply bound to the promise of fulfillment in the reward of the main prize.

One consequence of the thrust toward adaptation to an environment in which the person feels at home is the orientation toward action at the expense of reflection. The person will not hold problems in suspense pending thought and reflection. It is as though his or her mind is organized into an in-box and an out-box. Issues filed in the in-box must be acted upon and disposed of as finished business in the out-box. Action suspended provokes anxiety. The result of an orientation toward action is a too rapid acceptance of assumptions and the adoption of solutions that seem to have worked before. Without realizing he is functioning out of habit, he is bound to substitute repetition for innovation.

Managers are not prone to learn from mistakes. The habits of the mind, oriented toward action, will gloss over mistakes with the reflex notion that history has little to teach—a manifestation of the uneasiness with the reflective mode of thinking. Often the manager will resort to the cliché "that's history," said disdainfully, when she is urged to consider the causes of mistaken actions.

Sydney Finkelstein, a professor at Dartmouth's Tuck School of Business, wrote a book analyzing management errors. Finkelstein subscribes to the principle, well established in medicine, that learning from mistakes is a sure route to preventing the compulsion to repeat in the present what worked in the past. Doctors regularly attend "M and M" (morbidity and mortality) meetings to learn the causes of the cases that went wrong. Finkelstein's book, the message of which is that one must examine assumptions carefully before committing to a course of action, is a step in the right direction as applied to management.[6]

Action that bypasses reflection is bound to produce error. The reflective mind operates in a vertical manner, allowing the workings of preconscious and unconscious modes of thought. Vertical modes of thought avert premature action and increase the possibilities of insight and creativity without causing anxiety and the rigidity of ego defenses. The reflective mind is comfortable with regression to thinking akin to free association. There is no cost or penalty associated with thinking freely. Cost occurs to the obsessive, paralyzed, or morbid mind, rather than to the free-floating mind.

What is the missing link in the operational code of the manager? Is the educational experience of business school too limited to the orientation toward action? Perhaps schools of management need to rethink their mission. Solely training talented people in the use of problem-solving techniques might not be enough. Perhaps they must be trained to build on the imaginations underlying their gifts as well.

> A man who has been the indisputable favorite of his mother keeps for life the feeling of a conqueror.
>
> Sigmund Freud[7]

Part 4

The Empowerers

Martin Luther King, Jr., and Militant Nonviolence: A Psychoanalytic Study

It is an impediment to conducting a psychoanalytic inquiry into the life and work of Martin Luther King, Jr., that his heroic attributes are many and large. He was a charismatic leader of the black church; a tactician who forged an American version of Gandhi's nonviolent movement in India; a preacher and orator who electrified the black and white liberal community in overcoming racism; a winner of the Nobel Peace Prize in recognition of his struggle against the injustice of separatism and racial inequality; and a martyr who fell to an assassin's bullet and thereby became enshrined as a symbol of America's unsteady progress in perfecting a union dedicated to the proposition that all men are created equal. Yet above all, he was a human being, who recognized his own imperfection and who struggled with a sense of sin that was both personal and communal.

Sympathetic biographers often choose to overlook King's human imperfections to focus on idealizing this heroic figure. A notable exception is Michael Eric Dyson,[1] a professor at DePaul University and an ordained Baptist minister. Dyson, although he omits deep psychological interpretations of certain apparent flaws in King's character, takes up in detail King's plagiarism in writing his doctoral dissertation at Boston University and his sexual promiscuity. We have to acknowledge Dyson's courage in recognizing human failings in a national and international icon. Evidently, he enraged many worshipers of the King image, who accused him of demeaning a true hero. But for Dyson, an icon is no less human for struggling with his own sense of imperfection; the hero becomes more heroic as we view his struggles with sinfulness and what, to a conventional mind, are ordinary and distasteful failings in character.

A deeper and more perplexing question begs an answer: Do these so-called failings have anything to do with the calling King undertook in fostering militant nonviolence? Or, are they merely trivial footnotes to the story of a man with a vision, who was bent on restoring the dignity of human beings, both black and white?

King's assumption of leadership appeared to be an accident, the outgrowth of an event in Montgomery, Alabama, on December 1, 1955, when Rosa Parks refused to give up her seat on the bus. The bus boycott in Montgomery gave birth to the militant nonviolence movement that spread, under King's leadership, from the South to the North and expanded its reach into politics and the movement against the war in Vietnam. Inspired in part by Gandhi's passive resistance movement, which had overthrown Great Britain's colonialism in India, King relied on his deep belief in the message of Jesus Christ to love one's neighbor as oneself and when assaulted, to turn the other cheek. The power of this Christian love would transform the life of the oppressor as it would be redemptive in the life of the oppressed.

Martin Luther King, Jr., was born on January 15, 1929, the second child and first son of Martin Luther King, Sr., and Alberta Williams King. Christened Michael, he legally became Martin when he was issued a passport as an adult. ML, as his father called him, had a sister a year older. A second son, Alfred Daniel (called AD), was born a year and a half later to complete the family. Martin Luther King, Sr., called Daddy King, was an ordained Baptist minister who, along with his father-in-law, preached at the Ebenezer Baptist Church in Atlanta. King, Sr., had overcome a hard and deprived childhood. He managed to complete high school and graduated from Morehouse College. In the meantime he married Alberta Williams, whose father, A. D. Williams had founded Ebenezer. After graduating, King, Sr., joined his father-in-law as associate pastor of Ebenezer, and he and his wife (who he called Bunch) lived with her parents in their large house in a middle-class black section near the church. When the Reverend Williams died in 1931, King, Sr., became the pastor of Ebenezer, continuing to live in the Williams's house with his mother-in-law and his family. Mrs. Williams was a beloved grandmother, called "Mama," who evidently doted on Martin.

Daddy King was a stern man who dominated his household and family. He was a strict disciplinarian, meting out frequent spankings as punishment. The spankings lasted until King reached age 15. The strictness of the household and the punishment did not lead to his withdrawal or overt rebellion, and it did not cause him overtly to turn against his father. Probably, the maternal comfort he received from his mother, who supported Daddy King's dominant role in the family, as well as the loving attention of Grandmother Williams, soothed King without diminishing his masculine independence. The second son, AD evidently suffered under the influence of his stern father. While AD followed his father in becoming an ordained minister, he experienced psychological disabilities—as evidenced by alcoholism and an inability to hold a position in a church. AD also suffered from the effects of following a favored son, living in the shadow of his successful older brother and a domineering father against whom he had difficulty holding his own.

King had a privileged childhood, compared to that of the typical black child in a working-class family in the South. The family was well-off financially and the father of the household held a high-status position in the black community. But as Lerone Bennett, another of King's biographers, explains, based on his own background as a Negro growing up in the South:

> Childhood is a time of terrors and vague fears for all children. For a Negro child, who must come to terms not only with himself but with the uneasy knowledge that the world knows something about him and his past, something considered shameful and

delimiting, childhood is a period filled with monstrous shapes and shadows. . . . Like all Negro children, Martin felt the shadow before he saw it. There were places he could not go. There were things he could not do. There were instruments, objects, and people he had to avoid. Out there in the world was something monstrous and menacing, more terrible perhaps because no one could reduce it to words a little boy could understand. But it was out there, on the periphery of vision, and one day the shadow fell.[2]

Bennett and King were classmates at Morehouse College and friends. Bennett's insight not only grew out of the common experience of black youth in a dominant white society, but also from the empathic stance of an individual subjected to the same "shadow" in which his friend lived. There were specific events in King's childhood that made the shadow real and not simply an ominous presence. He describes to Bennett being told by the mother of his white playmates that her children could no longer play with him because they were white and he was black. He was reduced to tears and ran to his mother, who had to explain as gently as she could about the distant and strained relations of blacks and whites. She talked about the segregation of the races going back to slavery and the civil war. She concluded her talk with her six-year-old son by telling him to remember that he was as good as anyone and not to feel inferior.

There were other instances in which the young King came face-to-face with discrimination. His father once took him to a shoe store and sat down to be waited on. The sales clerk told King, Sr., he would wait on him but that he had to move to a seat in the back of the store. The father insisted on staying where he was and finally left the store because he could not be waited on there. On another occasion, a policeman stopped King, Sr., for a minor traffic infraction. The policeman called him "boy." King, Sr., replied that his son sitting next to him was a boy while he was a man. King, Jr., could take pride in his father's dignity and willingness to stand up for himself, but the backdrop of racism could not have escaped him. He could take pride also, as he grew older, that his father had risen from a difficult and deprived background, had achieved a good education at Morehouse, and become an ordained minister.

King had a relatively healthy childhood and upbringing. The love he received from his mother and grandmother sustained him as he achieved a masculine character in striving for a healthy independence in the face of a troubled identification with his powerful and successful father. He was a good student, who skipped grades, and graduated from Booker T. Washington High School at age 15. Despite his young age, he was well adjusted and had little difficulty fitting in with his classmates. As to his future, he appeared undecided although his father was keen on having him become a preacher and join him at the Ebenezer. King himself thought he would follow a career in medicine, which he viewed as a way to help people directly. But he was not gifted in science and turned away from this possibility and began to think about law.

He entered Morehouse College intending to become a lawyer, but not passionately convinced that the law was for him. He decided to major in sociology, then came under the influence of Morehouse president Benjamin E. Mays, who preached during chapel services. King was by then a budding orator, having won a competition, and would often practice oration in front of a mirror. Under the influence of President Mays, he decided to become a preacher. When he told his mother of his decision during his junior year at Morehouse, she urged him to talk to his father. King, Sr., showed no emotion when he told him of his choice of vocation, but, after hearing him out, said that he should deliver a sermon to test his commitment to being a preacher.

King delivered the sermon in a small room in the church. As he spoke, more and more people came to listen. "He was just seventeen," his father said, "and he started to give this sermon—I don't remember the subject—in the first unit of the church and the crowds kept coming, and we had to move to the main auditorium." Later, King, Sr., got down on his knees to thank God for his son's decision. King was immediately ordained as a minister, despite his youth and lack of formal education in theology, and named assistant pastor of his father's church.[3]

The decision to become a preacher came after considerable soul searching. He had to overcome inhibitions to following in his father's footsteps and to burying his distaste for the histrionics characteristic of black congregations. One part of him seems to have felt disdain for the emotionalism of black churches, and for blacks as being loud, boisterous, and unclean. He was fastidious in personal cleanliness and dress—he favored tweed suits during college (earning the nickname "Tweed"). His behavior was circumspect, except that he allowed himself some assertiveness in his relations with women. But he stood out as a serious and reserved young man who seemed much more mature than his age.

Graduating from Morehouse, King enrolled in Crozer Seminary, in Chester, Pennsylvania, where there were six Negroes in a class of 100. When he started there, he was self-conscious, disturbed:

> I was well aware of the typical white stereotype of the Negro, that he is always late, that he's loud and always laughing, that he's dirty and messy, and for a while I was terribly conscious of trying to avoid identification with it. If I were a minute late to class, I was almost morbidly conscious of it and sure that everyone else noticed it. Rather than be thought of as always laughing, I'm afraid I was grimly serious for a time. I had a tendency to overdress, to keep my room spotless, my shoes perfectly shined, and my clothes immaculately pressed.[4]

King excelled in his studies. He pursued an intellectual approach to the ministry and read widely. Hegel was one of his favorite philosophers in his dialectic of thesis, antithesis, and synthesis. King also studied the principle of reform and social justice through an active church and ministry. He became acquainted with Gandhi and passive resistance as a force enabling social change and political justice.

A number of currents in King's life came together during his years at Crozer. He found outlets for his intellectual approach to the ministry and came to the realization that he was ambitious for success through his intellect, and that he could more than hold his own with white students while enjoying a degree of social acceptance he had not realized until then. Ambitious to continue his studies in philosophy and to earn a PhD, he enrolled in the doctoral program at Boston University (BU). He began his doctoral work in philosophy and then continued in the School of Theology. Clearly, he was on a path to surpass his father through formal education and high academic achievement.

Continuing at BU the pattern of identification with teachers begun at Morehouse and Crozer, King studied with leading advocates of personalism, a philosophy centered on the primacy of the individual. He continued to pursue his studies in theology, but he came to the conclusion that his best chances for a successful career, using his talents to best advantage, lay in preaching and the active ministry.

While in Boston, King met Coretta Scott, a student in the New England Conservatory of Music and a talented singer intent on a concert career. He overcame her reluctance to give up her musical aspirations by persistent courtship. The couple married on June 18, 1953, at her parents' home in Marion, Alabama, with his father performing the ceremony. Although they requested that "obey" be omitted from the bride's marriage vows, to which King, Sr., agreed reluctantly, King clearly dominated the relationship—with Coretta King's compliance. She accepted his masculine assertiveness, claiming that in all respects, unlike many black males, he was completely comfortable as a man. In her memoir, Coretta King hints that their marital adjustment was complete; she doesn't mention his later sexual infidelities and seems to have ignored them.[5]

After completing his formal course work and his orals at BU, King and his bride moved to Montgomery, Alabama, where he was pastor at the Dexter Avenue Baptist Church. He wrote his doctoral dissertation while carrying out his ministerial duties and adjusting to married life, and in June 1955, BU awarded him a PhD in systematic theology. His doctoral dissertation later became controversial as a result of considerable plagiarism evidence.

It is difficult to reconcile King's academic achievements at Crozer and BU with his plagiarism. As a preacher, he used other preachers' sermons, but a common explanation for that, short of plagiarism, is the culture of black sermonizing. "In black oral culture black folk learn to refine rhetoric and shape identity by joining their voices to the voices of their ancestors and their contemporary inspirations. Thus King did not view such an art as verbal theft but as a time honored, community-based tradition with deep roots in black culture."[6] But in academic work, cribbing the words of others without quotation marks or footnotes is a serious matter.

Dyson sees King's plagiarism as a response to the negative identity that was a constant threat to a talented black student. Another way of speaking of this threat—which could be viewed as a projection of the dominant white culture—is to define the fear of failure. An ambitious and talented student, as King had proven himself in his work at Morehouse and Crozer, would carry little weight in his self-image in a sophisticated and competitive atmosphere such as one would find at BU's School of Theology. Wanting to succeed in his doctoral work, perhaps driven by the desire to exceed his father's accomplishments, he might constantly have been fearful that he could not compete in a rarified eastern academic atmosphere.

The fear of failure can also be converted into contempt for the standards of academic achievement by which King expected to be judged. To doubt one's own ability while simultaneously disparaging in one's own mind the process by which judgments of ability and achievement are reached could overcome ethical standards and lead to cheating.

There are some suggestions in what Dyson wrote about King, as well as in the work of others, that King could get away with plagiarizing in his dissertation because of the desire on the part of professors to overlook standards in the case of a black student. King's dissertation plagiarized the work of a PhD candidate who had submitted a thesis three years earlier. His doctoral supervisor had also been the professor in charge of the plagiarized dissertation. What was the probability that the professor consciously overlooked the ethical violation in order to protect a black candidate? The 2003 case of the black *New York Times* reporter Jayson Blair comes to mind. Blair's supervisors protected him and ignored reports that he falsified his stories, cribbed from sources without attribution, and reported conducting interviews that never took place. Given the strong desire to diversify its staff of reporters, the supervisors appear to have wanted so much for the reporter to succeed that they became lax or consciously overlooked the breach of journalistic ethics. In the case of King's supervisor at BU, there is no direct evidence that he knew of the plagiarism and suppressed evidence of it, but the suspicion remains.

In accepting the position at Dexter, King had disappointed his father, who wanted him to join Ebenezer as associate pastor. Here again, he was able to follow his own inclinations, disappointing his father, without creating a permanent rift in their relationship.

The Dexter Avenue appointment, along with marriage, marked significant gains in ego development for King. He found his vocation in the church and seems to have established his independence from his father while apparently maintaining his relationship with the elder King even though he had surpassed him in academic credentials. At Dexter, King relinquished his earlier desires for an academic career and followed in his father's footsteps in the Baptist ministry.

While he had absorbed the culture of the Negro and was sensitized to the problems of prejudice and inequality, little in his preparation for a career predicted the role he would play in the black protest movement against discrimination. Race riots in the 1940s following the migration of blacks from the South to northern cities such as Detroit, and the experience of blacks in the military during World War II, indicated that the days of passivity among blacks were coming to an end. Then along came Rosa Parks.

There were no role models for the movement. Booker T. Washington, founder and first head of the Tuskegee Institute (1881) believed in practical training for blacks to enable them to earn a living. Training at Tuskegee was not ideologically driven and did not seek to confront the white majority over civil rights. The emphasis on self-improvement through training and the cultivation of values such as thrift and high moral standards avoided confrontation over racial inequality. Another prominent black, W. E. Du Bois (1868–1963), differed from Washington in advocating confrontation with the white society to overcome racial injustice. Du Bois, a founder of the National Association for the Advancement of Colored People (NAACP) and a professor at Atlanta University, was a recognized sociologist who had earned advanced degrees at Harvard University and gained recognition for his writings—which included novels and poetry. But Du Bois could not be seen as a role model for the movement. He advocated separation from white society in the United States and a return to Africa. He moved to Ghana and lived his last years in exile from America.

Roger L. Shinn, of the Union Theological Seminary, in his foreword to *Roots of Resistance*, states:

> Among the mysteries of history is the appearance from time to time of leaders who defy all laws of probability. In the language of the Old Testament, God in times of human need some times "raises up" a prophet, a judge, a deliverer, a priest, or a shepherd. Today we think up intricate schemes of economic, social, and psychological causation to account for the emergence of unexpected leaders, but we do not do much better, and often we do worse, than the simpler language of the Bible.[7]

The essence of *Roots of Resistance* is King as a black preacher devoted to militant nonviolence through a profound identification with Jesus Christ. From a psychoanalytic point of view, identifications are familiar grounds for ego development and for the attachments between leader and led.

There was an event. Rosa Parks decided to remain in her seat on the bus home after a typical day of fatiguing work at her job as a seamstress in a department store. She would not move, despite the harassment of the bus driver, and in the end, she willingly went to jail to uphold her right to a seat on a segregated bus. This event ignited the movement of nonviolent protest and King's leadership in the bus boycott.

Rosa Park's decision to stay where she was on the bus seemed spontaneous, but Parks was active in the local NAACP and had prepared herself to protest bus segregation when the opportunity arose. December 1, 1955, presented the occasion. The police removed her from the bus, and booked and jailed her on charges of resisting arrest and violating the bus segregation statutes. The trial took place on Monday, January 5, and she was found guilty of the bus segregation charges. This conviction became the basis of appeal in the federal-court system resulting ultimately in the U.S. Supreme Court decision declaring bus segregation unconstitutional—a major victory for the Montgomery bus boycott, for King, and for the Montgomery Improvement Association (MIA).

The decision, immediately following Parks's arrest, to make a test of segregation on buses came from E. D. Nixon, the former head of Montgomery's NAACP chapter, and Mrs. Jo Ann Robinson, an activist in the black community of Montgomery, who had explored various ways to start a bus boycott. Both Nixon and Robinson believed that the jailing of Rosa Parks presented the opportunity.[8] King reluctantly went along with the decision to hold a meeting of black ministers, in his church, to formulate plans for a bus boycott. The meeting revealed serious discontent with the older leadership and as a quick fix, the group elected King to head the boycott—to begin on Monday, December 5. Leaflets announcing the Monday boycott appeared along with newspaper reports so that blacks would stay off the buses on Monday morning. The boycott was underway and would last for a little over a year.

King had little or no experience in leading a group movement such as the bus boycott. Mobilizing the black community to stay off the buses required logistical efforts to provide alternate transportation to and from work. It required negotiating skills in meetings with city and bus officials to resolve the boycott in the least amount of time. King had to rely on the MIA board, made up of other black ministers and community leaders, to counsel him on conducting the boycott. The counselors included Reverend Ralph David Abernathy, a close friend and advisor; E. D. Nixon of the NAACP; Jo Ann Robinson; Fred D. Gray, the lawyer for the MIA; and various preachers from the black churches. Apart from Nixon, Robinson, and Gray the members of the committee organized to plan strategy lacked experience in tactical matters.

King's advantages in his new found leadership position stemmed from the fact that, unlike other ministers, he had no critics or rivals. He was young but considered a fine preacher. The board of the newly formed MIA planned the strategy for the boycott and became the negotiating arm of the black movement. King addressed the boycott rallies held in various black churches, evoking the religious tone of nonviolence and Christian love. L. D. Reddick, another King biographer, says:

> Martin Luther King was the spokesman, the philosopher and the symbol of the Montgomery bus boycott. In these roles he was without a peer and the additional dimension to the movement that helped make the struggle epic. . . . There were many good speakers . . . but King was the best of the lot. He established close rapport with the people. No matter who gave the pep talk, the mass meeting audiences were never completely satisfied unless they heard from King. They believed in him. One "sister" said that when King spoke she felt that God himself was near; another testified that when she heard King's voice she could also hear the rustle of angels that she could see dimly, hovering over him.[9]

In its negotiating stance, the committee of the MIA adopted a conservative approach. The proposals it offered to end the boycott were very modest and did not initially seek to overturn segregation. But the negotiators for Montgomery and the bus company would not budge. The Montgomery officials increasingly adopted a hard stance in confronting the MIA, its negotiators, and the black community—whose members were refusing to ride the buses.

The Montgomery officials made a number of tactical errors that created the stage for nationwide—and worldwide—publicity for the boycott and the determination of the black community to continue it. As a result of the jailing of eighty or more leaders of the black community, including King, and a court trial in which the judge, immediately after testimony and summation, declared the defendants guilty of an illegal boycott, Martin Luther King, Jr., became a charismatic leader for the nation and the world. He became linked with Gandhi.

The black community in the United States has traditionally been steeped in an oral culture, arising especially from the preaching of black ministers.

In his famous address, delivered in Washington, D.C., on August 28, 1963, in front of the Lincoln Memorial, as the keynote speech to conclude the civil rights march, King achieved the pinnacle in eloquence, exemplifying the merging of an audience in identification with the speaker. It was no longer a mass audience listening to a speech, but a unity transformed from many, in an experience that was oceanic. King implored his audience not to "wallow in the valley of despair," but to join him as he exclaimed, "I have a dream." He repeated the phrase, "I have a dream," as he sought to overcome the despair of the blacks over racism and inequality. "I have a dream that one day every valley shall be exalted, every hill and mountain shall be made low, the rough places shall be made plain, and the crooked places shall be made straight and the glory of God will be revealed and all flesh shall see it together."[10] The climax occurs as he chants the plea to let freedom ring, concluding with the prayer-like Negro spiritual, "Free at last, free at last, thank God Almighty, we are free at last."[11]

The practical successes of militant nonviolence depended in large measure on eliciting violent responses from the movement's adversaries. The movement did not articulate the need for the sadistic response, it was implicit in the need for maximum public and press exposure of participants submitting passively to the violence engendered by their nonviolent protest. The effect was to sear the conscience of the white majority. In the instances, few in number, in which the sadistic response was not forthcoming, the protest tended to lose momentum and even disappear.

The protest movement in Albany, Georgia, failed to overturn segregation and became a defeat for King and the nonviolent movement when Police Chief Laurie Pritchett arrested protesters without using violence and with care to treat people politely. The few instances of violence in that city occurred outside the view of the press and the public so the authorities could maintain their position of meeting nonviolent protest with nonviolent legal proceedings. Pritchett jailed protesters but he sent them to outlying jails away from Albany. When protesters prayed before going to jail, Pritchett joined them in prayer, accentuating his nonviolent stance. There was no nationwide publicity because there was no violence, which meant that sympathetic Northerners remained relatively unaware of the Albany protest movement.

The movement in Albany had begun as a voters' rights movement under the auspices of leaders of the Student Nonviolent Coordinating Committee (SNCC). A group of local black leaders formed the Albany Movement in November 1961 to overturn segregation in public facilities. The head of the Albany Movement, without the knowledge and assent of the SNCC officials, asked King to come to Albany to lead a protest march. King along with Ralph Abernathy agreed to lead a march, and without conscious intent, assumed the prominent leadership position accorded to him given his reputation and national visibility.

The leaders of SNCC resented King's intrusion in the Albany protest. They referred to him as "De Lawd" and felt that they had done all the work and he was garnering all the credit. SNCC was not committed to nonviolence. They went along out of deference to King, but with resentment of his prominent position in the black civil rights movement.

William D. Watley, writing in 1985 on the nonviolent movement, understood the practical significance of the sadistic response without using the concept of sadism. "If Montgomery demonstrated that harsh repression by the adversary could generate sympathy and outside pressures on behalf of the victimized, then Albany taught King that an opponent who wears the façade of gentleness could halt the efforts of sympathetic outsiders and produce a sense of futility among the resisters."[12]

Birmingham, Alabama, was another instance of the usefulness of the sadistic response to the movement's momentum. When the demonstrations there began, including "sit ins" in lunch counters for whites only and marches to demonstrate against school segregation, the city authorities received a federal injunction prohibiting the demonstration. King decided to ignore the injunction and he, along with others, went to jail. There he wrote his famous "Letter from Birmingham City Jail" in response to a letter from eight leading white ministers opposing the black movement.

As an offshoot of the march from Selma to Montgomery, leaders of the SNCC in Selma opposed many of King's attempts to arrive at compromises with a representative of the United States' attorney general. SNCC leaders were critical of King and the Southern Christian Leadership Conference (SCLC), and presented a militant alternative to King's nonviolent approach. King prevailed in his approach to the marches, but he became increasingly fatigued and even depressed by the weight of his responsibilities. He had taken on a heavy schedule of speaking engagements aimed at eliciting support and funds for the SCLC and had to take time off for rest, and on occasion, had to check into hospitals for rest and recuperation.

The psychological pressure on King was not limited to an almost inhuman work and travel schedule, which he maintained while resolving conflict among his advisers and staff. The FBI under J. Edgar Hoover launched a campaign to discredit him and undermine his support in the civil rights movement. If King became somewhat paranoid in his fear of the FBI, it was not delusional, but in response to the reality of threats and harassment.

The incident that supposedly started the FBI attacking King was recorded by Cartha D. "Deke" DeLoach, Hoover's lieutenant at the Bureau:

> Hoover developed an intense animosity toward the civil rights leader, one that grew, like the biblical mustard seed, from a small kernel into a huge living thing that cast an enormous shadow across the landscape. That kernel was little more than a brief comment by King in a November 19, 1962, article about the civil rights movement in the South. . . . "One of the great problems we face with the Federal Bureau of Investigation in the South is that its agents are white Southerners who have been influenced by the mores of the community. To maintain their status, they have to be friendly with the local police and the people who are protecting segregation. Every time I saw FBI men in Albany [Georgia], they were with the local police force."[13]

Hoover had a knee-jerk reaction to any criticism of the FBI. He pointed out to Attorney General Robert Kennedy that only one of five agents in Albany was a Southerner, the rest were from the North. But this defense did not deal directly with the allegations that the FBI agents in Albany were close to the local police. To set the record straight, Hoover asked DeLoach to set up a meeting with King. DeLoach called and left a message. Either the message did not get to King, or he was too preoccupied to call back. DeLoach and Hoover took the failure to return the call as a snub and reacted angrily.

David Garrow, in his study of the FBI's hostility toward King, believes that the so-called snub had less to do with the FBI's increased surveillance of King than his association with Stanley Levison, a New York lawyer and trusted advisor, who was allegedly an active member and influential figure in the Communist Party. The FBI's wiretapping and bugging of the SCLC's offices and King's home, along with the taps on Levison, failed to obtain corroborating evidence of a communist plot, or Levison's involvement in the Communist Party, to justify their interest in the King-Levison relationship. Hoover continued to press his organization, and particularly the New York and Atlanta offices, to increase their surveillance of King.

Hoover's frustration with the bureau's inability to link King, the SCLC, and Levison as subversives under the influence of the Communist Party led him to issue a public condemnation of King. On November 18, 1964, he met in his office with a group of journalists who were members of the Women's National Press Club. In a monologue he defended the FBI against King's by then two-year-old charges that agents were Southerners who sided with local police against the Negro antisegregation movement. Evidently, Hoover warmed up to the subject as he noted the reporters' heightened interest in the meeting. He said, "In my opinion, Dr. Martin Luther King is the most notorious liar in the country." DeLoach, who attended the meeting, reacted with astonishment and near panic on hearing Hoover's words. He tried three times to get Hoover to declare these comments off the record. Hoover ignored DeLoach and announced that despite DeLoach's advice, he wanted his comments about King to remain on the record.[14]

Acting either on his own initiative or on the advice of his counselors, King arranged an appointment with Hoover, at which he was accompanied by Reverend Ralph Abernathy, Andrew Young and Walter Fauntroy of the SCLC. It was a conciliatory meeting, with Abernathy and King complimenting the FBI on its fine work in the South. No mention was made of King's earlier criticism of the FBI or of Hoover's statement that King was a notorious liar. The meeting produced no change in Hoover's attitude toward King and the black civil rights movement. Instead, taps and bugs continued to produce reports on conversations as well as sounds of sexual activity in motel rooms where King was staying.

The decision to meet with Hoover indicates a high level of psychological naïveté on King's part, and possibly on the part of his advisors. If King believed he could establish a conciliatory relationship with Hoover, he was sadly mistaken. Holding the meeting and conducting it as though the "liar" accusation had not been made played into Hoover's hands, allowing him to defend his bureau without retracting the insult. The attempts to discredit King as a leader in the black community continued. Instead of the attack based on allegations of sympathy, if not overt dependence, on a communist, the FBI pursued him based on the bugging information it accumulated. Hoover did not hesitate to distribute copies of tapes made from the taps and bugs. The distribution list included the president, the State Department, the Defense Department, and the Attorney General's Office.

One day, a package addressed to King arrived at his residence. Coretta King received it in his absence. The package contained an audio tape of King in his motel room leaving no doubt of sexual activity. The package also contained an anonymous letter, made to look as though a Negro had written it. It read, in part, "King, look into your heart. You know you are a complete fraud and a great liability to all of us Negroes . . . you are a colossal fraud and an evil, vicious one at that.

You could not believe in God. . . . Clearly you don't believe in any personal moral principles." The letter concluded with the threat that King had 34 days before the letter and accusations would be made public, and it concluded, "You are done. There is but one way out for you. You better take it before your filthy, abnormal fraudulent self is bared to the nation."[15] The one way out: suicide.

DeLoach reveals in his book that William C. Sullivan, assistant director of the FBI, was the author of the anonymous letter and had sent the letter and tape to King's house. DeLoach also states that Hoover had not authorized Sullivan to prepare the tape and letter and had no knowledge of Sullivan's action. King felt threatened and harassed by the FBI and became depressed and fearful.

King's sexual behavior outside of marriage was promiscuous and compulsive. Abernathy and other lieutenants in the SCLC were completely aware of the fact that King had many sexual liaisons while traveling away from home. King explained that he was away as many as 27 days a month and needed the sex to relieve the anxiety and the tensions of his demanding schedule. Abernathy tried to caution him about the possibility of scandal, but King had no intention of ending his relationships with women. Coretta King ignored her husband's philandering. Even when she received the FBI tape, she chose to act unconcerned about the evidence of her husband's extramarital sex.

Abernathy attributed King's sexual attractiveness to the power of his personality, his charisma as an orator, and his public prominence. Women came on to him and he could not resist, even where the attraction verged on the obvious and the FBI threatened public disclosure. There is some validity to King's own explanation, that he needed sex as a tranquilizer. But there is never a simple cause-effect relationship to compulsivity. His sexual habits contained a strong element of danger that he would be found out and subjected to ridicule. This danger probably enhanced the sexual excitement—another reason King could not control the behavior.

King's deeply religious feelings acted as a component of his sexuality. In Christianity, believers must accept their sinfulness. This sense of inherent sin is almost a condition of belief in God. King could preach on the virtues of marriage and the purity of being true to marriage vows. But his beliefs and preaching did not inhibit him from seeking satisfaction in sex outside of marriage. The inconsistency between belief and practice could be bridged by the acceptance of one's sinfulness. To seek perfection borders on arrogance. To accept one's sinfulness is humility, especially when it is accompanied by the desire to meet moral standards in the future—albeit with hardly any expectation that these standards can be met. But the recognition of sin does not provide a free ride, one does not have one's pleasure without a price. The price to be paid is in guilt—not easily dispensed with in a religious attitude.

King had periods of depression, particularly as he expanded his activity beyond the South into northern cities such as Chicago and Cleveland, and beyond geography into issues such as poverty (which to his mind created a unity of interest between blacks and poor whites), war, the Vietnam conflict, and colonialism. Along with his wife and his associates, he attributed his depression to excessive travel, public speaking, the pressures of managing SCLC, and the mounting discontent with nonviolence—particularly with the rise of the Black Muslim movement, which presented an alternative to the passivity of nonviolence. But perhaps unconsciously, he felt afflicted by what he perceived as shortcomings both in his work and his sexuality, and he labored over a sense of guilt. He seems to have taken little pleasure in winning the Nobel Peace Prize since his depression, compounded by Ralph Abernathy's feeling that he should have shared with King the prize and the money award, went unabated.

Masochism—the need to be punished—when enacted, is a sexual perversion. In the absence of the enactment, the fantasies underlying this need to be punished convert the impulse into a transformation of character. The effect seems to be remote from sexual impulses and appears as a highly developed, rigid morality. It may be unconscious to the individual and often takes the form of identification with the oppressed, the disadvantaged, and the underdog in society. It is frequently a partner to a deeply religious attitude, but without the feature of providing a path to redemption.

King identified with the blacks as an oppressed minority. His aggression toward the white majority took the form of nonviolence—which didn't mean it was less aggressive—for the purpose of engendering guilt. When King came to the pulpit or the platform, his oration promoted a sense of guilt in the wider community, while stimulating the moral masochism to which his listeners were already predisposed. The identification was with the sufferers, and the ultimate redemption for both blacks and whites lay in enacting reforms. The Civil Rights Act of 1964 and the Voting Rights Act of 1965 closed the gap separating whites and blacks and ameliorated the sense of guilt inherent in moral masochism.

For King, the moral masochism penetrated more deeply into his psyche than even he could recognize. During the 1960s his depression became more evident to his associates in the SCLC and to Coretta King. For King the sense of guilt manifested itself in the expectation that he would die at the hands of an assassin. There had been one attempt on his life when a demented black woman stabbed him during a book signing. He came close to death because the implement she used penetrated only a fraction away from his aorta. His morbid sense of his own assassination accompanied his depression. It was fulfilled on April 4, 1968, when he was shot as he stood on the balcony of the Lorraine Motel in Memphis.

The strength and faith of King, Sr., were severely tested by the murder of his firstborn son, the loss of the child who, while surpassing him in achievement and renown, had become a great source of pride to him. "My first son, whose birth had brought me such joy that I jumped up in the hall outside the room where he was born and touched the ceiling—the child, the scholar, the preacher, the boy singing and smiling, the son—all of it was gone."[16] During the funeral service, he cried out, "ML! Answer me, ML," but he had to accept his loss.[17] It left a void and hurt that scarcely could be healed.

On July 21, 1969, about a year after King's murder, his brother drowned in the swimming pool of his house, in the middle of the night. He had moved to Atlanta to become the associate pastor of the Ebenezer Baptist Church. Abernathy, in his autobiography, quotes King, Sr.: "I refused to be bitter. I refused to question God. At A.D.'s funeral, I told the world that 'I had lost much, but I thanked God for what I had left!'"[18]

King Sr.'s ordeal and the testing of his faith was once again challenged when his wife was shot to death. An assassin entered the church on the last Sunday of June, 1974. Bunch was at the organ playing before the start of the service. Suddenly a voice shouted out, "I'm taking over here this morning," and shots rang out hitting Bunch and wounding a deacon. She was rushed to the hospital where she died.[19]

King's assassination, the death by drowning of his younger brother and the murder of their mother while at the church organ provokes in us an eerie feeling of being unwilling witnesses to senseless death that we knew would happen, much as in a classical Greek tragedy. That King, Sr., could absorb the horror as a test of his faith and submission to God's will provides little by way of healing since the deaths are beyond comprehension.

King's depression consequent to his feeling weighed down by his responsibilities, manifested in a premonition that he did not have long to live, but he did not take precautions such as engaging bodyguards to protect him. He was vulnerable on the balcony of his motel where his assassin awaited him. He died a martyr to the cause of racial equality. Power rested heavily on his shoulders. He did not consciously covet the life of a hero, nor did he turn away from the calling that was to be his. He lived with the ambivalence of the hero figure, accepting the gift of oratory that was the main instrument of his leadership. His stature remains, awaiting a successor to rekindle the fire of racial justice.

Frantz Fanon: Purgation Through Violence

In 1973 Irene Gendzier published a book on Frantz Fanon, a black French-educated physician and psychiatrist who became the apostle of violence in the anticolonial movement in Algiers. In her preface Professor Gendzier states that she had intended at the outset of her research to write a psychohistory of Fanon, but "as I became more involved in the Fanon story, in the French, Martiniquean, and Algerian aspects of Fanon's life, I chose to concentrate more on the social and political dimensions of the man's world and less on the individual roots of his response to it."[1]

While remaining sensitive to the personal side of Fanon and his development, Gendzier concluded that to write what would amount to a case history would distort the main theme of Fanon's life, which was a protest against the white man's negative image of the black and the hatefulness of white colonialists against the native colonized. Yet the stories are intertwined, as Gendzier herself acknowledges, and to isolate the philosophical, the social, and the political from the developmental and personal does an injustice to the quest for Fanon in the midst of his anger and intellectualization.

The task of finding the man and relating him to his work is complicated by the fact that, despite his passion and hatred, he was a person who could manage to hide who he was behind his intellect. As a psychiatrist who read Freud, to him psychoanalysis was not a personal venture, but rather an aspect of his reading. He never sought a personal analysis, nor did he practice psychoanalysis, either privately or institutionally. He was action oriented. His training and practice as a psychiatrist followed the use of electroshock therapy and the liberal and humane treatment of patients hospitalized for psychotic disorders. He was a social psychiatrist who removed restraints from patients and engaged them in group activity—including involving them in the affairs of the hospital as a community. He was an advocate of getting patients back into their families and communities as quickly as possible, to continue treatment if necessary as outpatients. But increasingly, he turned his attention and interests to philosophy, and his writings had less to do with the practice of psychiatry and medicine than with the plight of the natives of the Maghreb and black Africa. Whatever introspection he experienced, the apparent effects were to direct his passion into intellectual works on anticolonialism.

He advocated violence against colonials, although he did not engage personally in violence or in terrorist activity, but used his writing to expound the theory of violence in overcoming racism and colonialism.

In 1944, at the age of 19, Fanon wrote a letter to his father deeply critical of his father's absence as a force in the family. This was an unusual letter, since other siblings seemed to accept the father's passivity as simply an aspect of the culture. But not Fanon. The letter said:

> Papa, you really have sometimes failed to perform your duty as a father. I allow myself to judge you in this way because I am no longer of this earth. These are the reproaches of someone living in life's beyond. Sometimes Maman has been unhappy because of you. We made her unhappy enough. In future, you will try to return to her one hundredfold all she has done for the equilibrium of the family. The word now has a meaning that was previously unknown. If we, the eight children, have become something, Maman alone should take all the glory. She was the spirit. You were the arm. That is all. I can see the face you will pull when you read these lines, but it's the truth. Look at yourself. Look back at the years that have passed, lay your soul bare and have the courage to say: "I deserted." And then, repentant parishioner, you will be able to return to the altar.[2]

Fanon wrote this letter while in the army in France during World War II. Death was realistically in the air. But was he still beset with an unresolved oedipal conflict? Freud had not dealt with racial problems and the implications that the cultural acceptance of detached fatherhood and a powerful matriarchy had for the universal validity of the Oedipus complex. Fanon used Freudian psychology to explain the gap between self and other and the negative identity of the black as a projection of the white's equation of black with dirt, primitive sexuality, and ignorance. But Freud and psychoanalysis held no place for him neither in the formation of a personal identity as a physician and psychiatrist nor as a method of gaining insight into one's own neurotic conflicts. He stated, "It is too often forgotten that neurosis is not a basic element of human reality. Like it or not, the Oedipus complex is far from coming into being among Negroes. It might be argued, as Malinowski contends, that the matriarchal structure is the only reason for its absence . . . it would be relatively easy for me to show that in the French Antilles 97 per cent of the families cannot produce one Oedipal neurosis. This incapacity is one on which we heartily congratulate ourselves."[3] If this view reflects impatience with psychological causation of mental disturbance, it is probably a reflection of his urgency for action. For Fanon, ideas should lead to action.

Frantz Fanon was born in Martinique, a French protectorate, on July 20, 1925. His father, Casimir, was in the civil service and relatively prosperous. His mother, Eleanore, was a mulatto and an illegitimate child with white ancestors originating in Austria and living in Alsace. Besides bearing eight children, Eleanore owned a small shop selling hardware and drapery, adding to the financial comfort of the family. Frantz was the fifth child in the family, to be followed by two sisters and a brother. He resembled his father, being darker than his siblings.

His mother stressed the value of education, and he and his siblings attended the best school available in Fort-de-France, the town in Martinique where the family lived. Besides education, his mother valued discipline, comportment, and family unity. She insisted that the children speak perfect French and avoid Creole as being beneath the family. If they lapsed into slang, she would say angrily, "Don't behave like a nigger."[4] On one occasion, a visiting uncle treated the children to ice cream. She joined the group after the ice cream vendor had left and asked one of her daughters for a taste. The daughter replied, "Why me?" Her mother reacted angrily and took the ice cream away and flung it against a tree, exclaiming, "What belongs to me belongs to you. What belongs to me belongs to you belongs to all of us. Put that into your head once and for all!"[5]

As a child, Fanon was active, rebellious, and mischievous. He and his friends would sneak into movie houses without paying. He assumed leadership of the group of boys, who were usually older than he. He loved to play soccer and was adept as a player. Among his siblings, he was closest to his older brother Joby.

With adolescence he became an avid reader, spending time at the local library searching for books on philosophy and French culture. He learned literature at Lycée Schoelcher, from the poet and politician Aimé Césaire, an impassioned teacher and a strong influence on his students. Césaire became the voice of negritude, striving to instill self-esteem in blacks—a philosophy that evoked ambivalent responses in Frantz. Another man, who became a surrogate father, was his uncle Edouard Fanon, a teacher with whom Fanon and Joby lived for two years at the behest of their mother because she was concerned over the lack of paternal influence and discipline of her sons.

When France fell to the Nazis and was divided, during World War II, remnants of the French navy moored off the coast of Martinique (which remained part of Petain's France). Under Admiral Robert's control of Martinique, the island became divided in sentiment with a strong attachment to the Free French under General Charles de Gaulle. Admiral Robert provoked hatred among the native Martinicans. According to David Macey, "Life in *Tan Robe* [referring to Admiral Robert's administration of Martinique] would bring [Fanon] his first serious encounter with racism."[6]

Because of the racism that Admiral Robert and his navy fostered, Fanon, at age 17, left the lycée and boarded a ship for Dominica to enlist in the Free French forces. After a short while he returned to Martinique and continued his schooling. But after graduation, he enlisted with the Free French forces and landed first in Casablanca (March of 1944) then transferred to Algeria to prepare for the invasion of southern France. The invasion took place in August, with American troops in the vanguard. Fanon's division landed in St. Tropez in October, by which time American troops were well into southern France, and the division moved rapidly north. After receiving a shrapnel wound, he was evacuated for treatment and convalescence and was soon playing soccer with other soldiers recovering from wounds. Fanon wrote the letter to his father that is quoted above, with intimations of death, while he was serving in the Free French army. In October 1945, six months after the German surrender, he sailed with his regiment for Martinique.

In a letter to his parents before the end of the war, he wrote:

Today, 12 April. It is a year since I left Fort-de-France. Why? To defend an obsolete ideal. I don't think I'll make it this time. During all the scraps I've been in, I've been anxious to get back to you, and I've been lucky. But today, I'm wondering whether I might not soon have to face the ordeal. I've lost confidence in everything, even myself.

If I don't come back, and if one day you should learn that I died facing the enemy, console each other, but never say: He died for the good cause. Say: God called him back to him. This false ideology that shields the secularists and the idiot politicians must not delude us any longer. *I was wrong!*

Nothing here, nothing justifies my sudden decision to defend the interests of farmers who don't give a damn.

They are hiding a lot of things from us. But you will hear them through Manville or Mosole. The three of us are in the same regiment. We've been separated, but we write to each other, and even if two of us die, the third will tell you the same dreadful truths.

I volunteered for a dangerous mission, and I leave tomorrow. I know I won't be coming back.[7]

His experience with racism in the Free French army had disillusioned him. He realized he was black and lived in a different world from the whites.

Contrary to his premonition, Fanon returned from the war and picked up his life. He went back to the lycée to prepare for his oral examinations for the baccalaureate, in order to continue his studies in France under a grant that was available to him as a veteran of the war under the Free French. In the summer of 1946, having passed his orals, he sailed for France. Initially, he was unsure of what career he wanted to follow. He toyed with the idea of law or dentistry, but settled finally on medicine. He had planned to study in Paris but once he got there he felt there were too many blacks living there. Not wanting to be part of the black Martinican community, he moved to Lyon and began his medical studies there.

In February of the following year, Fanon received word of the death of his father in January. To console himself he went to his sister Gabrielle, who was studying pharmacy in Rouen, and on the train back to Lyon, he wrote a letter to his mother. "It is very difficult for one to imagine the death of one's father. . . . Be kind enough, Maman, to send all the details of his death, did he have thoughts of me, you know, one always wants to know what one who gave you life thinks of you. It's this estimation that henceforth directs your life . . . your daily efforts."[8] He concluded the letter, "Without you, what are we, what are we?"[9]

His medical studies proceeded uneventfully, although he had difficulty with anatomy and dissection. While in secondary school, he had managed to sneak into an autopsy room where he had watched the procedure and become ill. His aversion to dissection continued through medical school, and as a result, he never contemplated a career in surgery or even general medicine.

While psychiatry appeared to be for him a residual choice among the medical disciplines, he was aware of his humanistic inclinations in his identification with the plight of the blacks living in an atmosphere of colonization both in Martinique and France. But at this early stage in his professional development, he had yet to evolve the philosophy that would ultimately lead to purging blacks and whites of prejudice through the enactment of violence.

Psychiatric training in Lyon was substandard. The emphasis was on organic diagnosis and treatment with a general usage of shock therapy even where not indicated, such as in the treatment of anxiety. Fanon took a post in a hospital outside of Lyon and commuted back to his residency on Saturdays to make rounds with his chief. He found little satisfaction with his psychiatric training in Lyon and left a negative impression on one of his supervisors in the hospital outside of the city—where he was the lone intern for 500 patients.

Facing the requirement of presenting a thesis to qualify for graduation with a medical degree, he decided to submit the manuscript he had been working on, which was an early draft of what was later to become *Black Skin, White Masks.* This manuscript was totally unsuitable as a medical dissertation, and his enraged professor rejected it, forcing him to produce something more appropriate for a psychiatric department with an emphasis on organic illnesses and psychosurgical treatment. The thesis he then submitted reported on a case involving a hereditary disease and was accepted following an oral examination in November 1951.

Fanon's training in psychiatry improved, as did his career, with his appointment to Saint-Alban hospital under the renowned psychiatrist François Tosquelles. Tosquelles was a Spaniard from Catalonia who opposed Franco and had had to leave Spain. He became Fanon's first real mentor in psychiatry. Fanon found the methods Tosquelles introduced enlightened, humane, and beneficial in the treatment of mental disorders. Patients were not incarcerated behind walls nor tied down in their beds. In order to overcome the wartime shortage of food, patients grew their own food and had managed to survive without the horrendous death rates found in other mental hospitals during World War II. Macey describes the treatment methods and atmosphere of Saint-Alban:

> The basic ambition of Tosquelles and the Saint-Alban group was to humanize their institution by recognizing and promoting what Balvet called the human value of its inmates. A variety of therapeutic techniques ranging from drug therapy and ECT to psychoanalytically influenced psychotherapy and encounter groups were used, but the central emphasis was on group work. The theories involved were also varied, almost to the point of eclecticism. Living together inevitably meant working together, and that implied breaking down the rigid hierarchies that divided doctors from nurses, and patients from staff. The key element was the therapeutic club, to which all patients belonged as of right. A general assembly elected delegates to a bureau and to the commissions responsible for the secretariat, the library, the film club and the all-important newspaper. The underlying thesis was that psychotherapy dealt with individuals who were *aliénés,* meaning "alienated" in both the clinical and the social sense. Their flight into psychosis or schizophrenia had led them to break the social contract, to become outsiders who were excluded from social life. Although the cause of their alienation was biopathological, and therefore to be treated as such, the club's existence was founded upon a gamble: the possibility of transfusing a social life into its patient-members, of reintegrating them into some form of symbolic exchange (it is this that provides the important link with Lacanian psychoanalysis). The gamble could be seen to have paid off when, for example, the schizophrenic took it into his head that he would like to drink a coffee in the canteen. In order to do so, he had to obtain money and in order to obtain money, he had to work. With the money he

had earned, he could go to the canteen, where he had to speak to whoever was serving. He then had to pay for his coffee, wait to be given his change and thank the canteen lady. The goal of all the preceding therapy was to bring the patient to the point where he could begin to enter a process of social exchange and intercourse by deciding that he wanted a coffee and starting the chain of events.[10]

Frantz found a place for himself in Saint-Alban, where he founded treatment protocols based on social psychiatry—for which he became renowned.

In order to qualify for a senior post in hospital psychiatry, Fanon had to take his postgraduate exam, which he did in June of 1953 after a brief stay in Martinique. Meanwhile, the year before, he had married Josie, a white 18-year-old student whom he had met in 1949. Josie helped him with his first book, *Black Skin, White Masks,* which he dictated to her since he could not type. To the day she died, Josie Fanon maintained her reluctance to discuss her husband with authors and journalists so there is no indication of how she reacted to the text she typed, including passages that refer to black hands caressing white breasts and the imagined reactions of a white Lyonnaise woman to the size of a black man's genitalia. When Gendzier was writing her biography of Fanon in the 1970s, she tried a number of times to interview Josie, but Josie always refused, claiming a surfeit of Fanon followers. She committed suicide in 1989, without leaving any evidence to suggest how she reacted, assuming she knew, that Frantz had fathered a daughter, Mireille, in 1948—the year before he met her—with a white woman who was also a medical student. Josie and Fanon had a son, Olivier, who tried in vain to have his father's body reburied alongside his mother's in Algiers.

Black Skin, White Masks, published in 1952, is an impassioned book mixing Fanon's outrage at the whites' treatment of blacks with despair at the acceptance by blacks of the negative image projected on them in white racism. Fanon was especially angered by the condescension he encountered in a white person complimenting a black on speaking French so well, the implication being "like a white person." He was outraged at the tendency of white Frenchmen in speaking to blacks to use "*tu,*" which is reserved for a child, instead of "*vous*" when speaking to an adult. "A white man addressing a Negro behaves exactly like an adult with a child and starts smirking, whispering, patronizing, and cozening. It is not one white man I have watched, but hundreds. . . . I have made a point of observing such behavior in physicians, policemen, and employers."[11] Whites talked "pidgin nigger" to blacks, a demeaning way of putting down the black. "You are on a train and you ask another passenger: 'I beg your pardon, sir, would you mind telling me where the dining car is?' 'Sure, fella. You go out door, see, go corridor, you go straight, go one car, go two car, go three car, you there.'"[12] Fanon gave a lecture in Lyon drawing a parallel between Negro and European poetry. "A French acquaintance told me enthusiastically, 'At bottom, you are a white man.'"[13]

There are two chapters in *Black Skin, White Masks* on the sexuality of mixed racial relations. Both of these chapters deal with the conscious and unconscious attraction and repulsion of sex relations in mixed races. Fanon is saying that for the black woman and the white man, the attraction is the conscious desire to be white, especially in mulatto women, who fear returning to being a Negress. A mulatto woman approached by a black man, according to Fanon, often feels insulted. She considers herself white and feels demeaned to be taken for a black woman. The desire is for "lactification," to be bleached and never to return to blackness.

For Fanon, the Negro is a victim of white civilization. For some writers and philosophers, the solution to this sense of being a victim was to espouse the unique identity of the black and this identity's contribution to culture. For Leopold Sedar Senghor, who became president of Senegal, and Aimé Césaire, poet and politician, negritude was a rallying cry for black self-esteem. The problem for the Negro was to take action to overcome the negative images derived from the white and the effects of these negative images in the collective unconscious of the black. In *Masks,* Fanon begins to allude to the problem of converting passivity and blanket unconscious acceptance of the negative images into action. But merely to accept and believe in negritude was not the answer for him. The Negro felt in his collective unconscious "one is a Negro to the degree to which one is wicked, sloppy, malicious, and instinctual. Everything that is opposite of these Negro modes of behavior is white. . . . In the collective unconscious, black = ugliness, sin, darkness, immorality. In other words, he is Negro who is immoral."[14]

Fanon uses Hegel to emphasize the importance to the black of restoring lost self-esteem by gaining the recognition of the other, the white man. To gain this recognition from the other, the black had to take action, and ideally, action (not yet defined in Fanon as violence) on both sides would result in mutual recognition. "But the Negro knows nothing of the cost of freedom because he has not fought for it. . . . The former slave needs a challenge to his humanity, he wants a conflict, a riot."[15] The result would be affirmation, saying yes to life, to love, and to generosity while saying no to scorn, to degradation, to exploitation. This yes and no was preparation for action. "Face to face with the white man, the Negro has a past to legitimate, a vengeance to exact."[16]

The conclusion of *Black Skin, White Masks* foretold what Fanon would write in *The Wretched of the Earth.* Before taking up writing this second book, he had to complete psychiatric training, after which he accepted a post in a psychiatric hospital in Blida, outside Algiers.

The psychiatric hospital in Blida, as with psychiatry in all of Algeria, was in a relatively primitive state. The surroundings were pleasant enough, but the treatment methods backward. Fanon set out to reform hospital treatment, applying the social psychiatry he had learned at St. Alban. He found some allies among the staff, but by and large, he encountered resistance. At the same time, he became aware of the political repression by the French colonials in Algeria and of the activity of the National Liberation Front (FLN), which he joined. Violence accelerated in Algeria on the part of the French military and the colonials, countered by the growing militancy of the FLN forces. The French employed torture to extract information about the FLN, and some of the patients Fanon attended were victims of the torture or enforcers who had become psychotic and depressive in reaction to having participated in or inflicted the torture. One policeman who was engaged in torture came to Fanon for treatment of his uncontrolled violence against his family. He wanted Fanon to treat him so that he could continue his work without guilt and without violence against his family—including a 20-month-old infant. Another case that came to Fanon was the killing of a French boy by two of his playmates. His interview with the 14-year-old perpetrator provided him a chilling example of the loss of humanity brought about by both sides in the struggle. The young Algerian had decided to kill his friend because he and his accomplice wanted to avenge the killing of Algerians. They chose their playmate because he was accessible.

In response to the violence on the side of both Algerians and Europeans, repressive measures reached Fanon who, because of his anticolonial writing, was suspected of aiding the FLN. In fact, he was active in the FLN primarily through his writing.

With threats against his life, his situation in Blida became untenable, and he submitted his resignation to the resident minister in Algeria:

> For almost three years, I have devoted myself completely to the service of this country and to the men who inhabit it. I have not been sparing in either my efforts or my enthusiasm. Every aspect of my actions demanded as its horizon the universally hoped for emergence of a viable world.
>
> But what is enthusiasm and what is a concern for men when, day by day, reality is being torn apart by lies, acts of cowardice and scorn for man? What are intentions when their embodiment is made impossible by emotional poverty, intellectual sterility and hatred of the people of this country?
>
> Madness is one of the ways in which man can lose his freedom. And being placed at this intersection, I can say that I have come to realize with horror how alienated the inhabitants of this country are.
>
> If psychiatry is a medical technique which aspires to allow men to cease being alienated from his environment, I owe it to myself to assert that the Arab, who is permanently alienated in his own country, lives in a state of absolute depersonalization.
>
> The status of Algeria? Systematic dehumanization. . . .
>
> For long months, my conscience has been the seat of unforgivable debates. And their conclusion is a will not to lose hope in man, or in other words myself.
>
> I have resolved that I cannot face my responsibilities at any cost on the fallacious grounds that there is nothing else to be done. For all these reasons, Monsieur le Ministre, I have the honour of asking you to accept my resignation and to bring my mission in Algeria to an end.[17]

The French authorities expelled Fanon from Algeria, although officially he was placed on a leave of absence. Before he left a bomb exploded outside his house, but caused no injuries. He went to Paris for a brief stay and then on to Tunis, where he officially joined the staff of the FLN. For all practical purposes, his career as a psychiatrist came to an end at this juncture. He devoted himself to work with the FLN and to writing anticolonial articles and *The Wretched of the Earth*.

If there remained any doubt in anyone's mind as to his intentions, either philosophical or political, *The Wretched of the Earth* dispelled any notions other than the outright espousal of violence to end colonialism. He declared his position in the first chapter of the book, entitled "On Violence." For the colonized, there was no choice other than killing to rid the land of the colonizer. There was no possibility for compromise. And on this score, he criticized the European, the colonizer, and the nationalist bourgeoisie for proposing compromise between the two. He broke with the Marxists, for whom the theory of revolution rested on the militancy of the working classes, and promulgated, instead, the militancy of the peasants as the force for revolution—but not by compromise or treaties.

> Compromise involves the colonial system and the young nationalist bourgeoisie at one and the same time. The partisans of the colonial system discover that the masses may destroy everything. Blown-up bridges, ravaged farms, repressions, and fighting harshly disrupt the economy. Compromise is equally attractive to the nationalist bourgeoisie, who since they are not clearly aware of the possible consequences of the rising storm, are genuinely afraid of being swept away by this huge hurricane and never stop saying to the settlers: "We are still capable of stopping the slaughter; the masses still have confidence in us; act quickly if you do not want to put everything in jeopardy." One step more, and the leader of the nationalist party keeps his distance with regard to that violence. He loudly proclaims that he has nothing to do with these Mau-Mau, these terrorists, these throat-slitters. At best, he shuts himself off in a no man's land between the terrorists and the settlers and willingly offers his services as go-between; that is to say, that as the settlers cannot discuss terms with these Mau-Mau, he himself will be quite willing to begin negotiations. Thus it is that the rear guard of the national struggle, that very party of people who have never ceased to be on the other side in the fight, find themselves somersaulted into the van of negotiations and compromise—precisely because that party has taken very good care never to break contact with colonialism.[18]

Dien Bien Phu became the prime example for Fanon of violence as the sole means to overturn colonialism. Just as the French (and later the Americans) were defeated in that epic battle for Vietnam, colonial rule would be overthrown as a result of violence and not statesmanship or compromise. As for prolonged colonizer occupation, Fanon declared, "The truth is that here is no colonial power today which is capable of adopting the only form of contest which has a chance of succeeding, namely the prolonged establishment of large forces of occupation."[19]

Fanon likened violence to receiving a royal pardon through which the colonized ultimately receive freedom. But this freedom depends upon the release from an inferiority complex that is overturned or cleansed through violence. Once violence achieves its end of freedom, both from the subjective inferiority complex and the oppression of the settler, socialism becomes the means for achieving economic freedom. "Capitalist exploitation and cartels and monopolies are the enemies of underdeveloped countries. On the other hand the choice of a socialist regime which is completely orientated [sic] toward the people as a whole and based on the principle that man is the most precious of all possessions, will allow us to go forward more quickly and harmoniously, and thus make impossible that caricature of society where all economic and political power is held in the hands of a few who regard the nation as a whole with scorn and contempt."[20]

His utopian vision of a postcolonial society under socialism reveals a level of naïveté on his part that does not encourage a more thoughtful view of man and society. His fixation on the evils of colonialism in perpetuating the inferiority complex of the blacks, and the cure through violence, prevented him from serious concern for the aftermath of violence. He could not look beyond violence to purge the hateful images internalized from the whites' projections on to the colonized.

The final chapter of *The Wretched of the Earth* allows Fanon to resume his psychiatric analysis of the effects of colonialism on the mental disorders he treated in Blida. (Reference to two of these cases appears earlier in this chapter.) Fanon had concluded in his brief practice as a psychiatrist, that curing mental disorders, apart from palliative methods, was frustrated by the causation, which he believed was colonialism. As a physician-psychiatrist, he had reached a dead end in his own mind and became an activist in the FLN—a revolutionary—although in his behavior he did not engage in violence.

Jean Paul Sartre wrote the preface to *The Wretched of the Earth,* which catapulted Fanon and the book to fame and notoriety. Fanon had long admired Sartre and Simone de Beauvoir through their writings, and he was anxious to have Sartre write the preface. He arranged to see him while Sartre and de Beauvoir were vacationing in Italy, where he presented him with the manuscript.

Sartre exclaimed in the preface that Fanon was fearless in his advocacy of universal socialism for the third world. "Europeans, you must open this book, and enter into it. After a few steps in the darkness you will see strangers gathered around a fire; come close and listen, for they are talking of the destiny they will mete out to your trading centers and to the hired soldiers who defend them."[21] As one of the leading intellectuals in France, when Sartre spoke, the French listened, even though at one level his message was seditious. (Once when French authorities wanted the government to bring Sartre to trial for sedition—which Sartre had challenged them to do—de Gaulle responded, "One does not arrest Voltaire."[22])

Fanon did not live long enough to see the effects of his book and to witness, if not enjoy, his notoriety. In 1960, while in Ghana, he was discovered to have an elevated level of leukocytes in his blood, and further tests in Tunis led to the diagnosis of leukemia. When he sought treatment in Moscow, where he felt he would be safe from assassination attempts, the doctors recommended that he go to the United States for treatment, and the U.S. Department of State, along with the CIA, arranged to bring him to The National Institute of Health in Bethesda for treatment. He entered the Clinical Center on October 10, 1961, and died on December 6. The CIA arranged to have his body flown to Tunisia, and he was buried just over the border in Algeria.[23]

The revolutionary war in Algeria, between the French and the FLN, broke out in 1954 and lasted until 1962. It proved to be bloody and cruel. The French army in Algeria bitterly opposed ending the battle and there were threats from the nationalists of carrying a coup d'état into France proper—including assassination threats against de Gaulle, who had assumed power in France in 1956. As bloodshed continued, there were various attempts at compromise, but the FLN wanted total independence from France. Recruits in the French army refused to serve in Algeria, and the French grew tired of the warfare. The French government finally gave in, and a conference in Evian beginning in March 1962 led to a peace treaty granting full independence four months later, on July 3.

Independence movements sprang up all over Africa. It seems as though the legacy of Fanon's writing and of his official duties in the FLN promoted the movement for independence. He had served for a brief period as Algeria's ambassador to Ghana, but his role in these independence movements was relatively minor. His work and reputation in the black movements in the United States also seems to have been minimal. Although a black power force emerged there, it proved minor in the granting of full rights to black people as compared with the results of Martin Luther King's nonviolent movement.

At the time of this writing, summer of 2003, violence and terrorism are no strangers to the world. Little is mentioned in the press and other media of Fanon, nor is he associated with violence throughout Asia, the Middle East, and Africa.

In the current conflicts, fundamentalism seems to have trumped Fanon and his theories of violence. The war is no longer racial or purely nationalistic. But for the proponents of violent fundamentalism, the same questions that are a major part of Fanon's legacy apply to the new terrorists. Is there a cost to violence, which must be taken into account in asking what kind of society is in store for the countries and people of the third world? Does the turmoil stop when ends appear to have been achieved? Or does violence become a way of life with untamed aggression searching for new aims and objects?

Fanon's vision was limited and his time horizon restricted. Perhaps his aggression could not be contained in a time horizon that was immediate and where the play of imagination cannot contain the pressure for purgation through terror. Perhaps, also, he sensed he had little time for thinking beyond the present. He died a silent and nonviolent death at age 37.

13

The Psychodynamics of Empowerment

The life and work of Martin Luther King, Jr., and Frantz Fanon represent radically different approaches to the problem of empowerment. Nonviolent confrontation and the outright espousal of violence both aimed through action to reverse the low self-esteem of blacks and the colonized of Africa and the Caribbean and to produce change, but under vastly different circumstances. In the case of nonviolence, or Gandhi's satyagraha, passive resistance will bring about change particularly if it creates a sense of guilt supported by a moral code as well as legal redress. The more the objects of nonviolent confrontation retaliate with violence, the more guilt is generated and, ultimately, the greater the possibility of change by legal means. A charismatic leader, supported by followers gifted with tactical acumen, is essential in the nonviolent movement and is the agent for change through the effects of mass psychology and identification.

Violent movements, whether through organized warfare, guerilla tactics, or random acts of terror, depend upon hatred to release aggression from the restraints of conscience. Terrorism in the Middle East, fostered by religious fanaticism that promises eternal paradise to suicide bombers, seems to depend upon dispersion of authority and even upon competing terrorist groups. Terrorists play upon the psychology of low expectation to instill the belief that there is little or nothing to lose through violence. Concern for the future is absent as is the value of attachment to family, friends, and a future.

Colonized countries that have gone through a period of violence to achieve independence face the question of what comes after violence. How does leadership reverse the psychology of low expectation and foster a reverence for life over death? Recent history provides little reassurance that it is easy to subdue and channel the aggressive impulses toward life-giving aims. Dictatorships, tribalism, and rivalries, with horrifying repressions and killings, seem to be the common answer to what follows violence in the name of empowerment. Fanon did not live long enough to see the results of his espousal of violence in the Africa that he hoped would cure the inferiority complex of blacks. He would have faced a bitter effort to deal with, if not rationalize, the barbarisms of an Idi Amin or the civil war in Liberia and in Mali. What would he have had to say about the economic deficiencies in oil-rich Algeria and the tribal warfare there after independence?

Sooner or later the focus has to shift into an inquiry into the true meaning of empowerment. Empowerment means the liberation of the individual from uncontrolled aggression, and from the subordination of the ego to mass psychology.

Individuals who are caught up in empowerment movements, both nonviolent and violent, substitute one form of dependency—on an authoritarian program or leader—for another—economic privation. Liberation, from these and other forms of dependency, requires freeing the ego from group psychology and from neurotic disabilities that restrict the development of the individual.

Once restrictive governments are replaced, new goals have to be developed with the aim of enhancing the ego through education, economic opportunity, and personal freedom. This is a tall order, one that has not been successfully implemented in the third world. We are in the midst of a contagion of violence and terror. Empowerment in the name of these repressive activities is an illusion, a false promise that chains individuals to abject dependency.

The problem of empowerment is not restricted to third world countries. Empowerment movements have sprung up in the United States and other developed countries with democratic institutions. Empowerment movements have been adopted in the name of feminine liberation and equality of the sexes. In complex organizations empowerment programs seek to alter hierarchies, to "flatten" the organizational structure, decreasing the authority of top levels while increasing the autonomy of the lower levels. These ideological approaches carefully avoid the fact that hierarchy is a form found in nature. Assemble a group, give it a purpose, and if left to its own devices, it will organize itself into a hierarchical structure in the shape of a pyramid.

True empowerment is a result of individual transformation from dependency to autonomy following the path of maturation from infancy onward. Ego development will be restricted as long as individuals are victims of dependency on groups or limited because of neurotic conflict, including a punitive structure of self-defense. Empowerment is a function of the liberation of the ego and thus, cannot be given to the individual, but must be self-engendered given the benefits of movements such as King's for nonviolent social and institutional change.

Education and training to develop competencies is the sure, albeit slow, route to empowerment through the enhancement of talents, whether in developed economies or third world nations. In underdeveloped nations the route toward self-engendered empowerment may be longer, and results may be slower to materialize, but whether in developed or underdeveloped economies, self-empowerment requires motivation. The desire to develop and strengthen the ego must be internalized, and this comes with the cultivation of talents.

Unlike mass movements under the leadership of a charismatic leader, empowerment of individuals through the development of talents comes through education and training. Identification with gifted teachers, who stimulate learning, is a microscopic process that occurs not only in the formal atmosphere of the classroom but also in the seemingly mundane activity in factories and offices—wherever people assemble to accomplish work.

Hisashi Shinto became head of Japan's IHI Shipbuilding Company, following the purge of wartime industrial heads. He prepared IHI for the shipbuilding boom by adapting American modular-construction methods to the production of ships. A key element in his modernization approach was the selection of graduate engineers for front-line supervisory positions. He stressed technical competence as a prerequisite for these front-line positions. It may not require a degree in engineering, but this level of competence and the ego strength inherent in having the knowledge for the job is the necessary prerequisite of empowerment.

Knowledge that gives supporting strength to the ego, for a supervisor, is not necessarily the same as the technical expertise of the engineer. A supervisor is more a generalist than he is a specialist. His technical knowledge may be derived from experience rather than from book learning. He may be compared to the *bricoleur*,[1] or handyman, utilizing a store of knowledge derived from hands-on experience with a variety of tools and techniques. Strengthened by an acute capacity for observation, this generalist can identify the cause of problems and provide solutions that can then be employed by specialists. Admiral Rickover is an example of the *bricoleur*, who uses the knowledge he derived from observation and experimentation and, as a byproduct, teaches, by example, how one can empower oneself.

The supervisor as *bricoleur* enjoys self-esteem to a degree that enables him to stand up to specialists and project a sense of personal power that is not easily shaken. Having this sense of personal power, he gains the respect of workers, who recognize that he is acting in their interests as well as his own. He is empowered by the strength of his ego.

Technological progress in an organization affects the individual as it affects the structure of authority and power in organizations. Loss of authority—the price of progress and increased productivity—tends to be greatest at the lower levels of the organization. Before the advent of mass production, skilled workers exhibited high degrees of autonomy in controlling their work. But with the advent of scientific management and the innovations of Frederick Winslow Taylor, a marked shift occurred in the distribution of authority and power. Taylor's system transferred authority from the supervisor and the worker to people who specialized in organizing manufacturing processes in factories. He saw from early experience, as apprentice and then skilled worker in machine shops, that factories lacked rational organization and methods. Individual workers were free to devise their own methods, leading to marked variations in the way individual machinists performed their work. Taylor asked, "Isn't there one best method?" He observed machinists at work and measured the time it took to perform the various steps in completing their tasks. To eliminate wasted motion was to eliminate the idiosyncratic arrangements of the workplace. Taylor standardized tools and methods and trained workers in the new approach. He invented the job of the industrial engineer, the specialist in time and motion studies and the microorganization of work.

Taylor did not see his invention as attacking the power and autonomy of the worker; he was liberating the worker from the irrational use of energy and providing the opportunity for enhanced earnings through the piecework-payment method he introduced. More important, he believed he was liberating the blue collar worker from the irrational and abusive authority of supervisors, who had little appreciation for the importance of rational methods and would arbitrarily castigate workers for shirking duty on the job. Instead of a personal relationship in a superior-subordinate structure, supervisors and workers alike became subordinate to the system of scientific management. In this way, the system achieved perfect justice—everyone was equally deprived of autonomy in the control exerted by the impersonal system.

The system of scientific management initially aroused hostile reactions from workers and management alike. But it endured and became the hallmark of management practice in the twentieth century. The residual effect in power relations is that it requires supervisors to enhance their autonomy and to become knowledgeable about work methods in order to challenge specialists where appropriate. The loss of power this engenders in lower-level supervisors is a challenge to the strength of their ego.

A supervisor would appear to have little formal authority in a modern structure with a highly articulated organization of specialists. As she or he advances in a hierarchy, possibly to reach the level of CEO of a corporation, she or he is granted formal authority. But successful performance depends on transforming formal authority into personal power, linking the top and lower levels of the hierarchy. The case of a CEO who could not accomplish this transformation reinforces the theme that empowerment is a self-generated strength of the ego.

The board of directors of a large corporation had to select a new CEO. There was considerable urgency in naming a successor, since a corporate raider had instituted a proxy fight to gain control of this corporation. A candidate surfaced from a successful company in which he had served as chief operating officer, the second position in the hierarchy. The challenge for him in his new position was to assume the number one post as CEO.

As soon as he finished negotiating the terms of his employment, the CEO devoted himself to winning the proxy battle. He worked hard, meeting with large shareholders and lenders to make the case for supporting the existing board and management. He was successful in this fight and now had to turn his attention to figuring out what to do in his role as CEO.

Shortly after the proxy fight, the CEO called an influential director to ask his opinion on hiring a consulting firm to undertake a study of the company and its competitive position. His intention, he told the director, was to get recommendations from the consulting firm for new strategies for the corporation. The director advised the CEO to hold off bringing in a consulting firm because he was new to the job, and, despite his success in the proxy fight, he was unfamiliar with the industry and with his key executives. Also, he had little firsthand knowledge of the strengths and weaknesses of the organization and the competitive environment. The director cautioned the CEO that to bring in a consulting firm as his first move would jeopardize his direct relationship with his key subordinates as well as lower-level staff.

The director soon realized that the CEO's solicitation of advice had been purely pro forma. Even before the telephone call, he had decided to engage the consulting firm, and the purpose of his call was to enlist the director's support for the idea even though the decision was well within the CEO's prerogatives.

Shortly after announcing the engagement of the consultant, the CEO called the director and asked him if he would be willing to read and comment on the consulting firm's proposal. The director agreed and soon read the proposal. His immediate reaction was that it was so general that it could apply to any firm and that it did not include the proposed diagnosis of the company's situation. He suggested that the consulting firm be asked to develop a proposal specific to this company. The CEO countered with a request: would the director prepare a set of questions to guide the consultation. The director complied and was surprised to learn that the consulting firm had adopted his questions without amendment or modification. The director's questions had become the consulting plan.

The director's prediction of the effects of the consultation on the CEO's authority proved correct. He had distanced himself from his people and effectively transferred his authority, and ultimately his power, to the consultants. He remained an unknown to his subordinates as well as to the board of directors, as the consultants occupied center stage. To make matters worse, he lacked an independent base for judging the recommendations that came before him. He merely accepted carte blanche the consultants' recommendations, and asked the board for its support. The board adopted a passive position and did not engage the CEO in an active discussion of the planned course of action, not unlike many boards in corporate America. The board's passivity resulted from a desire to avoid criticizing the CEO, because criticism could raise doubts about the CEO's ability and might be seen as a lack of confidence in him on the part of the board. The board preferred passivity to risking the appearance that it lacked confidence in the CEO—which could have been inferred had a vigorous discussion ensued.

The effects of the consultation were disastrous, since the consultants' recommendations, adopted without modification, were faulty and wasted corporate resources. After a brief time the board dismissed the CEO, and the company soon filed for bankruptcy.

Every role in an organization has some degree of authority. It is the right of the incumbent to initiate action and thinking on the part of subordinates. In most cases, subordinates accept this right as legitimate and will attempt to perform within the acceptable range of expectations. But in this formula, nothing worthwhile will happen until the initiation carries with it the sense of personal power of the incumbent.

Whether a lower-level supervisor or chief executive, the successful holder of a role in the organization provides a potential for action with both magnitude and direction. This potential carries with it the inner strength of the actor based on intellect and self-esteem. The use of personal power is the expenditure of resources on the part of the actor. If the action is successful, the power of the actor is enhanced, ensuring his or her confidence for future initiatives.

In psychoanalytic theory, the ego—the regulatory apparatus of the mind—evolves through conflict. The individual, from infancy through adulthood, is a pleasure-seeking entity. He or she must learn to regulate impulses, to delay gratifications, and to take account of reality in seeking to satisfy desires. The ego also performs defensive functions to regulate anxiety. Defenses ward off external dangers, but their main function is to exert control over impulses, which, if enacted without regard for reality, would endanger the person's safety and equilibrium.

Besides experiencing pleasure and providing defenses against anxiety, the ego is the agency for the development of talents, which in part are innate. These capacities of the ego are the result of acutenesses that evolve from the experience of conflict during development. Through the mastery of conflict come highly sensitized capacities of the senses such as sight and sound and, beyond the senses, mental attributes become recognized as talents. As individuals experience the honing of talents and gain reward and recognition for using them, their egos are enhanced, and the result is a growing feeling of personal power.

The dictionary definition of empowerment is "to give power to someone else." An institution may grant authority to an individual in a role, but only the strength of the ego can transform authority into power. Thus, the individual uses ego strength, made up in part from confidence in the uses of her or his talents, to take action and assert herself or himself in real situations.

A major element of this strength is talent—the innate capacities of the individual. These capacities, if undeveloped, or impeded by disabilities arising from neuroses, are wasted assets. To illustrate the restrictions that neurotic conflict exerts on the ego, and hence on the development of talents, we turn to one of Freud's celebrated cases—Dora.[2]

Dora was 18 years old when she began psychoanalytic treatment with Freud. She started treatment reluctantly, at the insistence of her father—who had become alarmed when he discovered a suicide note she had written. She suffered from an array of symptoms such as shortness of breath, an uncontrollable cough, loss of voice, and migraine headaches. These symptoms originated during her eighth year, and were severe during her adolescence and a cause of great concern for her father. With her disabling symptoms, she had little energy for or interest in her intellectual development, and there appeared to her parents to be little they could do to help her and to encourage her to engage her intellect.

Dora was deeply attached to her father and hostile to her mother. But the relationship with her father was complicated—not only by her longing for him and her repressed sexual desires, but also by her involvement in a sexual liaison between her father and Frau K, a family friend married to Herr K. When her father would arrange to meet Frau K in another town, Dora would go along, ostensibly to help look after Frau K's children. Dora knew that her father and Frau K were lovers, but this knowledge did not sever her relationship with her father. She willingly became involved in her father's love affair and to a considerable extent, allowed her presence during the trips to visit Frau K to facilitate her father's relationship with Frau K.

Dora had a precocious interest in sex and would read books that informed her fully on sexual anatomy and activity. But with all the knowledge she had, she repressed her own sexual desires. On one occasion during a visit with the Ks, Dora went on a walk with Herr K and he made sexual advances toward her. Reacting with disgust, she repelled his kisses and reported the incident to her father—who accepted Herr K's denial. She concluded that she was being offered to Herr K in exchange for her father's affair with Frau K. It was after this that Dora wrote the suicide note.

The analysis had lasted for three months when Dora abruptly broke off treatment. The conclusion was inescapable that transference of her sexual wishes toward her father on to Freud was the cause of her leaving analysis before a cure had been effected. But even during this brief treatment, Freud had elicited, and had helped Dora to become conscious of, her repressed sexual desires and the objects of these desires.

Her sexual desires seemed highly mobile when it came to the objects attached to them in her unconscious. Not only her father and Herr K, but Frau K had also become an object of sexual longing and homosexual attraction. If she could not have her father in the oedipal triangle, she would identify with him and replace him in his relationship with Frau K. For all of these repressed sexual wishes, and the repression of the various objects of these desires, Dora was substituting illness. The hysterical symptoms seriously interfered with her maturation, and restricted the development of ego capacities even in an era, seemingly, of already limited opportunities for a bright, attractive woman. For the price she paid in failing to develop talents and interests, she received compensation in controlling her parents through her illness. This trade-off, though to her disadvantage, compensated her neurotically in the agony she caused her parents, particularly her father.

Dora reported two dreams in the course of her treatment. The first dream revealed a reproach toward her father for not protecting his children—Dora and an older brother. The dream involved imagery of a locked door that could have prevented the father from saving his children from a fire. The associations to the dream revealed fantasies connected to masturbation and bed-wetting during her latency years, along with sexual desire, which she connected to Herr K, whom she slapped in the face when he made sexual advances.

The second dream had images of the death of her father and her difficulty in getting home for the funeral. In the dream, when she arrived home she learned that her mother and other mourners were already at the cemetery. She was too late for the burial. The interpretation of the dream led to her wish for revenge toward her father. The dream also foretold transference of wishes for revenge upon Freud, who in her unconscious, was thwarting her sexual desires. She did in reality get revenge by stopping treatment and preventing the cure Freud sought in his work as a physician.

As a postscript to the case, Freud reported that two years after the precipitate ending of the analysis, Dora came back with a symptom of facial neuralgia for which she sought help. She had achieved independence from her father and was no longer in the middle of his affair with Frau K. The neuralgia was easily cured when she told Freud that the symptom had appeared two weeks prior to her visit, and Freud connected this timing to the appearance in the newspaper that he had been appointed professor. The symptom seemed an act of remorse for having thwarted Freud in his attempt to cure her and at the same time, for having slapped Herr K—whom she had seen being run over by a carriage.

Without presenting details, Freud reported that Dora had pursued intellectual interests and that she had married the man in whom she became interested at the time she reported her second dream. Freud concluded, "Just as the first dream represented her turning away from the man she loved to her father—that is to say, her flight from life into disease—so the second dream announced that she was about to tear herself free from her father and had been reclaimed more by the realities of life."[3]

In writing the Dora case, Freud found ample evidence to support his theory of transference in the curative effects of psychoanalysis. The Dora case is not a detached accounting of the history of a neurosis. It is a case about transference, in which the patient experiences in her attachments to the analyst a fresh version of the infantile neurosis, the experience becoming the leverage for changing neurotic suffering into active living and striving for positive ego goals.

There is a popular notion about talent that seems to equate creative work with neuroses. Innate talent seems to take second place to neurotic suffering as the bedrock of outstanding performance. While this popular notion appeals to romantic fantasies about the underlying sources of gifted work, it fails to take into account the biological foundation of talent and the hard work required to cultivate and discipline innate gifts. The notion equating creative work with neuroses also badly underestimates the debilitating effects of unconscious conflict on the capacities to work, let alone to gain pleasure from the efforts involved. The case described below affords a closer look at how neuroses suspend progressive development and empowerment.

A man in his mid-twenties decided to undergo psychoanalytic treatment. The main symptoms he presented were excessive drinking and self-destructive behavior. He would experience a buildup of rage with undetermined cause. To relieve the rage and its accompanying anxiety, he would go on a drinking binge and do things like expose his arm to a lighted candle. It was as though the pain would drown the rage and allow him to restore his mental balance. These binges would occur with some regularity, and there was little he could do to control his rage and the self-destructive actions.

The analysis over a three-year period gradually centered on his ambivalent relationship with his father, a man of considerable accomplishment and status in the community. He spoke angrily of the demeaning behavior of his father toward him and his aspirations. But submerged in this conscious anger and felt rejection there appeared a deep longing for love and approval from his father. The father was himself a troubled man whose behavior, despite his achievement in work and community, reflected low self-esteem. The patient reported that his father had grown up in a troubled household without the love and support of his parents. When the father learned that his son was in analysis, he became intensely curious about what went on in analysis and made sarcastic comments about the procedure while revealing intense jealousy of his son's relationship with the analyst.

As the patient became conscious of his longing toward his father—clearly revealed in the transference—with the help of the analyst, he recognized that there was little he could do to gain the love and approval for which he longed. He could not change his father but he could change his expectations, and recognize without guilt that the problems of his father had little to do with his own actions and behavior.

The patient was in a career that paid well, but did not seem to challenge him or have a deep hold on his interests. He tolerated the career rather than immersing himself in it. One Monday he arrived for his hour, settled himself on the couch, and announced that he had decided to end the analysis, leave his job, and enroll in graduate school to prepare for a new career. Analysts are wary of a precipitous decision such as this. The concern is that perhaps the transference has become too intense and the patient is, in effect, fleeing the treatment in response to anxiety. Analysts are also concerned that a decision to leave is based on a "transference cure" in which the patient's positive feelings and desire to take action have grown out of positive feelings toward the analyst. Particularly in this case, the questions about the decision easily grow out of the nature of the patient's unrequited longing for a good father. He might have found this good father in the analyst and thus felt he had achieved what he had been looking for and was ready to move on in life. But if this were the case, he would be moving on without resolving deeper aspects of his unconscious wishes, such as the homoerotic aspects of his longing for a strong male figure in his life. And without this figure, he would remain angry, feeling that he could not sustain himself without this attachment.

The analyst did not pursue any of these lines of thought. He simply asked the patient how he had arrived at his decisions. The young man replied with some humor that the decisions had been easy for him. He had observed that when he read the literature in the field in which he had been working he would become sleepy and have difficulty concentrating. But when he read that in his prospective field, he felt alert, challenged, and stimulated. The analyst decided that the patient's decision should be respected. The patient and analyst agreed on a date for termination.

Several years after the conclusion of the treatment, the analyst received a request for a reference letter from the authorities responsible for certification in the field the patient had entered. He had concluded his training and awaited the credentials that would allow him to practice in his new profession. The patient had referred the authorities to him because in the qualifying procedure a psychologist evaluating the candidate had administered projective tests and believed he had uncovered fantasies that suggested problems that might interfere with the practice in this profession. The analyst responded with the opinion that these so-called negative fantasies would have no harmful effect on the young man's ability to work in his new profession. Several years after that, the former patient wrote to the analyst of his successful marriage and of advancement in his career.

In the presentation of this case as evidence of self-empowerment and enhanced ego capacities through the resolution of neurotic conflict, several questions deserve careful thought. Did the underlying strength of the positive transference mean that the individual finally achieved what he longed for and that the empowerment really came from the analyst and was not self-generated? Or did making conscious the repressed wishes liberate the individual so that he could make choices and pursue a life-plan reflecting self-empowerment? These and perhaps other questions cannot easily be answered. Controlled experiments cannot readily be conducted. But the critical issue in the problem of empowerment is the responsibility of the individual for the functioning of his or her ego. The scope of this responsibility includes the ownership of his or her own instinctual life and the control of his or her impulses. It also includes the honing of ego interests and talents and the ability to discard dependencies on groups. The autonomy of the ego is a universal issue relevant to both economically mature and third world nations. The insights of psychoanalysis are relevant to child rearing, education, and the building of institutions requiring strong individuals.

Martin Luther King, Jr., and Frantz Fanon were not notably psychologically minded nor likely ever to have entered analysis to explore respectively their sexuality and aggression. They were caught up in political movements with little time for self-reflection. King had an uncanny sense that he did not have long to live, and he seemed resigned to an early death. Even though there was a realistic basis for this preoccupation with death given the actual threats to his life as he led the nonviolent movement, one of the questions his life and death pose is whether unconsciously, he accepted death as a masochistic response to his own sense of sin.

Fanon paradoxically came face-to-face with a stealthy illness to which he passively succumbed. As a prophet of violence and terror, Fanon sought the expression of his aggression in writing. He participated not at all in acts of violence. His hatred was so dominant on the surface of his psyche that he had little capacity to reflect on the consequences for peaceful development of the individuals and societies in Africa and Martinique after they achieved independence. He believed in his theory that inferiority complexes result from oppression and left little room for the changes necessary in the individual and in society for the turn to progress and freedom. Even though he was trained as a psychiatrist, Fanon had no inclination for the nuances of self-reflection. He therefore became fixated on purgation of internalized inferiority feelings through violence. He expressed his aggression through writing and left violent acts to others. There is no evidence that beyond his writing he assumed leadership in overcoming the root causes and consequences of the negative images taken in by the projections of the colonizers.

Part 5

The Humanists

Joseph Conrad: Sharing the Secret of Command

Joseph Conrad lived command both in practice and in his imagined adventure stories. As a merchant seaman, Conrad qualified for a master's license in the British merchant marine and assumed his first command on the *Otago*, a vessel that plied the waters of the South Pacific. He was 31 years old at the time, and had served on merchant vessels for 14 years—starting as an apprentice seaman and gaining his master papers in 1886. He commanded the *Otago* for only one voyage and left the ship under mysterious circumstances. The owners were satisfied with his command of their vessel and expected to continue their contract with him.

He left the *Otago* ostensibly to work on his first novel, *Almayer's Folly,* but he was not done with the lure of adventure and command. In 1889 he captained a steamer and sailed up the Congo River (this adventure became the basis for *Heart of Darkness*). Imagination of adventure in Africa had been stimulated in him long before. He tells us in his autobiographical memoir that when he was nine, peering at a map, he put his finger on Africa and exclaimed, "When I grow up, I shall go there."[1] His fascination with Africa had been renewed as he read about Henry Morton Stanley and his African adventures in looking for another lost white man in 1888, replicating his search for Dr. Livingston in 1871. The publicity surrounding this successful search, according to Bernard C. Meyer in his psychoanalytic study of Conrad, renewed Conrad's childhood fantasy of adventure in the Congo, and it was this renewal that caused him to sign on for the tour of duty on the Congo steamer. Not long after this voyage, he gave up his career as a seaman and devoted himself to writing fiction stories based on his experiences, his fantasies, and his troubled psyche.

In Robert M. Armstrong's interpretive essay, command for Conrad was a renewal of deep psychological conflict.[2] The conflict centered on unconscious passive and active aims—to submit to his father, and to overpower him and take his place. Command represented the oedipal victory over his father, which Conrad could not tolerate, and reuniting with his mother, which also renewed conflict as a legacy of wishes stimulated and unresolved during the early years.

Another way of looking at Conrad's conflict in taking command is that it arose from his realization that life as a seafarer would not be true to his imaginative capacities. In *Typhoon*, his novel of the sea, Conrad wrote: "Captain MacWhirr had sailed over the surface of the oceans as some men go skimming over the years of existence to sink gently into a placid grave, ignorant of life to the last, without ever having been made to see all it may contain of perfidy, of violence, and of terror. There are on sea and land such men thus fortunate—or thus disdained by destiny or by the sea."[3]

Command stimulated Conrad's imagination, but left his true nature unresolved. On the one hand, he sought adventure to satisfy his wishes for an active life in command of men, standing above the ordinary pleasures of companionship among equals. Captaincy of a ship evoked images of the solitary, self-sufficient figure, the epitome of the drama of the loneliness of command. On the other hand, sailing the seas in command of a vessel was boring and the opposite of seeking expression of the inner voices of fantasy. At the core of Conrad's conflict in taking command was a clash between self-sufficiency, detachment, and isolation in the vision of command, and the force of fantasy and the need to give expression to the inner voices of the psyche. As expressed in his novel *Lord Jim*, "Imagination, the enemy of men, the father of all terrors, unstimulated, sinks to rest in the dullness of exhausted emotion."[4]

Conrad withdrew from the active life of the sea and command and found, with rare exception, the peace of mind and fulfillment that is supposed to accompany the practice of one's true vocation. As a writer, he seldom enjoyed freedom from psychological conflict; there were long periods of draught, when his imagination could not find the words to organize the fantasies into narratives. Also, he was ill for a good part of his adult life, suffering from gout, digestive problems, and depression. And his family life was troubled, his relationship with his wife and two sons were disturbed. Yet despite these travails, he continued to write, and savored those rare moments when his imagination and impulses came together to produce outstanding stories such as *The Secret Sharer, The Heart of Darkness,* and *Lord Jim*.

In *A Personal Record*, in 1912, he writes, "Only in men's imagination does every truth find an effective and undeniable existence. Imagination, not invention, is the supreme master of art as of life. An imaginative and exact rendering of authentic memories may serve worthily that spirit of piety towards all things human which sanctions the conceptions of a writer of tales, and the emotions of man reviewing his own experiences."[5]

Conrad set high standards for himself as a novelist. In his preface to *The Nigger of the Narcissus* he writes:

"A work that aspires, however humbly, to the condition of art should carry its justification in every line. And art itself may be defined as a single-minded attempt to
render the highest kind of justice to the visible universe, by bringing to light the
truth, manifold and one, underlying its every aspect. It is an attempt to find in its
forms, in its very colors, in its light, in its shadow, in the aspect of matter and in the
facts of life, what of each is fundamental, what is enduring and essential—their one

illuminating and convincing quality—the very truth of their existence. The artist, then, like the thinker or the scientist, seeks the truth and makes his appeal."[6]

The thinker, the scientist, and the artist seek the truth. Let us look at the example of Conrad to consider what drives those who aspire to command.

Joseph Conrad, who was of Polish descent, was born Jozef Teodor Konrad Nalecz Korzeniowski on December 3, 1857, in Berdichev in the Ukraine, then under Russian rule. His mother, Ewelina Nalecz Korzeniowski, was 13 years younger than her husband, Apollo, and the two had a long and troublesome courtship. The Bodrowskis had objected to Apollo for their daughter, believing he would be an unreliable husband. Shortly after her father died, Ewelina's mother consented to the marriage, and it took place when Ewelina was 23 and Apollo 36.

Apollo was a writer and a political activist opposed to Russian rule of Poland. He was financially insecure since his writing produced irregular income. His political views and Polish patriotism eventually got him into trouble with the Russian authorities, and he and his family were sent into exile in Northern Russia when Conrad was five. Life in exile was harsh, not only because of the severely cold winters, but also because Conrad was isolated, as he grew up, from children his age. His father educated him and exposed him to his writings and his translations into Polish of Shakespeare and other English authors. In his isolation, Conrad read. Particularly, he read adventure stories with themes of masculine assertion and dominance.

Ewelina was tubercular, and the cold winters of exile exacerbated her illness. Even with respite to visit her family, allowed because of her illness, her condition worsened and in 1865, when Conrad was eight, she died. Her death intensified the boy's attachment to his father who, in deep mourning, was often unavailable to him. The mourning continued, and every year, on the anniversary of Ewelina's death, Apollo would sit for a day staring at her photo, saying nothing, as though Conrad did not exist.

A year after his mother died, Conrad was sent to live with her beloved brother, Tadeusz Bobrowski, and they formed a close relationship. Three years later his father died (of tuberculosis; Apollo was given a hero's funeral in Cracow, with Conrad leading the funeral procession). Living with his uncle, who became more attached to him upon the death of his only child, Conrad continued with his schooling, but became obsessed with the desire to go to sea. This obsession shocked the uncle, and he did everything in his power to convince the 14-year-old that a life at sea was a poor choice, especially since, having lived all his life in a land-locked environment, he had had no realistic exposure to the sea and had no idea what it would be like to live the life of a sailor. Unable to dissuade him, the uncle enlisted Conrad's tutor to travel to with him in Switzerland, Germany, and Italy for Conrad's enrichment, but also to convince him to abandon the dream of a life at sea. The tutor tried to persuade him, but to no avail. Conrad left for Marseille in 1874 and entered the marine service at age 16 as an apprentice, the first step to advancement in the merchant navy.

During his service in Marseille, he undertook some daring and illicit smuggling of arms, fell into debt, and was also wounded by a gun shot—which some biographers interpret as a result of a duel, but others as a self-inflicted wound, a suicide attempt. The uncle went to Marseille to settle Conrad's debt and probably offered the duel as an explanation for his nephew's wound. (There was also some indication that Conrad had had an unhappy love affair during his stay in Marseille.) Leaving Marseille in 1878 for England, Conrad began the second phase of his maritime career—which culminated in achieving his master's license.

His career at sea progressed uneventfully. He secured papers as third mate and then first mate, sailing to Australia, Asia, India, Indonesia, and Bangkok over a ten-year period. His home port was London, and he became a naturalized British subject in 1886 just short of his thirtieth birthday. After he secured his master's papers, he vacillated in securing a command. He toyed with various options, some of which were unrelated to seafaring. He was restless, often at odds with his captains, and quarrelsome.

He did not secure a captaincy despite having attained the proper papers. He accepted a post as first mate on a ship sailing from Amsterdam to Java. Since the captain had not yet arrived, Conrad as first mate was responsible for the loading of cargo. Evidently, he made a mistake in the distribution of the cargo so that the ship, the *Highland Forest,* had a rough voyage. During a storm, a piece of the rigging fell on him and he was laid up under the care of the captain, who was at a loss to help him. At Singapore he entered a hospital for treatment, but the diagnosis was vague and the cure not forthcoming. Meyer, in his study, reports on the vagueness of the illness and says that Conrad "was presenting a foretaste of the flagrant hypochondriasis of his later years."[7] The fact that as first mate he had been responsible for loading the cargo and that he suffered the accident resulting in part from its having been loaded wrong, suggests to Meyer that Conrad doubted his ability as an officer—let alone as a captain.

Self-doubt notwithstanding, when Conrad took command of the *Otago* in 1888, he sailed from Bangkok to Australia with a call on Mauritius—a dangerous route, elected by him, that aroused concern on the part of his first mate as to Conrad's judgment. It was during the layover in Mauritius that Conrad met Eugenie Renouf, a 26-year-old woman, who engaged him in a flirtatious game of questions and answers, aimed at discovering his true nature.[8] Evidently, Conrad was attracted to Eugenie and called often at her family home in Port Louis. Impetuously, just before his ship was to leave Mauritius, he approached her brother to ask for her hand in marriage. The brother told him she was engaged and soon to be married. Conrad had displayed a marked naïveté in this impetuous courtship; he should have known she was unavailable.

He left Mauritius for Australia, the destination of the voyage. After this first voyage, the ship owners ordered the ship to another one calling on Mauritius, at which point Conrad resigned his command. It was then that he signed on to take a steam vessel up the Congo River. Once that voyage was finished, he returned to England, ill with dysentery. He did two more stints at sea and in 1894, became Joseph Conrad and settled in London to devote himself to writing novels. He wrote in English, not his first language, a remarkable feat for an author who relied on his experience enhanced by his imagination.

Conrad had begun writing his first novel, *Aylmer's Folly,* in 1889. The book was written in fits and starts aboard various vessels. In his autobiographical memoir, he recounts how he mustered the courage to ask a passenger on the *Torrens,* on which he was serving as first mate, if he would read the partially written manuscript. The passenger agreed. He returned the next day and handed over the manuscript without a word.

> He tendered (the manuscript) to me with a steady look but without a word. I took it in silence. He sat down on the couch and still said nothing. I opened and shut a drawer under my desk, on which a filled-up log-slate lay wide open in its wooden frame waiting to be copied neatly into the sort of book I was accustomed to write with care, the ship's log-book. I turned my back squarely on the desk. And even then Jacques never offered a word. "Well, what do you say?" I asked at last. "Is it worth finishing?" This question expressed exactly the whole of my thoughts. "Distinctly, " he answered in his sedate veiled voice, and then coughed a little. "Were you interested?" I inquired further almost in a whisper. "Very much." . . . "Now let me ask you one more thing: Is the story quite clear to you as it stands?" He raised his dark, gentle eyes to my face and seemed quite surprised. "Yes! Perfectly."[9]

This anxious conversation occurred in 1893. Conrad retired to London in 1894. He published *Almayer's Folly* in 1895, and thus, formally began his career as a writer.

The literary scholar Albert J. Guerard summarized Conrad's work as a novelist as follows:[10]

> Joseph Conrad was one of the most subjective and most personal of English novelists. And his best work makes its calculated appeal to the living sensibilities and commitments of readers; it is a deliberate invasion of our lives, and deliberately manipulates our responses.[11] This "invasion of our lives" was a risky venture for the novelist. For both the author and the reader, the work required an optimal involvement with, yet distance from, the work of fiction. Conrad's work evoked both for the author and the audience deep psychological conflicts. Issues of self-esteem, aggressive wishes reverberating from fantasies of passive surrender, can easily renew conflict of a universal nature. If these conflicts become reactivated in their primitive form both for the writer and the audience, the mechanisms of defense come into play. For the audience, one defense against the anxiety provoked is to withdraw, to become bored or sleepy as ways of distancing one's self from the conflict. For the author, the response of writer's block may stop progress on the book and may even prevent completing the work. As Norman Holland points out in his empirical studies of literary response, it is incumbent upon the author to provide in the work the optimal distance for the reader. The author provides auxiliary defenses while drawing the reader into the closeness necessary to appreciate the literary work.[12]

Conrad was not always successful in the creation of auxiliary defenses. He often experienced horrible blocks in his writing. He wrote to Marguerite Poradowska, who helped him secure his ship for the Congo adventure, "I am very discouraged. The ideas don't come. I don't see either the characters or the incidents. . . . I am in a constant state of irritation which does not allow me to lose myself in my story.

Consequently, my labors are worthless."[13] Robert Armstrong, noting the problems Conrad experienced in establishing the necessary distance from his own unconscious conflicts with his father, outlines the defenses he employed to allow himself to proceed with his writing:

> His need to establish distance between himself and his material is well known; he insisted that he could write creatively only in his third language; he had great difficulty in writing from the vantage point of the omniscient author, i.e. in his own person, and in most of his best fiction he works through a narrator; notoriously awkward in dealing with immediate action, he most often described events that had taken place in the past, even when his manipulations of time did not demand it; and finally, that impressionistic method itself through which he manipulated chronology and point of view allowed him to approach his material as indirectly as he felt necessary.[14]

In his memoir, Conrad writes, "I know that a novelist lives in his work. He stands there, the only reality in an invented world, among imaginary things, happenings, and people. Writing about them, he is only writing about himself. But the disclosure is not complete. He remains to a certain extent, a figure behind the veil; a suspected rather than a seen presence—a movement and a voice behind the draperies of fiction."[15] As Armstrong has noted, Conrad used a narrator as a veil, or a defense against the anxieties evoked in his stories—equally valuable for himself and his readers.

Critics largely agree on which of Conrad's works are his best: *Lord Jim* (1900), *Heart of Darkness* (1902), and *The Secret Sharer* (1912). These three stories invoke the idea of command and the psychological conflict of those seeking command. Each story presents the psychological challenges of mastering one's unconscious impulses as a condition for command and leadership.

In *Lord Jim,* the *Patna,* a ship taking 800 Muslims to a pilgrimage, strikes a submerged object and is badly damaged. The ship begins to take on water, and there are not enough lifeboats for the passengers and the crew. The captain and two officers secure a lifeboat and are about to cast off, leaving the pilgrims, who were asleep, to drown. Jim, the first mate, has remained on board and the officers call out to him to jump. As though responding to some will outside himself, without conscious intent, he jumps, and the boat casts away from the ship. Because the ship has turned away as a result of currents, the men in the lifeboat lose sight of it and believe it has sunk.

A French man-of-war comes upon the *Patna,* a vessel without officers and loaded with pilgrims, adrift on the sea, and takes her in tow into port. There, the story of the officers' abandonment comes out, and the captain and his officers, already having arrived in port, become the subject of an official inquiry assembled to try them for dereliction of duty. The captain takes flight, leaving the three officers, including Jim, to stand trial. The presiding officials, a magistrate and two maritime assessors, find the remaining defendants guilty and take away their maritime papers. Jim, the son of a parson, is in disgrace and forced to find livelihood as best as he can ashore.

Among the many ambiguities in this story, the fate of Captain Brierly, one of the assessors during the trial, stands out. Brierly finds Jim a disturbing presence, unknowable at any conscious level. Marlow, the narrator of the tale, says of Brierly:

> He seemed consumedly bored by the honour [of being named an assessor] thrust upon him. He had never in his life made a mistake, never had an accident, never a mishap, never a check in his steady rise, and he seemed to be one of those lucky fellows who know nothing of indecision, much less of self-mistrust. . . . The sting of life could do no more to his complacent soul than the scratch of a pin to the smooth face of a rock. This was enviable. As I looked at him flanking on one side the unassuming pale-faced magistrate who presided at the inquiry, his self-satisfaction presented to me and to the world a surface as hard as granite. He committed suicide very soon after."[16]

Observing Jim at the trial set in motion in Brierly, from deep within the unconscious, the loss of self-esteem. This collapse of an ego and the subsequent act of self-destruction is as inexplicable as Jim's act of jumping into the lifeboat.

Marlow keeps track of Jim's fate and helps arrange employment for him on the island of Patusan. Jim becomes godlike to the natives as he protects them by leading a battle to destroy their enemies. He is worshiped by them, and this restores his lost self-esteem. He takes a wife who, in her adoration of him, seems to complete the healing of his ego.

When Gentleman Brown and his marauders invade the island, Jim does not understand the threat Brown poses. In a battle Brown kills the native chief's son. Jim appears before the chief, looking straight at him as the chief, supported on his left side by one of his young men, lifts his right arm revealing the gun in his hand, aims at Jim, and shoots him. "They say that the white man sent right and left at all those faces a proud and unflinching glance. Then with his hand over his lips he fell forward dead."[17] The image of his hand over his lips symbolizes that Jim will not reveal the secrets of life and of command. We are left to our own imagination and mental devices to unravel this mystery. Why does Jim jump, and why does he hide from himself Gentleman Brown's true evil nature?

One interpretation is that Jim has never been tested, he has never been forced to endure and master the unconscious impulses that lead the ego to autonomy, or the freedom to make choices and to accept responsibility for these choices and their consequences. Early in the novel, we learn that Jim is:

> gentlemanly, steady, tractable, with a thorough knowledge of his duties; and in time, when yet very young, he became chief mate of a fine ship, without ever having been tested by those events of the sea that show in the light of day the inner worth of a man, the edge of his temper, and the fiber of his stuff; that reveal the quality of his resistance and the secret truth of his pretences, not only to others but also to himself.[18]

To this reader, "the secret truth of [Jim's] pretences" is a deeply held belief in the racial superiority of the whites. The pilgrims aboard the *Patna* are inferior, and thus, it is possible for Jim to be indifferent to their fate. The impulse to jump and save himself takes control as though by command from a voice outside himself. He does not know that it comes from his belief in his racial superiority as the son of a white minister. He is blind to Gentleman Brown's uncontrolled aggression because Brown, like him, is white and believes himself superior to the natives.

Unlike Brown, Jim can feel the effects, on his self-esteem, of ethical lapses and misjudgments. He welcomes the hearing and the magistrate's ruling that terminates his seaman's papers. He lives with the shame as just punishment for his impulsive act, just as he later accepts death for his blindness. While one might not be blamed for unconscious prejudices, in accepting command and responsibility for the fate of others, the imperative is to master these beliefs and prevent them from governing one's behavior.

In writing *Lord Jim,* Conrad leaves unexplained Jim's impulsive acts, first to jump, and second to act blind to Gentleman Brown's evil nature. It is left to the reader's imagination to provide explanations. Perhaps only in the twenty-first century would one conclude that at the core of Jim's unconscious mind there resided a racial prejudice that would impel him to save himself and suffer the pangs of lost self-esteem from failure in his duty. Shame and not guilt would undermine self-esteem in the failure to measure up to the standards of the ego of a man bound to the code of command. But guilt plays a part in the final episode of this novel of duty and command. In ignoring the threat of Gentleman Brown, Jim fails the test of conscience to protect his followers. Feeling his guilt, he willingly seeks the punishment of death, with his lips sealed as to the true causes of his failure in command.

In *Heart of Darkness* the narrator says, just as Conrad had said when he was nine, that as a youngster he would peer at maps and place his finger on a country that excited his imagination and exclaim, "When I grow up, I will go there." *Heart of Darkness,* which grew out of Conrad's journey up the Congo on a Belgian steamboat, tells the story of Marlow's search for and encounter with Kurtz, an agent engaged in the ivory trade for a Belgian company. Kurtz is a mysterious figure, who by reputation was on the ascendancy in the hierarchy of the company. The tension in the story heightens as Marlow approaches the station finally to meet Kurtz—the boat runs aground and needs repair; there is a long wait for rivets to repair it; once it is underway again and approaches Kurtz's station, the natives attack with bow and arrow, wounding the helmsman, who dies. Along with Marlow, the reader intensely awaits the encounter with Kurtz, and, along with Marlow, is horrified to find, surrounding Kurtz's home, poles mounted with human heads. "And there it was, black, dried, sunken, with closed eyelids, a head that seemed to sleep at the top of that pole, and, with the shrunken dry lips showing a narrow white line of the teeth, was smiling, too, smiling continuously at some endless and jocose dread of that eternal slumber."[19] Marlow realizes that Kurtz is a madman, mad with the power he wields over the natives and obsessed with collecting ivory—some for his own account. He is dying when Marlow meets him. Marlow is entranced with him despite the madness and the hints of cannibalism.

Kurtz entrusts to Marlow a manuscript he wrote for the International Society for the Suppression of Savage Customs. Marlow says of the report:

> It was eloquent, vibrating with eloquence, but too high strung, I think. Seventeen pages of close writing he had found time for! But this must have been before

his—let us say—nerves, went wrong, and caused him to preside at certain midnight dances ending with unspeakable rites, which—as far as I reluctantly gathered from what I heard at various times—were offered up to him—do you understand?—to Mr. Kurtz himself. But it was a beautiful piece of writing. The opening paragraph, however, in the light of later information, strikes me now as ominous. He began with the argument that we whites, from the point of development we had arrived at, "must necessarily appear to them [savages] in the nature of supernatural beings— we—approach them with the might as of a deity," and so on, and so on. "By the simple exercise of our will we can exert a power for good practically unbounded," etc., etc. From that point he soared and took me with him. The peroration was magnificent, though difficult to remember, you know. It gave me the notion of an exotic Immensity ruled by an august Benevolence. It made me tingle with enthusiasm. This was the unbounded power of eloquence—of words—of burning noble words. There were no practical hints to interrupt the magic current of phrases, unless a kind of note at the foot of the last page, scrawled evidently much later, in an unsteady hand, may be regarded as the exposition of a method. It was very simple, at the end of that moving appeal to every altruistic sentiment it blazed at you, luminous and terrifying, like a flash of lightning, in a serene sky: "Exterminate all the brutes!"[20]

Aboard the steamer heading home, in the throes of death, Kurtz cries out, "The horror! The horror!" When Marlow returns to England and meets with Kurtz's betrothed, he cannot bear to tell her the truth about Kurtz and his madness. She is devoted to Kurtz's memory and presses Marlow for his last words: "To live with, don't you understand I loved him—I loved him—I loved him!" Marlow replies, "The last word he pronounced was—your name."[21] It seems clear from Marlow's response to the betrothed that he is deeply attracted to Kurtz and his representation of megalomania. The horror is thoroughly mixed with the uncanny attraction to the madness associated with unlimited power. Marlow becomes our agent for experiencing the attraction and the dread, but sufficiently at a distance to allow us to remain immersed in this tale of power and command.

For Conrad, the heart of darkness resides nowhere but in the deepest levels of the individual's unconscious, a region familiar to him, and the wellspring of his creativity. Command is an encounter with risk. At the far end, command and its encounter with personal power can drive a person over the edge of sanity as megalomania takes control. The exotic scenes of Africa and the Congo may help make remote the dangers from within of the unbridled lust for power. Conrad himself, due to the loss at an early age of his mother and then his father, developed the need to escape the aftermath of tragedies. He left Poland to wander on the high seas, but he could not escape his own imagination and the need to master the aftermath of these childhood traumas. Command is one dominant theme in his writing in which his imagination sets the scenes for the striving for mastery and control.

In *The Secret Sharer*, a newly appointed captain faces the conflict of command as a dreamlike state of consciousness in which a man is tested before he can assume mastery of a ship and his own psyche.

She floated at the starting point of a long journey, very still in an immense stillness, the shadows of her spars flung far to the eastward by the setting sun. At that moment

I was alone on her decks. There was not a sound in her—and around us nothing moved, nothing lived, not a canoe on the water, not a bird in the air, not a cloud in the sky. In this breathless pause at the threshold of a long passage we seemed to be measuring our fitness for a long and arduous enterprise, the appointed task of both of our existences to be carried out, far from all human eyes, with only sky and sea for spectators and judges.[22]

The captain is unfamiliar with his ship and guarded in his relations with subordinates, who have been together for 18 months while he is a stranger to them and to the ship. "But what I felt most was my being stranger to the ship; and if all the truth must be told, I was somewhat of a stranger to myself." (p. 650)

Because Conrad has not used the familiar Marlow as narrator of this story, the reader directly confronts the challenge of command and the precursor to that challenge of knowing himself or herself. In the captain's first-person narration, the story takes on the immediacy and suspense of the question of whether or not the captain will achieve command.

One night the captain dismisses all hands and orders the men to go below deck, taking the late-night watch himself. He notices that a rope ladder set earlier for the tug captain to board has not been hauled in, and that a swimmer, almost an apparition, clutches the ladder. Once the captain has identified himself and assured the man that no one else is on the deck, the swimmer clambers on board. He identifies himself as Leggatt, first mate on the *Sephora,* which is anchored at some distance. He has killed a crewman during a storm when the ship was in peril. In a moment of uncontrollable rage, he throttled the man who refused to do his duty and prevented others from doing theirs. The captain of the *Sephora* panicked and failed to give the order to replace the damaged mainsail with a foresail. Leggatt gave the order and saved the ship.

When the captain of the *Sephora* comes on board looking for word of his first mate, who has escaped from his cabin where he was being held under arrest, the narrator captain keeps the secret.

Leggatt becomes a double for the new master. The two are as one, with Leggatt dressed in the captain's spare sleeping suit, hidden away in the captain's cabin. The captain hears a report that the wind has come up, which means the ship can get underway. This is a chance for Leggatt to leave the ship and swim to an island in the area. To increase Leggatt's chances of saving himself, the captain orders the ship to close in on the island, risking running aground and losing the ship. The crewmen are alarmed as the captain orders the course toward the island. Leggatt slips over the side as the ship approaches the island, wearing a hat the captain gave him to protect himself against the sun. The captain notices the hat floating on the water and orders the ship to turn in time to avoid disaster. Did Leggatt lose the hat, or did he set it in the water so the captain could judge the current? Just as the captain saved his double, Leggatt saves the ship and the captain's command.

As the ship sails safely away from the island and starts to draw ahead, "I was alone with her. Nothing, no one in the world should stand now between us, throwing a shadow on the way of silent knowledge and mute affection, the perfect communion of a seaman with his first command."[23]

The Secret Sharer is just one step away from a dream, at a level of awareness where the reader is emerging from a dream, conscious of fragments, but left to interpret an imperfect narrative. But the moral is clear. To command one must first be tested and found fit for the responsibility. The test is in part to measure one's technical competence—in this case, seamanship. It is also to assess one's self-confidence and to demonstrate that degree of certainty in issuing directives that other people are willing to follow, often automatically, without question or doubt. The test also measures the capacity for controlling one's own impulses, and here we are clearly in the realm of the unconscious.

Conrad's life and work as a novelist clearly place his preoccupations, if not his obsessions, with the underside of man's mental life. Bernard Meyer, in his perceptive psychoanalytic biography of Conrad, quotes Conrad's response to a man who tried to interest him in Freud's work: "I have no wish to probe the depths. I like to regard reality as a rough and rugged thing over which I can run my fingers—nothing more."[24] To voyage to the depths of the unconscious without the protections of his storytelling would have been intolerable for Conrad. He suffered enough as it is in the periodic breakthroughs of the darker impulses reflecting back on the loss of his mother—who in the unconscious had abandoned him—and in the unresolved rivalry with his father—who also died before Conrad reached manhood. While his uncle offered himself as a substitute for the missing father, Conrad could tolerate this caring from a man only at a distance. He seldom saw his uncle after he left Poland to become a seaman.

While living in Rye, England, Conrad developed a close relationship with the writer Ford Maddox Ford, who was 16 years his junior. The two met in 1898 and became literary collaborators. They remained close for the decade during which Conrad published most of his acclaimed work. When Ford fell in love with Violet Hunt and left his wife for her, Conrad felt betrayed, and the friendship between the two men was broken.

The relationship between Conrad and Ford had many levels of meaning psychologically for both individuals. Both were disturbed by the birth of their firstborns, suggesting jealousy stemming from the need for wife as mother. And although psychoanalytic writers do not explicitly infer an overt homosexual relationship, the closeness of the two men contained most of the elements of homoerotic attraction. Conrad probably saw in Ford reflections of himself, caught in the bind of unfulfilled needs for mother and father figures, as Ford, too, had missed the love and approval of his parents. The stories they produced in collaboration are clearly the work of misogynists. Unlike Ford, Conrad remained married, but his relationship with Jessie Conrad was for the most part unsatisfactory for both husband and wife. Ford fulfilled many needs in Conrad, and Conrad demanded loyalty, not to be displaced by another relationship. (When Conrad's firstborn son, Borys, married without Conrad knowing it, he reacted with the same sense of betrayal that he had experienced with Ford.)

The experience with personal power is obviously different for a novelist from that of a person in a formal position of authority. In the case of the novelist, the locus of the experience is in the realm of the imagination. Conrad as a novelist drew liberally for his stories on his years as a seafarer and briefly in command of a vessel, but these years found him oscillating between images of adventure and utter boredom. Since the conflict residing in his unconscious mental life could not easily be resolved, it was left for his imagination to provide, if only temporarily and sporadically, the materials he put to use as a great novelist. Had he remained a seafarer and captain, he probably would have ended his active years as a mediocre commander. The world was spared this mediocrity and gained instead an insightful and gifted novelist, who brought pleasure and self-understanding to a reading public.

Herman Melville's *Billy Budd:* A Study of Character

The evil that is in the world always comes of ignorance, and good intentions may do as much harm as malevolence, if they lack understanding. On the whole, men are more good than bad; that, however, isn't the real point. But they are more or less ignorant, and it is this that we call vice or virtue; the most incorrigible vice being that of an ignorance that fancies it knows everything and therefore claims for itself the right to kill. The soul of the murderer is blind; and there can be no true goodness nor true love without the utmost clear-sightedness.[1]

Herman Melville was born in 1819 and died in 1891. His *Moby Dick* (1851) sold poorly and garnered him little recognition during his lifetime. He stopped writing in 1866 when he took a job as a customs inspector in New York, When he died in 1891, he left an uncompleted manuscript entitled *Billy Budd: (An Inside Narrative).* His widow saved the story, along with other writings, mostly verse, and his granddaughter inherited the unpublished works. The publication of *Billy Budd* in 1924 created a Melville revival, and this last story was acclaimed a masterpiece, as was the earlier *Moby Dick.*

Melville's granddaughter, Mrs. Eleanor Melville Metcalf, permitted F. Barron Freeman to study the manuscripts for his book on *Billy Budd.* She subsequently gave the manuscripts Melville left behind to the Houghton Library of Harvard University, and two books appeared attempting to reconstruct Melville's work on *Billy Budd: Foretopman.*[2]

In the preface to his book, Freeman quotes a sentence that is underlined in Melville's copy of a Hawthorne short story: "It shall be yours to penetrate, in every bosom, the deep mystery of sin." At the end of his first chapter summarizing Melville's life and character, Freeman quotes from Melville, "Here ends a story not unwarranted by what sometimes happens in this incomprehensible world of ours. . . . Innocence and infamy, spiritual depravity and fair repute."[3]

Since its publication in 1924, *Billy Budd* has become an object of intense interest among literary critics. The story itself is spare, but the interpolations Melville used cause readers and critics to search for clues to his intent in the way he tells it and for ways to disentangle the underlying character of the three central figures in the narrative. For some, the story is an allegory of man's fall from innocence, a tale of good and evil that pits natural man against the repressive forces of civilization. For others, it depends on some real events. The mutinies of Spithead and the Nore in the British navy in 1797 provided the backdrop for the allegations of conspiring to mutiny aboard the *HMS Indomitable*. The fact that Melville describes the two mutinies in his introduction to the story suggests that these events propelled the action in *Billy Budd*. Closer to home and Melville's experience, a mutiny occurred aboard the U.S. naval training ship, the *Somers*, in 1842, following which, Midshipman Spence, the son of the secretary of war, and two seamen were hanged. The hangings caused an outbreak of criticism of the navy and the captain of the *Somers*, especially because there was no court proceeding leading to them; they occurred on the initiative of Captain Mackenzie, with the advice of several officers, but without any semblance of due process. Melville's cousin, Lieutenant Guert Gansevoort, was one of the officers Mackenzie consulted and may have played a principal part in the investigation leading to the hangings. While the *Somers* mutiny and Gansevoort's involvement may well have stimulated Melville's imagination, he clearly placed the story of Billy Budd in the British navy and in the late eighteenth century with reference to Spithead and the Nore, the French Revolution, and the war against France.

"Such a cynosure, at least in aspect, and something such too in nature . . . was welkin-eyed Billy Budd, or Baby Budd . . . he at last came to be called, aged twenty-one, a foretopman of the British fleet toward the close of the last decade of the eighteenth century."[4] (p. 9)

A party from the outward bound HMS *Indomitable*, a warship under the command of Captain Edward Fairfax Vere, boards the *Rights of Man*, a merchant vessel, to impress one or more members of its crew for service. The lieutenant in charge of the boarding party immediately spots Billy and impresses him. The captain of the *Rights* protests:

> Lieutenant, you are going to take my best man from me, the jewel of 'em. . . . Before I shipped that young fellow, my forecastle was a rat-pit of quarrels. It was black times, I tell you aboard the *Rights* here. I was worried to that degree my pipe had no comfort for me. But Billy came and it was like a Catholic priest striking peace in an Irish shindy. Not that he preached to them or said or did anything in particular, but a virtue went out of him, sugaring the sour ones. They took to him like hornets to treacle." (p. 11)

As the boat carrying Billy away passes the stern, and he waves farewell to the crew, he rises and exclaims, "And good-bye to you too, old *Rights of Man*." (p. 13). Melville selected for the name of the ship from which Billy is impressed the title of one of Tom Paine's essays. The irony of the ship's name and the act of impressing a merchant sailor does not come to Billy's awareness. He is portrayed as an innocent, incapable of satire in consciousness as in intent.

The ambiguity surrounding Billy deepens when the officer conducting the mustering asks him where he was born and receives the reply that he does not know and knows nothing of his father. He says, "But I have heard that I was found in a pretty silk-lined basket hanging one morning from the knocker of a good man's door in Bristol." (p. 16). The mystery surrounding Billy's birth and parentage is reminiscent of the mystery of the origins of heroic figures, such as Moses—found floating in a basket and rescued by a princess of noble birth; or Oedipus—found on a mountaintop where he was abandoned so he would not grow up to fulfill the oracle.[5]

The mystery surrounding Billy's beauty, which Melville describes as feminine, progresses in the description of the one mar in his makeup: the appearance of a blemish.

> [L]ike the beautiful woman in one of Hawthorne's minor tales, there was just one thing amiss in him. No visible blemish indeed, as with the lady; no, but an occasional liability to a vocal defect. Though in the hour of elemental uproar or peril he was everything that a sailor should be, yet under sudden provocation of strong heart-feeling his voice, otherwise singularly musical, as if expressive of the harmony within, was apt to develop an organic hesitancy, in fact more or less of a stutter or even worse. In this particular, Billy was a striking instance that the arch interferer, the envious marplot of Eden, still has more or less to do with every human consignment to this planet of earth. In every case, one way or another he is sure to slip in his little card, as much to remind us—I too have a hand in here." (pp. 17–18)

In introducing the other two characters in this tale, Captain Vere and John Claggert, the master-at-arms, Melville portrays them as sharply complex in contrast to the directness, innocence, and happy nature of Billy. He describes Captain Vere as a bookish man who never fails to bring into his cabin the store of books he will need for a voyage. The books favor history, biography, and other works that sustain his view of life and mankind, books that "in the spirit of common sense philosophize upon realities." (p. 25) Vere seeks and finds confirmation of his views of life in the books he reads.

> His settled convictions were as a dike against those invading waters of novel opinion, social, political, and otherwise, which carried away as in a torrent no few minds in those days, minds by nature not inferior to his own. While other members of the aristocracy to which by birth he belonged were incensed at the innovators mainly because their theories were inimical to the privileged classes, not alone Captain Vere disinterestedly opposed them because they seemed to him incapable of embodiment in lasting institutions, but at war with the peace of the world and the true welfare of mankind." (pp. 25–26)

Melville describes Vere as a detached and isolated individual. "Captain Vere, though practical enough upon occasion, would at times betray a certain dreaminess of mood. Standing alone on the weather side of the quarter-deck, one hand holding by the rigging, he would absently gaze off at the blank sea. At the presentation to him then of some minor matter, interrupting the current of his thoughts he would show more or less irascibility, but instantly he would control it." (p. 24) With officers equal in rank, Captain Vere is not a welcome companion. They find him "a dry and bookish gentleman." When out of earshot, his companions comment, "between you and me now, don't you think there is a queer streak of the pedantic running through him? Yes, like the King's yarn in a coil of navy rope?" (p. 26)

Melville introduces the third character in the story with the warning: "His portrait I essay but shall never hit it." (p. 27) John Claggert is the master-at-arms aboard the *Indomitable*. This title is a carryover from the days when naval vessels fought with small arms, and the master-at-arms trained sailors in the use of arms and in boarding attacks. With the advent of cannons, fighting was removed to a distance and arms became obsolete for sailors. The duty of the master-at-arms changed, then, to chief of police—to maintain discipline and report infractions. As one would readily imagine, the role was unpopular, especially since the master-at-arms used assistants who were seen as spies and reviled accordingly.

Mystery hangs over the head of Claggert. Nothing is known of his former life. He appears to be of aristocratic birth and upbringing not in keeping with the life of a seaman. His pallor, unlike the crew's ruddiness from exposure to the sun, "seemed to hint of something defective or abnormal in the constitution or the blood. But his general aspect and manner were so suggestive of an education and career incongruous with his naval function that when not actively engaged in it he looked like a man of high quality, social and moral, who for reasons of his own was keeping incog." (p. 27) Vague rumors circulate about Claggert's former life. He entered the navy as a mature man and at a low rank. Even the rank of master-at-arms implies some recognition of his superior upbringing and education. The rank he holds contrasts sharply with the rumors that he is of aristocratic birth and was charged with some swindle and brought before the King's Bench. Nothing can be verified about Claggert's alleged swindle, but the contrast between his persona, assumed education, aristocratic bearing, and a low-ranking position assumed when he entered the navy as a mature man heightens the mystery about him.

One day Billy along with the ship's crew observes the lashing of a sailor for some infraction of duty. Billy, horrified by this brutal punishment, resolves never to become the victim of a lashing. But he finds himself reported for minor infractions, such as improper stowing of his hammock. The crewmen jokingly urge him to sew himself into his hammock to find out why the corporals are reporting him. He decides to turn to an old sailor, called the Dansker, for advice. The Dansker warns Billy, "Baby Budd," (the affectionate term the Dansker uses for Billy and that has become the popular term, also used affectionately, when the crew speak of Billy) "Jimmy Legs (meaning the master-at-arms) is down on you." When Billy protests that the master-at-arms seems always to have a pleasant word for him, the Dansker says, "And that's because he's down upon you." (p. 33)

An incident occurs shortly after this interchange. The ship rolls while Billy is eating soup, and the soup spills just as Claggert is coming by. Claggert taps Billy lightly from behind with his rattan and says, "Handsomely done, my lad! And handsome is as handsome did it too." (p. 34) Billy takes this remark as a friendly comment, failing to notice the "involuntary smile, or rather grimace, that accompanied Claggert's equivocal words." (p. 34). The encounter leads Billy to protest that Jimmy Legs is friendly and not down on him.

Claggert approaches Captain Vere in private and accuses Billy of fomenting a mutiny. In disbelief, Vere calls for Billy to come to his stateroom and to hear Claggert repeat his accusation. Billy appears, and at Captain Vere's command orders Claggert to repeat his charge. When Claggert is finished repeating the accusation, Billy is dumbfounded and cannot speak in his own defense. He cannot get the words out of his mouth, stammers, and, even at the Captain's urging to speak out in his own defense, remains tongue-tied and cannot speak, as hard as he tries. Instead, he thrusts out with his arm and strikes Claggert on the forehead. Claggert drops to the floor, dead. Once the ship's surgeon has verified the death, Vere declares, "Struck dead by an angel of God! Yet, the angel must hang!" (p. 60)

Vere calls a drumhead court consisting of a lieutenant, the sailing master, and the captain of the marines. The surgeon thinks the captain deranged or reacting emotionally to the event. He believes, given the circumstances, that the captain should have ordered Billy held and transferred to a court martial once the ship landed. Members of the drumhead court agree with the surgeon, although he does not disclose the fact that he thinks the captain is deranged. But the court convenes, with Captain Vere present throughout. Billy's only defense is that he could not find the words to speak on his own behalf. To the question of whether there was malice between Claggert and himself, Billy replies, "No, there was no malice between us. I never bore malice against the master-at-arms. I am sorry that he is dead. I did not mean to kill him. Could I have used my tongue I would not have struck him. But he foully lied to my face and in the presence of my captain, and I had to say something, and I could only say it with a blow, God help me!" (p. 64)

Captain Vere, although testifying as the witness to the event, also maintains control of the proceedings and manipulates the thoughts of the drumhead court. He occupies the windward position, standing, while the officers sit on the leeward side below the captain. He does not excuse himself to allow the officers to deliberate. Instead, he lectures them on their duty to avoid feminine feelings and look only at the act and its consequence in the death of Claggert, not at intent. In response to the marine captain's comment that no one can shed light on the mystery behind what occurred, Captain Vere says, "Aye, there is a mystery; but to use a Scriptural phrase, it is 'a mystery of iniquity,' a matter for psychologic theologians to discuss. But what has a military court to do with it? Not to add that for us any possible investigation of it is cut off by the lasting tongue-tie—of him—in yonder . . . the prisoner's deed—with that alone we have to do." (p. 66) Vere will steadfastly play on the theme that the officers' duty is to judge the deed and to exact the only proper penalty: to hang Billy. Speaking no longer as a witness, but now as a coadjutor, Captain Vere says he detects in the officers a:

> troubled hesitancy, proceeding, I doubt not, from the clash of military duty with moral scruple—scruple visualized by compassion. . . . But your scruples: do they move as in a dusk? Challenge them. Make them advance and declare themselves. . . . If mindless of palliating circumstances, we are bound to regard the death of the master-at-arms as the prisoner's deed, then does that deed constitute a capitol crime whereof the penalty is a mortal one? But in natural justice is nothing but the prisoner's overt act to be considered? How can we adjudge to summary and shameful death a fellow creature innocent before God, and whom we feel to be so? . . . It is nature. But do these buttons that we wear attest that our allegiance is to Nature? No, to the King. . . . For suppose condemnation to follow these present proceedings.

Would it be so much we ourselves that would condemn as it would be martial law operating through us? For that law and the rigor of it, we are not responsible. Our vowed responsibility is in this: That however pitilessly that law may operate, we nevertheless adhere to it and administer it.

Sensing continuing doubt in the minds of the officers, Vere warns them not to let their hearts betray their heads. "Well the heart here denotes the feminine in man, is as that piteous woman and, hard though it may be, she must here be ruled out." (pp. 68–69) Billy is condemned to die by hanging at the yardarm.

In some of the most masterful and controlled writing in the novella, Melville describes the events leading up to the hanging. He portrays Billy's acceptance of death, without fear, and contrasts it with the chaplain's failed attempts to elicit a plea from Billy for God's mercy in the afterlife. But the chaplain accepts Billy's innocence in the ready acceptance of death, acknowledging that:

> innocence was even a better thing than religion wherewith to go to judgment ... but in his emotion not without first performing an act strange enough in an Englishman, and under the circumstances yet more so in any regular priest. Stooping over, he kissed on the fair cheek his fellow man, a felon in martial law who, though on the confines of death, he felt he could never convert to a dogma; nor for all that did he fear for his future. (p. 787)

Just before Billy is raised up the yardarm he exclaims, "God bless Captain Vere," to which the crew, stationed to witness the hanging, respond, "Without volition as it were, as if indeed the ship's populace were but the vehicles of some local current electric, with one voice from alow and aloft came a resonant sympathetic echo—'God bless Captain Vere!' And yet at that instant Billy alone must have been in their hearts, even as in their eyes." (p. 80) Billy's limp body hangs from the yardarm without spasm or motion except from the gentle roll of the ship, causing the ship's purser to question the surgeon. The surgeon cannot explain this phenomenon, and as the purser pursues the question, even offering the hypothesis of euthanasia, the surgeon rejects this metaphysical hypothesis as unscientific, and excuses himself to attend to a patient.

After the traditional burial at sea, still before daybreak, Captain Vere calls for the morning muster to divert the attention of the stunned crew from mournful reaction to the hanging of Billy Budd, commenting, "With mankind, forms, measured forms, are everything; and that is the import couched in the story of Orpheus with his lyre spellbinding the wild denizens of the wood." (p. 84)

In critical essays of *Billy Budd*, debate over two antithetical readings of the story and Melville's intent dominate. One reading is that the story is a testament of acceptance, the other that it is a testament of resistance.[6] Neither interpretation deals directly with a practical reading of *Billy Budd* as a tale inherently based on the idea of homosexuality as a fact of life aboard the sailing ships of the time. Melville cannot be accused of being a Freudian. He wrote well before Freud, and we can only postulate that he was an astute reader of the human psyche, experienced in the aura of the seafarer, given his own experience on whaling ships and naval vessels. It cannot be denied that he expanded his themes into the conflicts between "natural man" and "civilized man." Mankind pays a price for acculturation, a concept Freud later expanded in his essay, "Civilization and Its Discontents." For Freud, the price man paid was in repression and neuroses. For Melville, it was injustice in the name of rationality and the fear of disorder.

While literary experts, starting with Freeman, give due regard for sexual conflict in the characterization of Claggert and Billy Budd, they fail to develop a full explanation of the dynamics underling the depravity of the one and the unnatural innocence of the other. There is also a void in Captain Vere's character—as an aspect of repression, isolation of thought and feeling, and the defenses against anxiety in excessive attachment to form over reality—accounting for human behavior under conditions of command in the superior-subordinate relationship.

One of the problems critics encounter is the reluctance, or resistance to search for sexual themes in the work by referring to the author's own psychological development and conflict; this search is doomed to fail in explaining *Billy Budd*. There is little evidence to enable one, no matter how objective or expert, to explain the story in the context of the author's personal history. Here, speculation is a dead end. Furthermore, it detracts from the search for meaning in the tale. By focusing exclusively on the story much can be gleaned from the characterizations and the actions concerning the motivation and conflicts of the three leading figures. They are true to life and become even more true in the search for coherence in their psychological makeup.

Paranoia is a delusional state in which the subject believes he or she is the object of malevolent intentions on the part of mystical forces or concrete enemies. Thus, Freud, writing his case study of paranoia through the memoir of Daniel Paul Schreber published in 1903, noted that Schreber, a well-educated and accomplished jurist, believed he was put on earth to redeem the world and to save mankind. This mission came from God, and required that he gradually be transformed from a man into a woman. God would impregnate him, and he would give birth to a new species of man.

The remarkable features of this case included the ability to reason outside the realm of his delusions. In one of his hospitalizations, he would dine with the family of the head of the hospital and conduct himself in an exemplary manner, taking special care to be polite and fully reasonable with the female members of the family. He could reason well and speak lucidly in matters pertaining to his career as a jurist. Outside of the delusional sphere, he appeared completely normal and in fact convinced a court to have him discharged from a mental institution, whereupon he wrote the memoir that became the text for Freud's study of paranoia.

Schreber's belief that he was in the process of being transformed into a woman establishes the link between the delusional state of paranoia and homosexuality. (One must bear in mind that this link depends on clinical material, case by case, and should not be construed as a generalization that homosexuality and paranoia are in a cause-effect relationship.) Homosexuality may exist without pathological or delusional content or cause, but clinical study is the only route to discovering the generality of paranoia as a defense against homoerotic wishes, the case that Freud makes in his study of Schreber.

Freud's crucial idea in this study is that the delusional ideas are an attempt at recovery and should not be construed as the illness itself. They act as defenses against more catastrophic conditions such as severe depression and suicide, the extreme of self-loathing. In the Schreber case both morbid effects appeared in the progression of his illness. At the root of the symptoms, and the ultimate fantasy of his special relationship to God and his mission to save mankind lay Schreber's erotic attachment to his father and an older brother, both of whom had died. Thus, the delusional state represented the transformation of the objects of his homosexual wishes from father to son and, ultimately, to God, with more fantastic delusions at the expense of reality, but in an attempt at restoring psychic equilibrium.[7]

An incident, related by the unhappy captain of the *Rights,* who is about to lose Billy, begins when Red Whiskers, a former butcher, demonstrating to Billy the location for cutting a sirloin steak "insultingly gave him a dig under the ribs. Quick as lightning Billy let fly his arm. I dare say he never meant to do quite as much as he did, but anyhow he gave the burly fool a terrible drubbing." (p. 12) Red Whiskers becomes devoted to Billy following this drubbing, loving him as do all the crew—who darn his trousers and do his washing. In the story of Billy Budd, the reconstruction of Claggert's attack on Billy with the accusation that he is fomenting a mutiny is the transformation of homosexual love for Billy into hatred as a persecutor and perpetrator of Claggert's unacceptable wishes for an erotic relationship. In his paranoid delusions, Billy must be destroyed as a consequence of the feeling of persecution engendered by his unacceptable attraction to Billy. It is a transformation of a wish into a denial: "I don't love him; I hate him."

In the course of human development, as individuals pass through phases of both masculine and feminine sexuality, fixation may occur in which the individual gets stuck, so to speak, and is unable to shift erotic impulses to objects of the opposite sex. This fixation often leads to other stages, in which ideation becomes affected, and the individual displays depressive and even delusional thoughts. A case in a modern context may clarify the dynamics underlying delusional thoughts and homoerotic wishes.

The controller of a new enterprise faced a severe shortage of cash, which threatened the viability of the company. To deal with this crisis, he met frequently with the company president to plan moves to overcome the liquidity crisis. Normally, he had only infrequent face-to-face meetings with the president, who in the hierarchy was two levels removed from the controller (who reported directly to an administrative vice president). Once the crisis was resolved, there was a return to infrequent meetings between the president and the controller.

A change occurred in the demeanor and behavior of the controller. He would often sit in his darkened office for hours, uncommunicative and staring into space. He noticeably lost weight, but despite these observations, no one seemed to intervene in what was clearly odd behavior and outlook on the part of the controller.

One day, he walked into the president's office and said he was in love with the president's daughter, wanted to marry her, and hoped that religious differences would not stand in the way. The president was surprised, but instead of inquiring into the relationship either with the controller or later with his daughter, who was away at school and had not been in the office in over a year, he said that in this day and age, religion made little difference. The controller left and in a few days returned to the president's office with the same statement: he was in love with the president's daughter, wanted to marry her, and hoped that religious differences would not stand in the way. While again surprised, the president made reassuring noises saying that religious differences mattered little in this day and age. The president finally called his daughter and learned that the controller and had no relationship with his daughter. He was completely dumbfounded over the turn of events.

A week or so later, there was to be a luncheon including the president, the head of purchasing, and the controller to discuss procurement issues. Immediately, at the start of the luncheon, the controller repeated his desire to marry the president's daughter. This assertion was so out of place for the meeting that the president decided he had to do something. He sought professional advice and referred the controller and his mother—a widow who lived alone with this one son—to a physician. The mother reported that her son had been acting peculiarly and was uncommunicative, that he was the youngest child of four brothers and one sister, that he was 36 years old, and that he was unmarried. All of his siblings were married and living independently away from their mother.

The physician referred the controller to a psychiatrist, who immediately made arrangements for him to enter a psychiatric hospital where he was treated for severe depression. Reconstruction of the underlying causes of the illness revealed that the controller had valued his close relationship with the president during the liquidity crisis, and with its abatement, and the now only infrequent meetings with the president, the controller suffered a severe loss. The activity during the crisis had hidden the fact of a developing erotic attachment to the president, which in turn had led to the reversal of objects: it is not he that I love, it's his daughter. This delusional idea defended the controller against homosexual longings for a man who served as a surrogate father figure to him. By incorporating the daughter as the object, the controller could preserve a relationship with a father figure while defending himself against homosexual longings. The depression resulted from regression in the face of the failure of his delusional ideas to preserve attachment to the president through the daughter.

The peculiar behavior of the president in not immediately asking his daughter about the supposed relationship, but instead intellectualizing the so-called conflict over religious differences involved him directly in what seems to be an ego defense against emotional involvement in a human conflict. This avoidance and intellectualization brings us back to Captain Vere and his role in the Claggert-Budd psychodrama.

One of the most satisfying aspects of *Billy Budd*, the characterization of the ship's captain—the Honorable Edward Fairfax Vere—instructs the reader on a central dilemma of command. In the conflict between the head and the heart, between thought and emotion, which side of man's nature prevails? Or does command require an integration of thought and emotion to achieve a higher level of rationality than thought alone, detached from feeling, will allow?

Captain Vere reflects a personality who employs a split between thought and emotion. He represses emotion and elaborates, in his position of command, a detached intellect seemingly uninformed of the responsibilities of human relationships. The isolation of thought from emotion is an ego defense, beautifully displayed in Vere's manipulation of the drumhead court to reach the conclusion that Billy must hang and earlier, when Vere says, after the blow that has killed Claggert, "Struck dead by an angel! Yet the angel must hang." (p. 60) The absence of doubt, and the haste with which Vere concludes that Billy must hang, suggest that some automatism in Vere's ego controls his reaction, putting aside the need for deliberation. The sequence of events suggests that Vere is acting under the influence of an inner impulse, as though he believes he is being tested in his capacity for command. To appear decisive and even courageous in affirming the responsibility of wearing the king's buttons leads to the impulsive conclusion to hang Billy.

Melville argues both sides of the issue, leaving the reader to decide whether Vere is, if only temporarily, in an agitated and deranged mental state. Melville argues that the need for haste is apparent, given the recent mutiny at the Nore. Therefore, he is not quick to question whether Vere was really a brave captain acting under a strict military code. He is of two minds, or so he positions his readers. "The essential right and wrong in the matter, the clearer that might be, so much the worse for the responsibility of a loyal sea commander inasmuch as he was not authorized to determine the matter on that primitive basis." (p. 62) And: "a true military officer is in one particular like a true monk. Not with more self-abnegation will the latter keep his vows of monastic obedience than the former his vows of allegiance to martial duty." (p. 62)

But the doubt remains. Melville tells us Vere guarded against publicity.

> Certain it is, however, that subsequently in the confidential talk of more than one or two gun rooms and cabins he was not a little criticized by some officers, a fact imputed by his friends and vehemently by his cousin Jack Denton to professional jealousy of "Starry Vere." Some imaginative ground for invidious comment there was. The maintenance of secrecy in the matter, the confining all knowledge of it for a time to the place where the homicide occurred, the quarter deck cabin—in these particulars lurked some resemblance to the policy adopted in those tragedies of the palace which have occurred more than once in the capital founded by Peter the Barbarian. (p. 62)

During the scene of the drumhead court proceedings, Melville suggests another aspect of Vere's character: the pleasure in manipulating less verbal and intellectual officers of the court. These individuals have doubts both as to the legitimacy of the proceedings and the inevitable conclusion to which Captain Vere directs them when he suggests that they are in danger of falling under the sway of feminine feelings. None of the officers has the stamina or self-esteem to argue with Vere, especially in view of his likening a moral view to femininity.

Captain Vere portrays the dominance of a role in determining the behavior of an individual. The person lurking behind the role has little or no volition. Vere speaks the language of the role of the commander that is totally imbued in his personality and behavior. Here is full compliance between the requirements of the role and the inner man. This compliance comes about through the socialization of the individual as he is indoctrinated into the role. In this sense, Melville becomes a modern writer since with the advent of the large organization, role compliance is not restricted to the military. To suggest that there is conflict inherent between the role and the individual misses the point. To advance in a hierarchy seems to require subordinating one's inner imperatives to the pressures exerted by the role.

Compliance has hidden rewards. Not only status and advancement, the acceptance of the imperatives provides an auxiliary to the individual's defensive structure in guarding against anxiety. Whatever the level of power a conforming individual experiences, is borrowed from the organization and its structure of roles. Power is never personal.

Melville, writing, in the late nineteenth century, a story set toward the end of the eighteenth in the milieu of the British navy, speaks to us as living in and observing the modern organization. He invites us to experience the dilemmas of command and to search within ourselves for a way to assert the primacy of the individual who exists within the many roles society provides.

Not content to allow us to ponder the hanging of Billy Budd, Melville provides three kinds of afterthoughts. The first is a report of Captain Vere's death. The *Indomitable*, returning to a base following the account described in the story, falls into an engagement with the French warship the *Athéiste*. Vere is hit by a musket as his ship starts a boarding maneuver and is taken below deck. He dies ashore after the successful battle. The description of Vere's demise contrasts with the earlier account of Admiral Nelson's death festooned in full regalia, tempting the enemy to destroy him. The last words Vere utters before he dies are "Billy Budd, Billy Budd."

The second afterthought is a news account that appears in a naval weekly reporting on an incipient mutiny aboard the *Indomitable* and the hanging of Billy Budd who, in the report, was the ringleader. The report states that Billy was no Englishman but of some devious origin not uncommon among the impressed sailors.

The third afterthought perpetuates the memory of Billy. Sailors follow the movement of the spar from which Billy is suspended. "To them, a chip of it was as a piece of the cross . . . they instinctively felt that Billy was a sort of man as incapable of mutiny as of willful murder. They recalled the fresh young image of the Handsome Sailor, that face never deformed by a sneer or subtler vile freak of the heart within." (p. 87) A foretopman of Billy's watch writes a ballad entitled, "Billy in the Darbies," which concludes with these lines:

> But me they'll lash me in the hammock, drop me deep.
> Fathoms down, fathoms down, how I'll dream fast asleep.
> I feel it stealing now. Sentry, are you there?
> Just ease these darbies at the wrist, and roll me over fair,
> I am sleepy, and the oozy weeds about me twist. (p. 88)

16

Identity, Imagination, and Command

Both Conrad and Melville were fascinated by the ambiguity that presents itself in the attempt to understand human nature. Conrad was compelled by his need to find the truth in the human condition. As he wrote in his preface to *The Nigger of The Narcissus,* "And art itself may be defined as a single-minded attempt to render the highest kind of justice to the visible universe, by bringing to light the truth, manifold and one, underlying its every aspect. . . . The artist, then, like the thinker or the scientist, seeks the truth and makes his appeal."

For Melville, most of us have only a superficial knowledge of human nature. This superficial knowledge may serve an ordinary purpose. In his own voice, without narrator or character in his novel *Billy Budd,* Melville adds, "But for anything deeper, I am not certain whether to know the world and to know human nature be not two distinct branches of knowledge, which, while they may coexist in the same heart, yet either may exist with little or nothing of the other." (p. 36) The search for the truth about human nature is elusive, but for the humanist, the quest goes on reaching for an ever-closer approximation, fully recognizing that to pass from a normal nature, "one must cross 'the deadly space between.'"

The crossing of this deadly space between is a hazardous enterprise at best. The hazard for the novelist is journeying into a realm where he or she may get lost and become prey to his or her unconscious conflicts—resulting in the affliction called writer's block. On the other hand, the reader seeking immersion in the novel may experience less than optimal exposure in his or her ability to empathize with the characters or the story. To be forced into a regressive mental state by overexposure to unconscious conflict leads to withdrawal from the work of art through the familiar responses of boredom or sleepiness and the inability to get into the story. The novelist must provide for the reader the auxiliary defenses against the anxiety inherent in exposure to the deadly divide that seems to separate the so-called normal personality from the pathological. And defending too well may result in failed recognition of character and plot and the inability on the reader's part to see himself or herself in the narrative. Thus, the humanist is engaged in a test, not unlike the one Conrad provided in *The Secret Sharer,* the net result of which is the deepening of self-knowledge.

For the humanist and the audience, the experience of writing and enjoying a novel depends on optimal psychological regression from the control of rational thought processes to loosely structured and "free-floating" adventure in the service of the ego. Regression in the service of the ego, a somewhat ambiguous concept brought to our attention in the work of the psychoanalyst Ernst Kris,[1] suggests that without experiencing the state of a free-floating imagination, the ego, or perhaps more specifically, identity and character, becomes rigid and incapable of imaginative enterprise.

Among those who function in and study modern organizations, a debate about the nature of leadership that was underway for most of the twentieth century continues to this day. Some will say that the truth about command begins, and may even end, with Socrates' dictum "Know thyself." Conrad would seem to subscribe to this dictum, without reducing command to this one piece of advice, in his exquisite use of the notion that fitness for command depends on successfully dealing with an event that is a test of one's character. Melville is more cautious about the notion of testing. Does Captain Vere accept the test in deciding on Billy's fate, or does he escape the personal test by relying on the structure of rules and the obligation, as he sees it, that comes with wearing the king's buttons?

Some will say that the truth about command is no simple matter of accepting the so-called loneliness of command. The loneliness of command implies the condition of narcissism, in which the individual loves no one but himself. Narcissism, not defined as a borderline or psychotic mental state, but as the absence of the feeling of dependency, has an inherent advantage in relation to subordinates and others. Not feeling dependent enables an individual to integrate authority and convert it into personal power. With this integration, the individual becomes an object of identification. He or she projects the image of a presence, an object of intense interest on the part of others as well as an object with whom others identify. The hazard is the tendency to cross the line into megalomania, so dramatically portrayed in the character of Kurtz in Conrad's *Heart of Darkness*.

Modern day socialization carries with it an aversion to narcissism especially as it is applied to the idea of command. This aversion results from the idealization of the organization and the importance put on teamwork and cooperation over individualism and self-assertion. To be known as a team player is a sure way to get ahead in organizations. It seems that the price to be paid in conformity is small compared to the rewards gained in being recognized as a team player. For the humanist, this is a bargain to be avoided.

Erik Erikson in his essay "The Problem of Ego Identity"[2] cites George Bernard Shaw's autobiographical preface to his early writings, in which Shaw describes his youthful efforts to forge a personal identity. Shaw started out in early adulthood in a career destined to make him into a banker. He writes, "I made good in spite of myself, and found, to my dismay, that Business, instead of expelling me as the worthless imposter I was, was fastening upon me with no intention of letting me go. Behold me, therefore, in my twentieth year, with a business training, in an occupation which I detested as cordially as any sane person lets himself detest anything he cannot escape from. In March, 1876, I broke loose."[3]

In breaking loose, Shaw did not enter a life of purposelessness. He had acquired the habit of hard work and turned to writing, in which the discipline acquired in his business training, and probably earlier in life, enabled him to practice a new craft and become the famous writer the world recognized.

Erikson is using this incident as an example of what he came to call a "moratorium" from the imposition of a role that Shaw cordially detested, but what Shaw had reacted to was the visceral experience of displeasure and despair one feels when one is untrue to one's talents and the capacities of one's ego. The concept of identity refers to an integrative experience of the ego. The crisis of adolescence, in which identity is diffuse, leads to multiple identifications. These identifications are experiments in finding one's true self. The resolution of the identity crisis presupposes the end of experiments with various roles. The resolution is supposed to occur when the person finds an occupation and a place in society.

The concept of identity coupled with the norm of integration as opposed to diffusion is a bit simplistic. By itself it may give more weight to finding a role than to understanding and using one's talents or interests. Observations of people with distinctive talents often reveal that such people do not have a coherent sense of identity. Instead, their talents tend to obliterate the distinction between work and play, with their imagination leading the way in continual mental experimentation involving a type of fantasy. In the world of science, this type of fantasy finds expression in formulating and carrying out thought experiments that lead to experimentation and the testing of hypotheses. In works of art, including novels, the experiments are not entirely in one's mind, but lead to trial narratives that might take their form in novels.

But what is the equivalent mental activity in the realm of command? Is it testing oneself by reflecting upon the action that one is part of in dealing with complex human and economic issues? For some people in positions of authority, reflection soon leads to anxiety-ridden fantasy and the test falls by the wayside as these people lose their identity in a role. They seek the safety of the repetition compulsion—finding the path of activity that has provided reward in the past with the expectation that it will succeed in the future.

In the later Victorian era, during which Conrad wrote his best work and Melville withdrew into a mundane occupation as a customs inspector, there existed an implicit and enduring faith in order and stability. Nurtured by a deep belief in authority, sustained in optimism derived from growing imperial and industrial power, both embedded in the sense of righteousness that comes from being at one with God and society, the establishment expected and reinforced the need for control of the instincts. From the distance of the twenty-first century, it may seem strange that writers such as Conrad and Melville, whose work comes out of such an era, can be read and experienced as a venture into the ever-present primitive side of man. The defense against the anxiety this venture might cause in the reader is the distancing that exists in the manifest content of the stories (man against the sea and nature), in the settings of the stories, (exotic lands evoking a dreamlike state), and in the absence of the familiar sides of everyday life such as family and community.

In contrast to the novelist, Freud, writing as scientist and physician, does not enable any detachment from the conflicts he evokes in describing the unconscious and sexual development of the infant and in setting out the family romance of the Oedipus complex. He inadvertently assaults the most familiar experiences, attaching to them an underside of primitive impulses. Primitive man is not relegated to dark Africa, but is ubiquitous; order and stability are like a veneer, and control of the instincts a battle to be fought and won in each individual and in every generation anew. Nor is the control of instincts—particularly of man's aggressive impulses—far from conscious awareness in the twentieth and early twenty-first centuries. Bloody warfare, terrorism and civil war, substance abuse, and senseless homicide that invades communities and the family, are so commonplace as to anesthetize humanity to its own primitive nature.

The way to escape from the terrors of the unconscious is to belong, to find membership in some established occupation and organization. Identity can be borrowed in a recognizable role. But the comfort of this identity comes at the price of suppressing imagination. A divide exists between the humanist, who lives by imagination, and the rest of us, who assiduously accept and cultivate a role. Irving Kristol, the neoconservative, writing in *Fortune,* says that the artist will endure all kinds of suffering, including the hypochondria and depression Conrad experienced, but will avoid at all costs the boredom of the mundane and the ordinary. The justification of this position, if it needs one at all is, in the words of the literary critic Albert Guerard, that "art induces greater sympathies (but also sterner judgments) than most of us are capable of in the daily conduct of our lives; it compels us to live less indifferently, and frees us from the irrelevant."[4]

Command in contemporary society, and the power that goes with it, is an experience in the progression through various roles in formal organizations. Whether in the military, in government, or in business individuals face the problem of establishing an identity through a role and moving up a hierarchy. The hierarchy defines the authority and responsibilities accorded to role descriptions, some of which are explicit in themselves, but some implicit in the traditions of the organization. Along with the definitions of roles go the rewards that adhere to different levels of responsibility in an organization. The degree of freedom to maintain individual autonomy and identity while enacting a role, is limited by the authority accorded to the role and the ability of the individual to transform this authority into personal power. Most people accept a trade-off, in which the role becomes an attribute of their identity. In exchange for this conformity, their defensive structure is supported in the recognition accorded them. And it is this exchange that talented individuals find offensive and that Shaw rejected when he became aware that business had its hold on him and would not let go. His problem was success in playing a role that would not allow for the full expression of his imagination. The same rejection of this exchange applies to Conrad's so-called failure in taking command. He probably would have performed acceptably as a ship's captain, doomed to live as Captain MacWhirr, who "had sailed over the surface of the oceans as some men go skimming over the years of existence . . . without ever having been made to see all it may contain."[5]

In discarding command in the role of a ship's captain, Conrad lived instead at high personal risk of overexposure to unconscious conflict. He suffered from various physical illnesses and from depression, and endured lengthy periods during which he could not write. His writing deteriorated in quality and in characterization over time. In his biography of Conrad, Dr. Meyer writes, "[T]he fluctuations in the quality of Conrad's writing were often closely correlated with his varying capacity to hold his art free from the contamination of immediate concurrent mental suffering. . . . Psychologically it would appear that he could no longer afford those introspective journeys into the self that constitute the greatness of the impressionistic art he created."[6] (Despite the personal and neurotic suffering, in the intervals during which Conrad felt liberated from psychological conflict, he produced great narratives. He achieved wide acclaim as a novelist and his work continues to provide enormous pleasure and insight for his readers.)

Subordinacy, the other side of the coin of command, is a theme that appears in the characters and plots of both Conrad's and Melville's stories. Even characters who hold positions of command are, in a sense, subordinates, if not to someone immediately above them in the hierarchy, then to an idea or image of final authority. Thus, when Captain Vere invokes the duty inherent in wearing the King's buttons, he is reinforcing the demands of subordinacy, the obligations to higher authority.

Melville brings to the fore the theme of attention to the obligations of subordinacy in his subtle short story, "Bartleby, The Scrivener." Being a scrivener is a mind-numbing occupation, in Bartleby's case involving proofreading legal documents in a law office, and Melville makes clear the idiosyncrasies of the scriveners in the office—idiosyncrasies that evidently exist to exert some shred of individuality. But none of these men is as eccentric or as puzzling as Bartleby, the newest employee in the office. To be a subordinate, one must meet expectations, willingly and without complaint. The way subordinates meet expectations often involves finding a space in their psyches in which the core sense of identity is not at risk. Thus, compliance with directives that fall within the individual's "zone of indifference" is automatic, requiring little expenditure of mental energy.[7] If a person with authority issues a directive that falls outside the zone of indifference, however, as becomes evident with Bartleby, there will be resistance to the directive and even failure to comply. When Bartleby is asked to help proofread a document he replies, "I prefer not to." The owner of the office is dumbfounded. How can one prefer not to follow a directive that is central to the duties for which he is employed and for which he receives compensation? This behavior is in clear violation of the implicit employment contract. If it persists, as it does in Bartleby's case, employment will be short lived.

The owner's bewilderment and reluctance to take action in firing the subordinate creates a tension in the story. Is he intrigued with Bartleby's extraordinary behavior, or himself fearful of acting in line with his power and ultimately firing Bartleby? He finally moves his offices to rid himself of Bartleby, and Bartleby ends up in The Tombs, where he dies refusing food. In the end, the reader is left to speculate on the character of Bartleby and his employer.

The story is a brilliant account of the turmoil a passive-aggressive personality can create. By recognizing the effects of the aggression underlying Bartleby's seemingly passive behavior, the reader can learn much about the dynamics of subordinacy, including the subtleties of control.

In a modern narrative that appeared in a study of group behavior in a machine shop,[8] a different kind of behavior in subordinate and superior is in evidence. Len, age 41 and unmarried, worked as a skilled machinist in the tool shop of a medium-sized company and also happened to be the city's chess champion. He taught his fellow workers chess during their rest breaks and also posted chess problems on the shop's bulletin board. Then he began to post notices criticizing shop practices, and indirectly the supervisor, for not having the proper tools available for machining. His supervisor removed these notices and issued a directive that only he—the supervisor—and management could post notices on the bulletin board. In response, Len placed a small bulletin board next to his lathe and tool chest, where he continued to place chess notices along with criticisms of shop practice—a direct affront to management and his supervisor. The supervisor tried to engage him in discussing why he persisted in using the bulletin board to criticize shop practices, and the conflict escalated to the point where Len told his supervisor to go to hell; he would continue to use his bulletin board as he saw fit. The supervisor told Len to go collect his pay; he was fired. Management supported the supervisor, and the episode of a failed superior-subordinate relationship came to an end.

The supervisor was a reasonable man who had tried his best to avoid the final confrontation that led to Len's termination. He was also a cold individual, seemingly an obsessive-compulsive type personality—a type that isolates feeling from thinking. Len's provocative behavior, in the face of the supervisor's approach to the issue, turned into open anger, with none of the subtlety that usually goes along with attempts to hide hostility toward authority with the blandness and seemingly innocent behavior of a passive-aggressive type of personality. One can only surmise that Len's confrontation with the supervisor was a fresh version of a legacy of ambivalence toward authority figures. With Len's type of personality, beneath the overt hostility lies a deeper wish for closeness and dependency, along with the expectation that these wishes will go unfulfilled.

Individuals have their first experiences with the politics of authority, power, and command in the family. Much of the dynamics of these experiences become repressed, but continue to exert their influence in all of the person's relations with others. In the case of authority relationships, the past may be activated through transference—that is, the content and coloration of past relationships with parents and siblings can become invested in present relationships, without the individual being consciously aware of the sources. Contemporaneous relationships become infused with the emotions and meanings of the past, and past conflicts resume their intensity in the present and are repeated in the enactment of superior-subordinate relationships.

One of the underlying functions of the modern organization is to take the personal out of relationships that are based on authority, thereby muting transference. The idea of command in superior-subordinate relationships is buried in the mechanisms that disguise power; it is embedded in the logic of efficiency, for example, a logic in which superior and subordinate are equally constrained in complying with directives from the system.

Under Frederick Winslow Taylor's system of scientific management, which, as we have seen, was based on the need to eliminate personal command from management practice, supervisors no longer issue directives and tell subordinates how to perform. Rather, directives and instructions reside in the system, to which superior and subordinate are equally bound. The idea is that in exchange for the loss of discretion and autonomy, supervisors and employees are governed equally through the impersonal management system.

Inventions such as scientific management often grow out of the effort of individuals to solve their personal problems through their work. The link between the humanism of the novelist and innovation in organizations is the imagination of the creative personality. This imagination is forged in neurotic conflict that finds expression in original work. Taylor suffered from an obsessional neurosis that derived from unconscious conflict in his attachment to his father. His decision to forgo education to become an apprentice in a machine shop was a suspension of the obligations of a traditional role; it abandoned a life path and the established roles consistent with his social status. Taylor resembles George Bernard Shaw in rejecting a life that threatened to take a hold on him. Instead of that life, he applied his imagination to revolutionizing the way work gets performed in factories and to eliminating the personal power of command in superior-subordinate roles.[9]

The humanist temper is different from the imagination of the innovator in modern organizations, and the difference can be seen also in the character of leaders who use command for creative purposes. An article published in *The Harvard Business Review* in 1977 posits a difference between managers and leaders,[10] in that managers act indirectly, favoring process over substance, while leaders are direct and focus on substance, placing their personal power on the table, so to speak, instead of hiding behind the formalities of process. By their directness and focus on substance, leaders release aggression converted to the service of work and innovation. Like humanists, they are artists (although the two have different types of imagination underlying their gifts). Both achieve independence and both are narcissistic. The narcissism of the leader enables him or her to speculate freely and imagine how the world might change through innovation.

The narcissism of leaders grows out of their having worked through some major disruptive experience, usually in their early years. The untimely death of a parent, some illness, or other form of disappointment has caused them to fall back on themselves and engage in introspection. For manager types, on the other hand, who have a more limited imagination, the disruption and its concomitant depression will result in rapid investing in roles and relationships and quickly avoiding reworking the life issues presented by the crisis. Managers are once-born personalities for whom conventional roles and relationships provide satisfactions and reinforce defenses. Leaders are twice-born personalities, who have endured the depression accompanying disappointment and loss and emerge with a healthy degree of narcissism.

The artistry of leadership often appears as a tactical imagination that accompanies a substantive talent. Leading a formal organization, outside of the military or the captaincy of a ship, requires a deep understanding of human motivation. Relying less on tradition and role imperatives than on this understanding, leaders form a vision that goes beyond maintaining the status quo. When Douglas Southall Freeman, the historian and biographer, delivered a speech on leadership to the War College in 1949, he said that a person in command who is a leader has to follow three personal rules: first, know your stuff; second be a man; and third, take care of your men (the three "C's" of leadership, Competence, Character, and Compassion). The way one achieves a defined level of accomplishment in these three C's opens an adventure in getting to know oneself. A leader thinks like a humanist in creating and enacting narratives that embody a vision to which other people may subscribe and which they may help achieve.

It is the exceptional person who, freed from the common dependencies of ordinary life, is able to live aggressively and comfortably with the personal power that is inherent in command. This person should not be confused with the authoritarian described in the work of Adorno and others.[11] The level of aggression needed to perform work belongs not exclusively to the person in command. The need for aggression invites others to find and utilize their own aggressive impulses in the service of work. True leaders are not threatened by the aggressiveness of subordinates. They welcome it and only experience discomfort in the passivity or sycophancy of subordinates. In this sense, leaders, like humanists, liberate people from conformity—if the freed ones have the personal resources to experience and use this freedom.

Conclusion

17

Character and Fitness for Command

What it takes in competence and character to command will depend to a significant extent on the forces at work, both in the environment and internally, in the particular organization. In government organizations, political factors tend to dominate thinking and action. In private enterprise, the aim of leadership is to avoid if not eliminate politicization. There is a Gresham's law applied to organizations: politics drives out realistic thinking. President Reagan's effort to produce a budget in February 1982 is a good case in point.

It might be tempting to say that President Reagan's budget message of February 8, 1982, and the budget process during the spring of 1982 are exceptional specimens of what the man and his presidency were all about. But although this is an accurate way of characterizing the presidency, it does not characterize the man.

The budget message crystallized all the problems President Reagan had in balancing the demands of his many constituencies. This is the essence of being a president. It is playing a role that has to make sense to a variety of constituencies with conflicting interests and concerns. They all want their special piece of the president's program, but not the whole thing. How does the president make each piece attractive enough so that each constituency will overlook or swallow what it doesn't like? By giving the conservatives a sizable defense budget, Reagan initially forced them into accepting the prospect of record-breaking deficits. At the same time, he put the squeeze on the Congress, which, along with business, hated the idea of large deficits—which meant that it had to face cuts in social spending. Reagan invited the Congress to go after the entitlement programs and, by indirection, the defense budget, as a way of trimming the deficits.

The last thing the Congress wanted to do in an election year was to increase taxes. So, Reagan managed to box in the Congress. As for the far left, particularly the poor and the minorities, he forced them to look to the states for satisfaction, which was a brilliant way to defuse a time bomb. By setting up multiple channels for complaint, he reduced the amount of discontent that could be focused on the White House. In the language of psychoanalysis, he could be the good and compassionate father, while the governors of the states took over the less pleasant image of the bad and withholding father. It was a brilliant performance of a role, but it says almost nothing about the man. He must have had inner motives, psychological conflicts, and defenses, but whatever his true self was, it was hidden behind the role. Reagan's personality may have needed a role—not only to hide behind but also in order to express his particular attachment to power.

After World War II, a new breed became CEO of corporations, universities, and our nation. Reagan may have been the best example of this breed, although Eisenhower was also formidable in this regard. The essence of the personality of this new breed was to be reasonable, optimistic, and above all, low-key and in control of their emotions. This was not playing a role. It was the personality of the new breed. Don't become an object of other people's love or aggression. Be friendly, but don't stir people's passion at the risk of stirring your own. It makes a marvelous fit between the person and the job.

The way to work this job is to select a point man for the controversial issues. The point man is the lightning rod for aggression and hostility. Having a lightning rod gave these presidents plenty of room to be the decent, friendly sort who kept out of the way of the love-hate reactions that seem to go along with the charismatic leaders—like FDR, Churchill, and de Gaulle. People were surprised in the 1980s that Reagan could espouse the conservative cause, having once been president of a union and an active Democrat. The case to make here is that his convictions regarding both liberal and conservative causes were not important to him, as his conservative admirers wanted them to be. He could admire FDR not because he, Reagan, believed in the New Deal, but probably because he admired the way FDR manipulated power and people.

Harold Lasswell, a political scientist in the mid-twentieth century, believed, along with the psychoanalyst Alfred Adler, that power serves the individual as a compensatory motive, helping to overcome the individual's feelings of inferiority and his or her sense of deprivation that comes from his or her past. This idea is an oversimplification, but it is a way to start looking into the question of what power means in the psyche of a chief executive. There are a lot of positive and altruistic reasons for people to seek power, including the desire to be of service and to help humankind. But one cannot ignore the fact that power is also a thick screen that allows people who have it to ignore their personal history. (Henry Kissinger said that power is a great aphrodisiac.) Power is a great defense. With power, not only do people believe they can put their history behind them, they can even entertain the illusion that they gave birth to themselves.

Not only that, but power can be a shield. The presidency is a goldfish bowl, where every act is visible and an object of intense scrutiny. Reagan could not even buy his wife a new set of china without it becoming everybody's business. People focused on trivia and as a result, gave the man tremendous freedom of action. Political scientists call it maximizing the number of options available to a chef executive. In the psychoanalytic view, the role, or image of the president, is a projective device. People make of him what they want him to be and interpret his actions in the light of their own needs and fears. As a result, he is home free. He does not need to plumb the depths of his personality to act in his role because his actions are always on the surface. The meaning of his actions, psychologically speaking, comes from the projections people put upon them.

The role is like a mirror. The reflection of the image prevents whoever is looking at it from seeing what is behind the mirror. This theme is important to the analysis of command, as in the case of Reagan, not just to portray Reagan but to tell the story of the new breed of leader mentioned above. The novelist Jerzy Kosinski, writing during the time Reagan was in the White House, created in *Being There* a clever character who, whatever Kosinski's intentions, gives us a lead into the psychology of the new breed and their followers. The main character, named Chance, is a gardener, who, besides being mentally retarded, has been isolated from the world and from people all his life. He has tended a garden in a rich man's house from his childhood days, and the only way he knows what lies beyond the walls of his cloister, his paradise, his womb, is through television (which incidentally is the perfect symbol of the mirror). People attribute wisdom to Chance's stupid words because they have to believe in the possibility of omnipotence as the ultimate wish fulfillment. The funniest and also the most pathetic part of the book occurs in Kosinski's reduction of sexuality. Chance has no libido, but neither do the other characters. Their sexual drive no longer belongs to them but is an attribute of an ambiguous "other," the magical mirror that turns people on. Chance can arouse a male stranger just as easily as a woman. In both cases the man and the woman satisfy themselves, but believe their pleasure results from Chance or Chauncey Gardiner as he comes to be known in the high flying world of power and politics.

This phenomenon is not new. Transference is something Freud discovered around 1900. In transference, a person attaches himself or herself to someone else, but that someone else is really a fantasy figure from the past—for example, his or her mother or father. But the mirror idea goes beyond transference in two senses. First, it is even more archaic than an image of one's parents, and second, the mirror exists as a cohesive force capable of becoming a political vector as well as a social fact. The power of the mirror is a direct consequence of the secularization of society and the unconscious. People once had various outlets for their fantasies, both individual and collective. Religion, for example, took care of some people's fantasies, but lost its way as a force because it became politicized. (The Catholic Church was about the only Christian religion that held onto the understanding that the spiritual and the profane needed to be separate.) The Moral Majority of Reagan's time drew Christianity, particularly the radical sects, into politics and succeeded in destroying the foundation of religion while exaggerating the only thing left for collective expression: namely, politics.

The mirror is ideally suited for mass politics because it does away, once and for all, with individuality. Religion, in raising the God image to consciousness, reinforced individuality because there was always this vast chasm between the person and God. The mirror is totally subliminal, and people do not realize they are seeing their own projection reflected back to them. It is like the sexual act in *Being There*. The act is totally autoerotic, but the person believes in the sexual potency of this ambiguous "other," the nonentity called Chauncey Gardiner.

You cannot fault a chief executive for not anticipating all the consequences of his actions. But you can fault him or her for failure in, or lack of, imagination. CEO's tend to become enmeshed in the tactical aspects of their job, so that the strategic or policy aspects are given short shrift. When crises occur, such as the terrorist attack on September 11, 2001, or Hurricane Katrina, the pressures on those in command force them to fall back on tactical concerns and to ignore the broader issues.

What is singular about President Reagan and the other leaders of the late twentieth century is their lack of imagination. Their vision seems to have been limited, and they seem to have suffered from the delusion that leadership is equated with managing crises. Nixon certainly liked to dramatize crises. And even John Kennedy, who was supposed to be charismatic, related to crises as though the image, if not the test, of his leadership would result from his appearance of being cool under fire as in the case of the Cuban missile crisis. The Kennedy revisionists had a field day showing how he provided a mirror of machismo, to allow the American people to strut, after the quiet years that president Eisenhower provided. The revisionists loved to quote the portion of Kennedy's inaugural address where he said, "Let every nation know, whether it wishes us well or ill, that we shall pay any price, bear any burden, meet any hardship, support any friend, oppose any foe, in order to assure the survival and the success of liberty." As a statement of national policy to guide foreign affairs, this is an absurdity. But as a reflection of the wish for power, control, and masculine dominance, it could not be more powerfully descriptive or more evocative.

Reagan's mirror was different in that it played down emotions and played up a kind of congeniality that was supposed to minimize the pain experienced in the fight against inflation. Those were tough times and people were amazingly placid and accepting of the changes underway. The mirror behind which Reagan hid his character, such as it was, encouraged the kind of passivity that in other circumstances would have led to protesting against the deceleration of social programs.

The line of investigation that would pursue the theme of Reagan's and his predecessors' lack of imagination ignores the question of how much and what kind of talent these presidents had. For example, it will not be productive to say they were mediocre intellects, but rather to investigate the question of how power figures become trapped in their own programming. Too often heads of organizations and of governments are genuinely awestruck by their position. They may feel they come by their power illegitimately, or they may feel insecure about making decisions, because they might possibly make poor ones and display poor judgment. This insecurity leads to self-programming, a survival formula designed to keep one's head above water in a sea of complexity and powerful expectations. The power-holders do not realize how they are boxing themselves in by this self-programming, which becomes a prophecy fulfilled in its very conception. With all the responsibility, the burdens of effort and decision, people at least ought to get pleasure from holding power. But in formulating and abiding by a survival formula, the power-holder begins to realize that the job is not fun—there is little pleasure in performing in the office of the chief executive. The chief executive may survive, but to what end, other than getting by and getting through.

Reading the histories of institutions of the late twentieth century is a lesson in how the power-holders of that era opted for minimum solutions. Their decisions were, for the most part, based on the principle that errors of commission are dangerous, because the discrepancy between promise and actuality is calculable. (The Vietnam War is a good case in point.) To risk errors of commission is to act, but also to find that one may have made a terrible mistake, as in the case of Argentina and the Falkland Islands. The power-holders in question in these situations tended to take the safe position and opt for errors of omission—who was to know that the failure to act would result in calamity a few generations later? In Reagan's case, the failure in imagination led his subordinates to act for him with calamitous results. The Iran-Contra scandal almost cost him his presidency. In this episode, the mirror projecting amiability and good intentions failed and only reflected Reagan's psychological defense of denial as he asserted repeatedly, "I did not trade arms for hostages." Advisors, including his wife, Nancy, could not seem to get through his character armor of amiability and passivity the recognition that he was under threat of losing his office. The way he behaved during this crisis in his presidency raises the possibility that underlying denial as a defense lay hidden another aspect of his character, grandiosity—a belief that nothing bad could happen to him. Even being kicked out of his first marriage could not penetrate the aura of grandiosity that protected him from formidable depressive reactions.

Grandiosity can be very destructive. People who have grandiose images of themselves and what they should, or are expected to, accomplish will be inhibited by those images. If the grandiose image can be dissolved, the individual will be able to complete work and get a lot of satisfaction from the work itself rather than the illusion of invulnerability and the anticipation of winning great prizes.

The responsibility of command is (besides truthfulness) competence in decisions and actions. To role-play competence without its substance is to widen the perception of inauthentic performance: that the person in charge is not to be trusted. A gap between performance and authenticity violates the principles of liberty, as they were named by John Adams: "Liberty cannot be preserved without the general knowledge among people who have a right. . . . an indisputable, unalienable, indefensible, divine right to that most dreaded and envied kind of knowledge. I mean of the characters and conduct of their rulers."

So much has happened since 2000 in the presidency of George W. Bush to question his approach to leadership, power, and command, particularly in terms of truthfulness and competence in decisions and actions. The outcomes of his presidency are unclear, and he has, perhaps without intention, put himself and the nation to a profound test—a test of our role in the world and our fate as a nation. Our discussion will be built around three critical incidents in his presidency to date.

The first is the way he or his advisors carried out a campaign that reached the Supreme Court, invalidating a recount of the vote in Florida. This campaign and the Supreme Court action gave Bush the presidency. While one might surmise that Bush entered the office with his legitimacy in doubt, his behavior suggested that he was acting without a shred of doubt about his legitimate hold on the office, and he proceeded with a complete right-wing agenda with tax cuts and deficits reminiscent of Reagan's agenda.

The second critical incident is his having led the nation into the war in Iraq following the terrorist attacks on the World Trade Center and the Pentagon. He did not falter when it became evident that he and his administration had lied to the nation by asserting that the basis for the attack on Iraq was Iraq's possession of weapons of mass destruction and Saddam's alliance with Osama bin Laden. As events in Iraq unfolded, it turned out that there were no weapons of mass destruction there and there was no alliance, manifest or covert, with bin Laden. Even before the attacks of September 11, the evidence was strong that Bush and his right-wing ideologues were planning on a war with Saddam and looking for an excuse or a rationale for attacking Iraq.

The third critical incident is Hurricane Katrina and the destruction of New Orleans and parts of Mississippi. The continuing insurgency in Iraq, and the casualties suffered by American troops, suggested that a shift was occurring in the balance of confidence in Bush on the part of the American public. His approval rating began to slip, and, with the errors he and his administration committed in responding to Katrina, the rating dipped below 30 percent (Pew and other polls). The failure in selecting competent subordinates undermines the constituents' confidence in the leader's fitness for command. Right after Katrina struck, Bush said to the head of the Federal Emergency Management Administration (FEMA), Michael D. Brown, "Brownie, you are doing one heck of a job." In a matter of days, Brown was removed from direct control of the federal response, and right after his removal, he submitted his resignation. It became obvious that he had no background or experience in managing an emergency or even other organizations. His job before Bush appointed him head of FEMA was to run an Arabian horse organization. He had put on his resume that he was an assistant in some organization, when in fact he was "an assistant to." In a press conference right after Brown's resignation, Bush said that he, himself, was responsible for any failures in the federal government's response to Katrina and that he would launch an investigation into what had gone right and wrong in the response—empty words further undermining his credibility.

Earlier in the history of the Iraq War, he was quick to make himself prominent in taking credit for the fall of Saddam. He landed a plane on an aircraft carrier, proclaiming with a large sign hanging from the superstructure, "Mission Accomplished." It should have been evident to the press and to the American public that he was staging a victory celebration that subsequent events in Iraq proved to be premature. He and his cabinet had failed to anticipate and plan for a post-Saddam uprising or turmoil.

These three critical episodes raise important questions about leadership and command. It does not require a deep exploration of personal history to examine the relationship between actions taken as a leader and character. The link between character and action is cognitive style, the way the mind works—which can be inferred from the actions and the approach to reality that underlies them as an aspect of the way the ego works.

Bush is ideologically driven. In that sense, he is a hedgehog and not a fox, to borrow Isaiah Berlin's typology. He knows one big thing, one all encompassing idea, that applies to the reality he faces. He uses ideology as a shortcut to making decisions, and this allows him to distance himself from involvement in working through problems or crises to policies and decisions. A hedgehog as a leader becomes dependent on his organization since he maintains a low level of involvement with others in making policy. Some people would credit this low involvement as an asset, applying the principle of delegation. But there are risks to this distancing and dependence. It weakens the leader's grasp of the issues involved in arriving at policy positions and decisions. And also, it allows the leader to appear to be long on posturing and short on a grasp of issues, events, and a historically deepened perspective. Bush and many of his subordinates lack an appreciation of history and even show a disinterest in the antecedents to crises. Their ability to articulate the reasoning behind policies and decisions is weak, as a consequence of the distance they maintain. They commit the fatal error of substituting ideology for reality testing and thinking.

Bush avoids press conferences and the relatively freewheeling interchange with reporters. When he speaks, it is usually from a prepared script. With the September 11 attacks and Katrina, he was slow to respond and initially appeared perplexed. When his handlers gave him a script, he then tried to enact the role of the brave leader facing a crisis.

People with this style are disdainful of the cautionary idea of the past as prologue. They have a deep aversion to introspection. While Socrates' advice to leaders, "know thyself," is a precondition for the educated mind, this advice may be studiously ignored on the part of leaders who choose to remain detached from the give and take of decision-making.

Leadership style is the visible manifestation of character. If, as we have said, character is the result of development, the legacy of the crises of childhood, the manifestation of character becomes the habitual response to any experience that might arouse anxiety. It is a regulatory function to maintain inner stability and the outer appearance that makes one recognizable to others. Given these considerations as a basis, a psychoanalytic study of a leader on public display such as George W. Bush would be valuable, but not without the data necessary to an inquiry in depth about how his character was formed through early childhood development. There is not much chance of considering information about his early childhood experience without speculating—which would be fruitless and irresponsible. But there are two facts about Bush that further inquiry into the study of his character.

First, he was born into a family distinguished by wealth and a record of political influence and election to public office. Such families seem to pass on to heirs either a sense of noblesse oblige leading to public service and philanthropy, or a sense of entitlement. The Rockefeller family is a good example of the sense of obligation that comes through wealth and status. Bush's lackluster career before politics and the use of others to accumulate wealth, suggests that he developed a sense of entitlement rather than responsibility during his adolescence and early adult years.

Second, he had a serious substance abuse problem for about twenty years, lasting well into his adult life. He is an alcoholic and presumably stopped drinking as a result of family intervention. The Reverend Billy Graham led him in an evangelical conversion. He became a born-again Christian and stopped drinking. These two facts about Bush are incontrovertible and beyond speculation. And they are important in the formation of character and his fitness for command in the presidency.

Because Bush's style is to distance himself from the process of decision-making, it is reasonable to assume that the call for a war on terrorism was not solely his invention. Starting with Vice President Cheney, he has a politically astute staff of advisors, with Karl Rove as a primary enabler specializing in building Bush's image as a commander who takes charge. The initial response to the terrorist attacks on September 11, the segment shown on TV of Bush in a classroom looking perplexed when an advisor whispered in his ear about the World Trade Center strike, shows an image of an adolescent about to have an anxiety attack. The footage of him inspecting the Katrina ruins from the air, designed to create an image of a take-charge president, was foolish. What could an air survey accomplish? A picture showing Bush leading a meeting of his cabinet and advisors would have been more to the point, showing real work.

As President Kennedy advised Robert McNamara in persuading him to take a cabinet job, there is no training program on being a president, but there is a prerequisite in the quality of the individual's character. In the absence of the requisite intelligence, sense of history, tolerance of anxiety, skepticism of oversimplified solutions to complex problems, the ability to communicate one's understanding of problems and courses of action, and above all, the skill to appeal to people's better nature in the face of diverse self-interests, there will be failed leadership and command. Formal education, while helpful, is not the primary prerequisite. It is a quality of mind in which the subtleties of psychological intelligence reign supreme.

Notes

Chapter 1

1. Sigmund Freud, *Group Psychology and the Analysis of the Ego* (New York: Bantam Books, 1960), p. 78.
2. Isaiah Berlin, *The Hedgehog and the Fox: An Essay on Tolstoy's View of History,* with an introduction by Michael Walzer (New York: Simon & Schuster, 1986), p. 1.

Chapter 2

1. Quoted in Stephen E. Ambrose, *Eisenhower, Soldier and President* (New York: Simon & Schuster, 1990), pp. 201–202.
2. Ibid., p. 185.
3. Ibid., pp. 178–179.
4. Ibid., p. 180.
5. Ibid, p. 165.
6. Ibid., pp. 165–167.
7. Dwight David Eisenhower, *At Ease: Stories I Tell to Friends* (Garden City, New York: Doubleday, 1967), p. 187.
8. Emmet John Hughes, *The Ordeal of Power: A Political Memoir of the Eisenhower Years* (New York: Dell, 1964), p. 39.
9. Ibid., pp. 40–41.
10. Ibid., p. 39.
11. Richard E. Neustadt, *Presidential Power: The Politics of Leadership* (Toronto: New American Library of Canada, 1964), pp. 69–83.
12. Ibid., p. 71.
13. Herbert S. Parmet, *Eisenhower and the American Crusades* (New York: Macmillan, 1972), p. 510.
14. Ambrose, *Eisenhower*, pp. 542–543.
15. Parmet, *Eisenhower*, p. 578.
16. Ambrose, *Eisenhower*, p. 49.
17. Ibid., p. 65.

Chapter 3

1. Donald T. Regan, *For the Record: From Wall Street to Washington* (New York: Harcourt Brace Johanovich, 1988), p. 142.
2. Nancy Reagan with William Novak, *My Turn: The Memoirs of Nancy Reagan* (New York: Random House, 1989), p. 333.

3. William Greider, "The Education of David Stockman," *The Atlantic*, December 1981.

4. David Stockman, *The Triumph of Politics: Why the Reagan Revolution Failed* (New York: Harper & Row, 1986), p. 9.

5. Nancy Reagan, *My Turn*, p. 61.

6. Lou Cannon, *President Reagan: The Role of a Lifetime* (New York: Public Affairs, 1991, 2000), p. 165.

7. Michael K. Deaver, *Behind the Scenes* (New York: William Morrow, 1987), pp. 85–88.

8. Ibid., p. 183.

9. Ibid., p. 255.

10. George Pratt Schultz, *Turmoil and Triumph: My Years as Secretary of State* (New York: Scribner's; Toronto: Maxwell Macmillan Canada; New York: Maxwell Macmillan International, 1993), p. 801.

11. Ibid., p. 3.

12. Ibid., p. 9.

13. Ibid., p. 10.

14. Reagan, *My Turn*, pp. 242–243.

15. Shultz, *Turmoil and Triumph*, p. 725.

16. Ibid., p. 773.

17. Cannon, *President Reagan*, p. 691.

18. Frances Fitzgerald, *Way Out There in the Blue: Reagan, Star Wars, and the End of the Cold War* (New York: Simon & Schuster, 2000), p. 212.

19. Ibid., pp. 353–354.

20. Quoted in ibid., p. 367. Taken from Admiral Crowe's memoir, *The Line of Fire* (New York: Simon & Schuster, 1993).

21. Shultz, *Turmoil and Triumph*, p. 1011.

22. Ibid.

23. The Tower Commission Report (New York: Bantam Books and Times Books, a division of Random House, 1987). See Section B, "A Failure of Responsibility," pp. 79–83.

24. Cannon, *President Reagan*, p. 661.

25. Lou Cannon, "To Tell the Truth: Will the Real Ronald Reagan Please Stand Up," Book Review section, *Los Angeles Times*, October 3, 1999, p. 1.

26. Garry Wills, *Reagan's America: Innocents at Home* (Garden City, New York: Doubleday, 1987).

27. Ronald Reagan with Richard G. Hubler, *Where's the Rest of Me* (New York: Duell, Sloan, and Pearce, 1965).

28. Ibid., p. 201.

29. Cannon, *President Reagan*, p. 191.

30. Ibid., p. 190.

31. Wills, *Reagan's America*, p. 284.

32. M. Brewster Smith, *Opinions and Personality* (New York: Science Editions, 1956), p. 39.

33. Leon Festinger, *A Theory of Cognitive Dissonance* (Stanford, CA: Stanford University Press, 1957).

34. Cannon, *President Reagan*, p. 655.

35. Wills, *Reagan's America*, pp. 30–33.

36. Stockman, *Triumph*, p. 355. Stockman uses this story to detail the president's denial of the reality of his flawed economic programs. See Chapter 12, "The President and the Pony," pp. 355–375.

37. Cannon, *President Reagan*, p. 431.

38. Ronald Reagan, *Rest of Me*, pp. 7–8.

39. Michael K. Deaver with Mickey Herskowitz, *Behind the Scenes: In which the Author Talks about Ronald and Nancy Reagan . . . and Himself* (New York: William Morrow, 1987), pp. 252–253.

40. See Hedrick Smith, *The Power Game: How Washington Works* (New York: Random House, 1988). Also, Richard E. Neustadt, *Presidential Power and the Modern Presidents: The Politics of Leadership from Roosevelt to Reagan* (New York: Free Press, 1990), p. 111.

41. Cannon, *President Reagan*, p. 374.

Chapter 4

1. John J. O'Connor, "A Portrait of Churchill," Cultural Desk, *New York Times*, June 18, 1986, p. 26.

2. "Halo Effect," Editorial Desk, *New York Times*, January 30, 1982, p. 22.

3. William James, *The Varieties of Religious Experience* (New York: Modern Library, 1994), pp. 80–184.

4. Ibid., p. 93.

5. Ibid., p. 95.

6. Ibid, p. 182.

7. George E. Kennan, *Around the Cragged Hill* (New York: W. W. Norton, 1994), p. 27.

8. Isaiah Berlin, *Four Essays on Liberty* (London, New York: Oxford University Press, 1969), p. 19.

9. Nicholas Lemann, "The Provocateur: Others Think as George Kennan Does but Don't Dare to Say So," *The New Yorker*, November 13, 2000, p. 94.

10. Sigmund Freud, *Group Psychology and the Analysis of the Ego* (New York: Bantam Books, 1960), p. 65.

11. James MacGregor Burns, *Leadership* (New York: Harper & Row, 1978), p. 40.

12. Ibid.

13. Abraham Maslow, *Motivation and Personality* (New York: Harper & Row, 1970), p. 80–92.

14. Freud, *Group Psychology*, p. 66.

15. Alexander L. George, *The "Operational Code": A Neglected Approach to the Study of Political Leaders and Decision-Making* (Santa Monica, CA: Rand, 1967), p. 191. Also in Alexander L. George, "The 'Operational Code': A Neglected Approach to the Study of Political Leaders and Decision-Making," *International Studies Quarterly* 13, no. 2 (June, 1969): 190–222.

16. Sigmund Freud, *An Outline of Psychoanalysis*, trans. and ed. James Strachey (New York: W. W. Norton, 1989).

17. Helene Deutsch, "Some Forms of Emotional Disturbance and Their Relationship to Schizophrenia," *Psychoanalytic Quarterly* 11 (1942): 301–321. Reprinted in Manfred F. R. Kets de Vries and Sidney Perzow, eds., *Handbook of Character Studies: Psychoanalytic Explorations* (Madison, CT: International Universities Press, 1991).

18. Ibid., 389.

19. Isaiah Berlin, *The Hedgehog and the Fox* (Chicago: Elephant Paperbacks, Irvin R. Dee, 1993), p. 1. The original edition was published in 1953 by George Weidenfeld & Nicholson.

20. Ibid.

21. Lou Cannon, *President Reagan: The Role of a Lifetime* (New York: Simon & Schuster, 1991), p. 250.

Chapter 5

1. Bart Barnes, "Adm. Hyman Rickover was Tenacious Visionary," Obituary, *The Washington Post*, July 10, 1986.
2. Interview with Robert Rickover.
3. Ibid.
4. Clay Blair, *The Atomic Submarine and Admiral Rickover* (New York: H. Holt, 1954), p. 70.
5. Hedrick Smith, *The Power Game: How Washington Works* (New York: Random House, 1988).
6. Interview with Theodore Rockwell.
7. Theodore Rockwell, *The Rickover Effect: How One Man Made a Difference* (Lincoln, NE: IUniverse, 2002), p. 118.
8. Elmo R. Zumwalt, *On Watch: A Memoir* (New York: Quadrangle, New York Times Book Co., 1976), p. 85.
9. Ibid., p. 95.
10. Interview with Harry Mandl and Theodore Rockwell.
11. Rockwell, *The Rickover Effect*, p. 324.
12. John F. Lehman, *Command of the Seas* (New York: Scribner, 1988), p. 1.
13. Rockwell, *The Rickover Effect*, p. 388.
14. Ibid., p. xvii.

Chapter 6

1. Sir Edward T. Cook, *The Life of Florence Nightingale* (London: Macmillan, 1913), p. 100.
2. Ibid., p. xi.
3. Ibid., pp. 41–42.
4. Cecil Woodham-Smith, *Florence Nightingale, 1820–1910* (New York: McGraw-Hill, 1951), p. 12.
5. Ibid., p. 34.
6. Cook, *Life*, pp. 109–110.
7. Woodham-Smith, *Florence*, p. 46.
8. Sir Edward Cook, quoting a letter from Florence to her sister.
9. Woodham-Smith, *Florence*, p. 60.
10. Ibid., pp. 77–78.
11. Ibid., p. 78.
12. From a poem by Lady Lovelace, Lord Bryan's daughter in honor of Florence Nightingale, quoted in Cook, *Life*, p. 142.
13. Ibid., pp. 146–147.
14. Ibid., p. 188.
15. A letter from the Keeper of the Queen's purse quoted in ibid., p. 216.
16. Ibid., p. 254.
17. From a letter to Selina Bracebridge, May 5, 1855, quoted in ibid., p. 255.
18. Ibid., p. 274.
19. George Pickering, *Creative Malady* (New York: Delta, 1974), p. 177.
20. Donald R. Allen, "Florence Nightingale: Toward a Psychohistorical Interpretation," in Raymond G. Hebert, *Florence Nightingale: Saint, Reformer, or Rebel* (Malabar, FL: Robert E. Krieger, 1981), pp. 64–83.
21. Ibid., p. 83.

Chapter 7

1. Sigmund Freud, "Some Character Types Met With in Psychoanalytic Work," *Writings on Art and Literature* (Stanford, CA: Stanford University Press, 1997).
2. Friedrich Nietzsche, "The Pale Criminal," *Thus Spoke Zarathustra* (New York: Modern Library, 1995), pp. 37–40.
3. Sigmund Freud, "Group Psychology and the Analysis of the Ego," *Standard Edition* 18 (1955): 129.
4. James Risen and David Johnston, "Traces of Terror: The Intelligence Reports; Agent Complaints Lead FBI Director to Ask for Inquiry," New York Times Abstracts, *New York Times,* May 24, 2002, p. 1.
5. Robert King Merton, *Social Theory and Social Structure* (New York: Free Press, 1968), p. 200.
6. Niccolò Machiavelli, *The Prince,* trans. and ed. Mark Musa (New York: St. Martin's Press, 1964), p. 191.

Chapter 8

1. Robert S. McNamara, *In Retrospect: The Tragedy and Lessons of Vietnam* (New York: Random House, 1995), p. 3.
2. Ibid., pp. 216–217.
3. Deborah Shapley, *Promise and Power: The Life and Times of Robert McNamara* (Boston: Little, Brown, 1993), p. 9.
4. For interesting details on Robert McNamara's early years, see Henry L. Trewhitt, *McNamara* (New York: Harper and Row, 1971), pp. 26–34.
5. David Halberstam, *The Reckoning,* (New York: William Morrow, 1986), pp. 204–223. (*The Best and the Brightest,* Halberstam's earlier book, tells the story of the U.S. involvement in the Vietnam war and was a book that fueled the fire of protest against the war.)
6. Ibid., p. 222.
7. Shapley, *Promise and Power,* pp. 52–57.
8. Robert S. McNamara, "McNamara Defines His Job," *New York Times Magazine,* April 26, 1964, p. 108.
9. For a brief and astute comparison of the philosophies adopted by various secretaries of defense, starting with James Forrestal, see James M. Roherty, *Decisions of Robert S. McNamara: A Study of the Role of Secretary of Defense* (Coral Gables, FL: University of Miami Press, 1970).
10. Robert N. Anthony, "McNamara Management," unpublished speech, p. 19.
11. Shapley, *Promise and Power,* p. 216.
12. McNamara, *In Retrospect,* p. 18.
13. Ibid., pp. 39–40.
14. Ibid., p. 332.
15. George W. Ball, *The Past Has Another Pattern: Memoirs* (New York: W. W. Norton, 1982), p. 369.
16. Clark Clifford, with Richard Holbrooke, *Counsel to the President: A Memoir* (New York: Random House, 1991), p. 460.
17. Ball, *The Past Has Another Pattern,* p. 383.
18. Clifford, *Counsel to the President,* p. 485.

Chapter 9

1. "Future Lessons from Yesterday's Man," *The Financial Times (London)*, August 21, 1997, USA edition, p. 8.
2. From the dedication in Harold Geneen with Brent Bowers, *The Synergy Myth* (New York: St. Martin's Press, 1997).
3. Harold Geneen with Alvin Moscow, *Managing* (Garden City, New York: Doubleday, 1984), p. 53.
4. Ibid.
5. Ibid., p. 55.
6. Ibid., p. 56.
7. Ibid., p. 68.
8. Ibid., p. 70.
9. Ibid., p. 71.
10. Ibid., p. 73.
11. Ibid., p. 75.
12. Robert J. Schoenberg, *Geneen* (New York: W. W. Norton, 1985), p. 95.
13. Ibid.
14. Geneen, *Managing*, p. 87.
15. Ibid., p. 96.
16. Ibid.
17. Ibid., p. 101.
18. Ibid.
19. Schoenberg, *Geneen*, p. 90.
20. Anthony Sampson, *The Sovereign State of ITT* (New York: Stein and Day, 1973), p. 92.
21. Geneen, *Managing*, p. 24.
22. U.S. Congress. House Committee on Interstate and Foreign Commerce Subcommittee on Investigations, *Legislative Oversight of SEC: Agency Independence and ITT Case* (Washington, D.C.: U.S. Government Printing Office, 1973), pp. 151–152.
23. Schoenberg, *Geneen*, p. 267.
24. Sampson, *Sovereign State of ITT*, p. 13.
25. Schoenberg, *Geneen*, pp. 321–324.
26. Ibid., p. 333.
27. Freud, *Group Psychology and the Analysis of the Ego* (New York: Bantam Books, 1960), p. 71.

Chapter 10

1. See Nathan Leites, *Kremlin Thoughts: Yielding, Rebuffing, Provoking, Retreating* (Santa Monica, CA: Rand Corporation, 1963); Nathan Leites, *Kremlin Moods* (Santa Monica, CA: Rand Corporation, 1964). See also Alexander L. George, *The Operational Code: A Neglected Approach to the Study of Political Leaders and Decision Making* (Santa Monica, CA: Rand Corporation, 1967).
2. See Abraham Zaleznik, *The Managerial Mystique* (New York: Harper & Row, 1989), pp. 28–29.
3. Chester Barnard, *The Functions of the Executive* (Cambridge, MA: Harvard University Press, 1938), pp. 168–169.
4. Helen Tartakoff, "The Normal Personality in Our Culture and the Nobel Prize Complex," in *Psychoanalysis: A General Psychology*, ed. Rudolph Lowenstien, L. Newman, M. Schur, and A. Solnit (New York: International University Press, 1966), pp. 222–252.

5. Ibid, p. 225.
6. Sydney Finkelstein, *Why Smart Executives Fail* (New York: Portfolio Press, 2003).
7. Sigmund Freud, *Gesammelte Werke. chronologisch geordnet*, vol. 12 (London: Imago, 1940–1952), p. 26.

Chapter 11

1. See Michael Eric Dyson, *I May Not Get There With You* (New York: Simon & Schuster, 2000).
2. Lerone Bennett, Jr., *What Manner of Man: A Memorial Biography of Martin Luther King, Jr.* (New York: Pocket Books, 1968), pp. 14–15.
3. Ibid., p. 22.
4. Ibid., pp. 25–26.
5. Coretta Scott King, *My Life With Martin Luther King, Jr.* (New York: Holt Rinehart and Winston, 1969), p. 91.
6. Dyson, *I May Not Get There*, p. 140.
7. William D. Watley, *Roots of Resistance: The Nonviolent Ethic of Martin Luther King, Jr.* (Valley Forge, Pa.: Judson Press, 1985), p. 7.
8. David J. Garrow, *Bearing the Cross: Martin Luther King, Jr., and the Southern Christian Leadership Conference* (New York: Vintage Books, 1986), pp. 54–55.
9. L. D. Reddick, *Crusader Without Violence: A Biography of Martin Luther King, Jr.* (New York: Harper & Brothers, 1959), p. 131.
10. Ibid., p. 219.
11. Ibid., p. 229.
12. Watley, *Roots of Resistance*, p. 69.
13. Cartha D. DeLoach, *Hoover's FBI: The Inside Story by Hoover's Trusted Lieutenant* (Washington, D.C.: Regnery, 1995), pp. 200–201.
14. Ibid., pp. 204–205.
15. Garrow, *Bearing the Cross*, pp. 125–126.
16. Martin Luther King, Sr., with Clayton Riley, *Daddy King: An Autobiography*, foreword by Benjamin E. Mays, introduction by Andrew J. Young (New York: William Morrow, 1980).
17. Ibid, p.190.
18. Ibid., p. 193.
19. Ibid., pp. 200–201.

Chapter 12

1. Irene L. Gendzier, *Frantz Fanon: A Critical Study* (New York: Pantheon Books, 1973), p. v.
2. David Macey, *Frantz Fanon: A Biography* (New York: Picador USA, 2001), p. 57.
3. Frantz Fanon, *Black Skin White Masks* (New York: Grove Press, 1967), pp. 151–152.
4. Patrick Ehlen, *Frantz Fanon: A Spiritual Biography* (New York: Crossword), pp. 26–27.
5. Ibid., pp. 21–22.
6. Macey, *Frantz Fanon*, p. 71.
7. Ibid., pp. 103–104.
8. Ehlen, *Frantz Fanon*, p. 90.
9. Ibid.
10. Macey, *Frantz Fanon*, pp. 150–151.

11. Fanon, *Black Skin*, p. 31.
12. Ibid., pp. 35–36.
13. Ibid., p. 38.
14. Ibid., p. 102.
15. Ibid., p. 221.
16. Ibid., p. 225.
17. Macey, *Frantz Fanon*, p. 299.
18. Fanon, *Black Skin*, p. 62.
19. Frantz Fanon, *The Wretched of the Earth*, preface by Jean-Paul Sartre, trans. Constance Farrington (New York: Grove Weidenfeld, 1991), p. 75.
20. Ibid., p. 99.
21. Ibid., p. 13.
22. Quoted in Macey, *Frantz Fanon*, p. 452.
23. Ibid., pp. 488–492.

Chapter 13

1. See Claude Levi-Strauss, *The Savage Mind* (Chicago: The University of Chicago Press, 1966), pp. 116–136.
2. Sigmund Freud, *Fragment of an Analysis of a Case of Hysteria. The Standard Edition of the Complete Psychological Works of Sigmund Freud*, vol. 7 (London: Hogarth Press, 1953), pp. 7–122.
3. Ibid., p. 122.

Chapter 14

1. From Joseph Conrad's autobiographical memoir, *A Personal Record*, quoted in Bernard C. Meyer, MD, *Joseph Conrad: A Psychoanalytic Biography* (Princeton, N.J.: Princeton University Press, 1967), p. 94.
2. Robert M. Armstrong, MD, "Joseph Conrad: The Conflict of Command," *The Psychoanalytic Study of the Child*, ed. Ruth Eissler, et al., vol. 26 (New York: Quadrangle Books, 1972), pp. 485–534.
3. Joseph Conrad, "Typhoon," *The Portable Conrad*, ed. Morton Dauwen Zabel (New York: The Viking Press, 1947).
4. Joseph Conrad, *Lord Jim*, (New York, The New American Library, 1961), p. 15.
5. Joseph Conrad, "A Personal Record," *A Conrad Argosy*, (Garden City, New York: Doubleday, 1942), p. 680.
6. Joseph Conrad, "The Condition of Art," in *The Portable Conrad*, ed., Morton Dauwen Zabel (New York: The Viking Press, 1947), p. 705.
7. Meyer, *Joseph Conrad*, p. 55.
8. Ibid., pp. 72–73.
9. Conrad, "A Personal Record," p. 677.
10. Albert J. Guerard, *Conrad the Novelist* (Cambridge, MA: Harvard University Press, 1958), p. 1.
11. Norman N. Holland, *The I* (New Haven: Yale University Press, 1985), pp. 100–106.
12. Armstrong, "Joseph Conrad," p. 134.
13. Ibid., p. 35.
14. Conrad, "A Personal Record," p. 666.

15. Armstrong, "Joseph Conrad," pp. 48–49.
16. Ibid., p. 307.
17. Joseph Conrad, *Lord Jim* (Garden City, New York: Doubleday, 1990), p. 308.
18. Conrad, *Lord Jim*, p. 6.
19. Joseph Conrad, *Heart of Darkness*, ed. D. C. R. A. Goontilleke, 2nd ed., (Peterborough, Ont.: Broadview; Hadleigh: Brad, 1999), p. 573.
20. Ibid., pp. 561–562.
21. Ibid., p. 603.
22. Joseph Conrad, *The Secret Sharer*, in *The Portable Conrad* (New York: The Viking Press, 1947), p. 649.
23. Ibid., p. 699.
24. Meyer, *Joseph Conrad*, p. 10.

Chapter 15

1. Albert Camus, *The Plague*, trans. Robin Buss, introduction by Tony Judt (London: Allen Lane, 2001).
2. F. Barron Freeman, ed., *Melville's Billy Budd* (Cambridge, MA: Harvard University Press, 1948). See also Herman Melville, *Billy Budd, Sailor: (An Inside Narrative)*, ed. Harrison Hayford and Merton M. Sealts, Jr. (Chicago: University of Chicago Press, 1962).
3. Freeman, *Melville's Billy Budd*, p. 27.
4. All quotations from the story are from the New American Library edition, with an afterword by Willard Thorp (New York: A Signet Classic, 1961). Page references will follow the quote in parentheses.
5. Otto Rank, *The Myth of the Birth of the Hero and other Writings*, ed., Philip Freund (New York: Alfred Knopf, Vintage Books, 1959), pp. 4–96.
6. See E. L. Grant Watson, "Melville's Testament of Acceptance," *The New England Quarterly* 6, no. 2 (June, 1933): 319–327 for the argument supporting the interpretation that Melville at last accepted the fact of evil and was no longer a rebel. For the counter argument, see Paul Within, "The Testament of Resistance," *Modern Language Quarterly* 20, no. 2 (June, 1959): 115–127.
7. Sigmund Freud, "Psycho-Analytic Notes on An Autobiographical Account of a Case of Paranoia," *Standard Edition*, vol. 12 (London: The Hogarth Press, 1958), p. 77.

Chapter 16

1. Ernst Kris, *Psychoanalytic Explorations in Art* (New York: International Universities Press, 1952).
2. Erik H. Erikson, "The Problem of Ego Identity," *Psychological Issues* 1, No. 1 (New York, International Universities Press, 1959), pp. 101–164. See also Norman Holland, *The I* (New Haven: Yale University Press, 1985), pp. 56–67.
3. Ibid., p. 103.
4. Albert J. Guerard, *Conrad, The Novelist* (Cambridge, MA: Harvard University Press, 1958), p. 129.
5. Joseph Conrad, "Typhoon," in *The Portable Conrad*, ed. Morton Dauwell Zabel (New York: The Viking Press, 1947), p. 208.
6. Bernard C. Meyer, M. D., *Joseph Conrad: A Psychoanalytic Biography* (Princeton, NJ: Princeton University Press, 1967), pp. 242–243.

7. Chester Barnard, *The Functions of the Executive* (Cambridge, MA: Harvard University Press, 1938), p. 168–169.
8. Abraham Zaleznik, *Worker Satisfaction and Development* (Boston, MA: Division of Research, Harvard Business School, 1956), pp. 83–91.
9. Abraham Zaleznik, *The Managerial Mystique* (New York: Harper and Row, 1989), pp. 62–76. See also Sudhir Kakar, *Frederick Taylor: A Study in Personality and Innovation* (Cambridge, MA: MIT Press, 1970).
10. Abraham Zaleznik, "Managers and Leaders: Are They Different?" *Harvard Business Review,* (May–June, 1977).
11. Theodore W. Adorno et. al., *The Authoritarian Personality* (New York: Harper, 1950).

Bibliography

Abernathy, Ralph David. *And the Walls Came Tumbling Down*. New York: Harper & Row, 1989.

Adorno, Theodor W., Else Frenkel-Brunswik, Daniel J. Levinson, and R. Nevitt Sanford. *The Authoritarian Personality*. New York: Harper & Row, 1950.

Allen, Donald R. "Florence Nightingale: Toward a Psychohistorical Interpretation." In *Florence Nightingale: Saint, Reformer, or Rebel*, by Raymond G. Herbert. Malabar, FL: Robert E. Kreiger, 1981.

Ambrose, Stephen E. *Eisenhower, Solider and President*. New York: Touchstone, Simon & Schuster, 1990.

Anthony, Robert N. "McNamara Management." Unpublished speech.

Armstrong, Robert M., M.D. "Joseph Conrad: The Conflict of Command." In *The Psychoanalytic Study of the Child*, edited by Ruth S. Eissler, Anna Freud, Marianne Kris, and Albert J. Solnit. Vol. 26. New York: Quadrangle Books, 1972, pp. 485–534.

Ball, George. *The Past Has Another Pattern: Memoirs*. New York: W. W. Norton, 1982.

Barber, James D. *The Presidential Character: Predicting Performance in the White House*. Englewood, NJ: Prentice-Hall, 1972.

Barnard, Chester. *The Functions of the Executive*. Cambridge: Harvard University Press, 1938.

Bennett, Lerone, Jr. *What Manner of Man: A Memorial Biography of Martin Luther King, Jr.* New York: Pocket Books, 1968.

Berlin, Isaiah. *The Crooked Timber of Humanity: Chapters in the History of Ideas*. New York: Alfred A. Knopf, 1991.

———. *The Hedgehog and the Fox*. New York: Simon & Schuster, 1968.

Blair, Clay, Jr. *The Atomic Submarine and Admiral Rickover*. New York: Henry Holt, 1954.

Brinkley, Douglas. *Rosa Parks*. New York: Viking Press, 2000.

Bruner, Jerome S., M. Brewster Smith, and Robert W. White. *Opinions and Personality*. New York: John Wiley, 1956.

Burns, James MacGregor. *Leadership*. New York: Harper & Row, 1978.

Camus, Albert. *The Plague*. Translated by Robin Buss with an introduction by Tony Judt. London: Allen Lane, 2001.

Cannon, Lou. *President Reagan: The Role of a Lifetime*. New York: Public Affairs, 2000.

———. "To Tell the Truth: Will the Real Ronald Reagan Please Stand Up." *Los Angeles Times*, October 3, 1999, Book review section.

Chodorow, Nancy. *Feminism and Psychoanalytic Theory*. New Haven: Yale University Press, 1989.

Clifford, Clark (with Richard Holbrooke). *Counsel to the President: A Memoir*. New York: Random House, 1991.

Colaico, James A. *Martin Luther King, Jr.: Apostle of Militant Nonviolence*. New York: St. Martin's Press, 1988.

Conrad, Joseph. *Heart of Darkness.* 2nd ed. Edited by D. C. R. A. Goontilleke. Peterborough, ON.: Broadview; Hadleigh, WA: Brad, 1999.

Conrad, Joseph. *Lord Jim.* New York: The New American Library, 1961.

Conrad, Joseph. "A Personal Record." In *A Conrad Argosy.* Garden City, NY: Doubleday, 1942.

Conrad, Joseph. "The Secret Sharer." In *The Portable Conrad.* New York: Viking Press, 1947.

Cook, Edward T. *The Life of Florence Nightingale.* London: Macmillan, 1913.

Cope, Zachary. *Florence Nightingale and the Doctors.* London: Museum Press, 1958.

Copeland, Melvin T. *And Mark and Era: The Story of the Harvard Business School.* Boston: Little, Brown, 1958.

Davis, Gerald L. *I Got the Word in Me: A Study of the Performed African-American Sermon.* Philadelphia, PA: University of Pennsylvania Press, 1985.

Deaver, Michael K. *Behind the Scenes.* New York: William Morrow, 1987.

DeLoach, Cartha D. *Hoover's FBI: The Inside Story by Hoover's Trusted Lieutenant.* Washington, DC: Regnery, 1995.

Du Bois, W. E. B. *The Souls of Black People.* New York: Penguin Books, 1989.

Duncan, Francis. *Rickover and the Nuclear Navy: The Discipline of Technology.* Annapolis, MD: Naval Institute Press, 1990.

Dyson, Michael Eric. *I May Not Get There With You: The True Martin Luther King, Jr.* New York: Simon & Schuster, 2000.

Ehlen, Patrick. *Frantz Fanon: A Spiritual Biography.* New York: Crossword, 2000.

Eisenhower, Dwight D. *At Ease.* Garden City, NY: Doubleday, 1967.

Erikson, Erik H. *Psychological Issues.* Vol. 1, no. 1. New York: International Universities Press, 1959.

Fanon, Frantz. *Black Skin White Masks.* New York: Grove Press, 1967.

———. *The Wretched of the Earth.* 1st Evergreen ed. New York: Grove Weidenfeld, 1991.

Festinger, Leon. *The Theory of Cognitive Dissonance.* Evanston, IL: Row, Peterson, 1957.

Financial Times (London), U.S. edition, Thursday, August 21, 1997.

Finkelstein, Sydney. *Why Smart Executives Fail.* New York: Portfolio Press, 2003.

Fitzgerald, Frances. *Way Out There in the Blue: Reagan, Star Wars, and the End of the Cold War.* New York: Simon & Schuster, 2000.

Frady, Marshall. *Martin Luther King, Jr.* New York: Viking Press, 2002.

Freeman, F. Barron, ed. *Melville's Billy Budd.* Cambridge: Harvard University Press, 1948.

Freud, Anna. *The Ego and the Mechanisms of Defense.* New York: International Universities Press, 1946.

Freud, Sigmund. *Fragment of an Analysis of a Case of Hysteria. The Standard Edition of the Complete Psychological Works of Sigmund Freud.* Vol. 7 and vol. 18. London: Hogarth Press, 1953.

———. Edward Bibring, Willi Hoffer, Ernst Kris, and Otto Isakower. *Gesammelte Werke. chronologisch geordnet.* [Hrsg. Von Anna Freud et al.] London: Imago, 1940–1952.

———. "Group Psychology and the Analysis of the Ego." *The Standard Edition of the Complete Psychological Works of Sigmund Freud.* London: Hogarth Press, 1955.

———. *Group Psychology and the Analysis of the Ego.* New York: Bantam Books, 1960.

———. "Psycho-Analytic Notes on an Autobiographical Account of a Case of Paranoia." *The Standard Edition of the Complete Psychological Works of Sigmund Freud.* Vol. 12. London: Hogarth Press, 1958.

———. "Some Character Types Met with in Psychoanalytic Work." *The Standard Edition of the Complete Psychological Works of Sigmund Freud.* Vol. 14. London: Hogarth Press, 1957.

Freund, Philip, ed. *The Myth of the Birth of the Hero and Other Writings By Otta Rank.* New York: Alfred A. Knopf, Vintage Books, 1959.

Gabriel, Richard A. and Paul L. Savage. *Crisis in Command: Mismanagement in the Army.* New York: Hill and Wang, 1978.

Garrow, David J. *Bearing the Cross: Martin Luther King, Jr., and the Southern Christian Leadership Conference.* New York, William Morrow, 1986.

———. *The FBI and Martin Luther King, Jr.: From "Solo" to Memphis.* New York: W. W. Norton, 1981.

Gendzier, Irene L. *Frantz Fanon: A Critical Study.* New York: Pantheon, 1973.

Geneen, Harold (with Alvin Moscow). *Managing.* New York: Doubleday, 1984.

——— (with Brent Bowers). *The Synergy Myth.* New York: St. Martin's Press, 1997. (See Dedication.)

George, Alexander L. *The "Operational Code": A Neglected Approach to the Study of Political Leaders and Decision-Making.* Santa Monica, CA: Rand Corp., 1967.

Greider, William. "The Education of David Stockman." *Atlantic.* December 1981.

Guerard, Albert J. *Conrad The Novelist.* Cambridge, MA: Harvard University Press, 1958.

Halberstam, David. *The Reckoning.* New York: William Morrow, 1986.

Hayford, Harrison, and Merton M. Sealts, Jr., eds. *Herman Melville, Billy Budd: Sailor.* Chicago, IL: University of Chicago Press, 1962.

Hewlett, Richard G., and Francis Duncan, *Nuclear Navy: 1946–1962.* Chicago: University of Chicago Press, 1974.

Holland, Norman N. *The I.* New Haven, CT: Yale University Press, 1985.

Hughes, Emmet J. *Ordeal of Power.* New York: Dell, 1964.

James, William. *The Varieties of Religious Experience.* New York: Modern Library, 1994.

Kakar, Sudhir. *Frederick Taylor: A Study in Personality and Innovation.* Cambridge: MIT Press, 1970.

Kennan, George E. *Around the Cragged Hill.* New York: W. W. Norton, 1994.

King, Coretta Scott. *My Life With Martin Luther King, Jr.* New York: Holt, Rinehart and Winston, 1969.

King, Martin Luther, Sr. (with Clayton Riley). *Daddy King: An Autobiography.* Foreword by Benjamin E. Mays, with an introduction by Andrew J. Young. New York: William Morrow, 1980.

Lehman, John F., Jr. *Command of the Seas.* New York: Charles Scribner's Sons, 1988.

Leites, Nathan. *Kremlin Moods.* Santa Monica, CA: Rand Corp., 1964.

———. *Kremlin Thoughts: Yielding, Rebuffing, Provoking, Retreating.* Santa Monica, CA: Rand Corp., 1963.

———. *A Study of Bolshevism.* Glencoe, IL: Free Press, 1953.

Levi-Strauss, Claude. *The Savage Mind.* Chicago: University of Chicago Press, 1966.

Lewis, David L. *King: A Critical Biography.* New York: Praeger, 1970.

Lewis, John (with Michael D'Orso). *Walking With the Wind: A Memoir of the Movement.* New York: Harcourt Brace, 1998.

Lowenstien, Rudolph, ed. *Psychoanalysis: A General Psychology.* New York: International Universities Press, 1966.

Macey, David. *Frantz Fanon: A Biography.* New York: Picador USA, 2001.

Machiavelli, Niccolò. *The Prince.* Translated by Mark Musa. New York: St. Martin's Press, 1964.

Maslow, Abraham. *Motivation and Personality.* New York: Harper & Row, 1970.

Merton, Robert K. *Social Theory and Social Structure.* Glencoe, IL: Free Press, 1957.

McNamara, Robert S. *In Retrospect: The Tragedy and Lessons of Vietnam.* New York: Random House, 1995.

———. "McNamara Defines his Job." *New York Times Magazine,* April 26, 1964.

Melville, Herman. *Billy Budd.* Afterword by Williard Thorp. New American Library Edition. New York: Signet, 1961.

Meyer, Bernard C. *Joseph Conrad: A Psychoanalytic Biography.* Princeton, NJ: Princeton University Press, 1967.

Morris, Edmund. *Dutch: A Memoir of Ronald Reagan.* New York: Random House, 1999.

Neustadt, Richard E. *Presidential Power.* New York: New American Library, Signet, 1964; Glencoe, IL: Free Press, 1990.

Nietzsche, Friedrich. "The Pale Criminal." In *Thus Spoke Zarathustra.* New York: Modern Library, 1995.

Parmet, Herbert S. *Eisenhower and the American Crusades.* New York: Macmillan, 1972.

Pickering, George. *Creative Malady.* New York: Delta, 1974.

Polmar, Norman and Thomas B. Allen. *Rickover, Controversy and Genius: A Biography.* New York: Simon & Schuster, 1982.

Powell, Colin (with Joseph E. Persico). *My American Journey.* New York: Random House, 1995.

Reagan, Nancy (with William Novak). *My Turn: Memoirs of Nancy Reagan.* New York: Random House, 1989.

Reagan, Ronald (with Richard Hubler). *Where's the Rest of Me?* New York: Duell, Sloan and Pearce, 1965.

Regan, Donald T. *For the Record: From Wall Street to Washington.* New York: Harcourt Brace Johanovich, 1988.

Reddick, L. D. *Crusader Without Violence: A Biography of Martin Luther King, Jr.* New York: Harper & Row, 1959.

Rickover, Hyman G. Editorial. *The Journal of Reactor Science and Technology* 3, no. 3 (1953).

Rockwell, Theodore. *The Rickover Effect: How One Man Made a Difference.* Annapolis, MD: Naval Institute Press, 1992.

Roethlisberger, F. J., and W. J. Dickson. *Management and the Worker.* Cambridge, MA: Harvard University Press, 1947.

Roherty, James M. *Decisions of Robert S. McNamara: A Study of the Role of Secretary of Defense.* Coral Gables, FL: University of Miami Press, 1970.

Sampson, Anthony. *The Sovereign State of ITT.* New York: Stein and Day, 1973.

Schlesinger, Arthur M., Jr. *A Thousand Days: John F. Kennedy in the White House.* Boston: Houghton Mifflin, 1965.

Schoenberg, Robert J. *Geneen.* New York: W. W. Norton, 1985.

Shultz, George P. *Turmoil and Triumph: My Years as Secretary of State.* New York: Scribner, 1993.

Shapley, Deborah. *Promise and Power: The Life and Times of Robert McNamara.* Boston: Little, Brown, 1993.

Sheehan, Neil. *A Bright Shining Lie: John Paul Vann and America in Vietnam.* New York: Vintage Books, 1988.

Small, Hugh. *Florence Nightingale: Avenging Angel.* New York: St. Martin's Press, 1998.

Smith, Hedrick. *The Power Game: How Washington Works.* New York: Random House, 1988.

Smith, M. Brewster. *The Pentagon Papers.* New York: Bantam Books, 1971.

Spector, Ronald H. *At War At Sea: Sailors and Naval Combat in the Twentieth Century.* New York: Viking Press, 2001.

Stockman, David. *The Triumph of Politics: Why the Reagan Revolution Failed.* New York: Harper & Row, 1986.

The Tower Commission Report. New York: Bantam Books, 1987.

Trewhitt, Henry L. *McNamara.* New York: Harper & Row, 1997.

Tyler, Patrick. *Running Critical: The Silent War, Rickover and General Dynamics.* New York: Harper & Row, 1986.

U.S. Congress. House Committee on Interstate and Foreign Commerce Subcommittee on Investigations. *Legislative Oversight of SEC: Agency Independence and ITT Case.* Washington, DC: U.S. Government Printing Office, 1973. pp. 151–152.

Washington, James M. ed. *The Essential Writings and Speeches of Martin Luther King, Jr.* New York: Harper Collins, 1991.

Watley, William D. *Roots of Resistance: The Nonviolent Ethic of Martin Luther King, Jr.* Valley Forge, PA.: Judson Press, 1985.

Watson, E. L. Grant. "Melville's Testament of Acceptance." *The New England Quarterly* 6, no. 6. 1933.

Weinberger, Casper W. *Fighting for Peace: Seven Critical Years in the Pentagon.* New York: Warner Books, 1990.

Within, Paul. "The Testament of Resistance." *Modern Language Quarterly* 20, no. 2. (June 1959).

Woodman-Smith, Cecil. *Florence Nightingale, 1820–1910.* New York: McGraw-Hill, 1951.

Young, D. A. B. "Florence Nightingale's Fever." *British Medical Journal* 311 (December 1995): 23–30.

Zabel, Morton Dauwen, ed. *The Portable Conrad.* New York: Viking Press, 1947.

Zaleznik, A. *Foreman Training in a Growing Enterprise.* Boston: Division of Research, Harvard Business School, 1951.

———. *The Managerial Mystique.* New York: Harper & Row, 1989.

———. "Managers and Leaders: Are They Different?" *Harvard Business Review,* May–June 1977.

———. *Worker Satisfaction and Development.* Boston: Division of Research, Harvard Business School, 1956.

Zuckerman, Lord. *Six Men Out of the Ordinary.* London: Peter Owen, 1992.

Zumwalt, Elmo R. *On Watch.* New York: New York Times Book Co., 1976.

Index